EXPERIENCES IN RESEARCHING CONFLICT AND VIOLENCE

Fieldwork Interrupted

Edited by
Althea-Maria Rivas and
Brendan Ciarán Browne

P

First published in Great Britain in 2018 by

Policy Press
University of Bristol
1-9 Old Park Hill
Bristol
BS2 8BB
UK
t: +44 (0)117 954 5940
pp-info@bristol.ac.uk
www.policypress.co.uk

North America office:
Policy Press
c/o The University of Chicago Press
1427 East 60th Street
Chicago, IL 60637, USA
t: +1 773 702 7700
f: +1 773-702-9756
sales@press.uchicago.edu
www.press.uchicago.edu

© Policy Press 2018

British Library Cataloguing in Publication Data
A catalogue record for this book is available from the British Library

Library of Congress Cataloging-in-Publication Data
A catalog record for this book has been requested

ISBN 978-1-4473-3768-3 hardcover
ISBN 978-1-4473-3771-3 ePub
ISBN 978-1-4473-3772-0 Mobi
ISBN 978-1-4473-3770-6 ePdf

The right of Althea-Maria Rivas and Brendan Ciarán Browne to be identified as editors of this work has been asserted by them in accordance with the Copyright, Designs and Patents Act 1988.

The statements and opinions contained within this publication are solely those of the editors and contributors and not of the University of Bristol or Policy Press. The University of Bristol and Policy Press disclaim responsibility for any injury to persons or property resulting from any material published in this publication.

Policy Press works to counter discrimination on grounds of gender, race, disability, age and sexuality.

Cover design by Hayes Design
Front cover image supplied by 123RF.com 123. The front image of stacked stones is known as a 'cairn' and is used to denote areas of significance, including to mark out pathways or to highlight places of danger.
Printed and bound in Great Britain by CPI Group (UK) Ltd, Croydon, CR0 4YY
Policy Press uses environmentally responsible print partners

MIX
Paper from
responsible sources
FSC
www.fsc.org   FSC® C013604

Contents

Acknowledgements

We would like to thank Pamela Kea and Liat Radcliffe Ross, who offered critical feedback and commentary on earlier versions of the book chapters, Roger Saul and Shelley Lauren Robinson for their continuous support and advice on the ideas, aesthetics and format of the book. Invaluable mentorship was provided throughout various stages of the writing and publishing process by Professor David Mutimer at the York University, Toronto, and Susan Johnson and colleagues at the Centre for Development Studies, University of Bath. We would also like to acknowledge the postdoctoral fellowship programme of the Centre for Development Studies at the University of Bath for the funding that made possible the presentation of the ideas underpinning this book in its initial stages.

We are grateful to the editorial staff at Policy Press for their belief in the message of the book, guidance and above all, their patience. Finally, we would like to acknowledge and thank those who inspired this book, the scholars, researchers and practitioners, who honestly shared their uncomfortable moments with us, and the colleagues, partners, researchers and research participants who live in the many countries mentioned in this book who have and continue to support and direct our work and ultimately, educate us.

On a more personal note, Brendan would like to thank those dedicated and committed colleagues at Al Quds (Bard) University who provided both professional and personal camaraderie during challenging times spent working and living in the West Bank. His parents, Marie and Paul, for inspiring the confidence to conduct difficult research in uncomfortable spaces. Finally, a special thank you is reserved for Emma for being the never-ending source of support, love, guidance and inspiration when living and working together in Palestine.

Althea-Maria would like to thank Alriguez Sebastian and Kathleen for everything.

Notes on the editors and contributors

Editors

Althea-Maria Rivas is a Lecturer in the Department of Development Studies at the University of Sussex, UK. Her research interests are race and global politics, gender insecurity and development, humanitarian intervention and post-conflict reconstruction, migration, feminist and postcolonial theory and pedagogy. She has lived, worked and conducted research for over 15 years in a number of countries in West and East Africa and Central Asia. She is also a Research Associate at the Harriet Tubman Institute for Research on Africa and its Diasporas at the Centre for Refugee Studies at the University of York, UK.

Brendan Ciarán Browne is an Assistant Professor in Conflict Resolution, Trinity College Dublin, Ireland. His research interests centre on conflict transformation, growing up in conflict, commemoration in conflict and transitional justice in Northern Ireland and Palestine. He has conducted extensive fieldwork in both settings, working with political representatives, youth and community workers, non-governmental organisations (NGOs) and former combatants. He is also a Research Fellow at the Centre for Post-Conflict Justice, Trinity College Dublin.

Contributors

Fathima Azmiya Badurdeen is a PhD candidate at the Department of Social Sciences, Technical University of Mombasa, Kenya. She has a Master's degree in Public Policy from the University of York, UK, and another Master's degree in Development Studies from the Open University of Sri Lanka. Her main areas of research are on terrorism studies and forced migration. She has held research fellowships and published research papers at the Refugee Studies Centre, University of Oxford and Mahanirban Calcutta Research Group, India.

Laurel Borisenko completed her PhD in conflict studies through the University of Amsterdam in the Netherlands. Her field-based research in three African communities focused on peacebuilding using the arts. Her research and publications are informed by many years as a practitioner, working in complex emergencies with United Nations (UN) agencies and international non-governmental organisations (NGOs). She works with the UN High Commissioner for Refugees (UNHCR) and teaches at Regent College, Vancouver, Canada.

Michael Broache is an Assistant Professor of Government and World Affairs at the University of Tampa in the USA. His research and teaching focuses on international relations and comparative politics, with a substantive focus on international law and a regional focus on sub-Saharan Africa.

Fabio Cristiano is a PhD candidate and Lecturer at the Department of Political Science, Lund University, Sweden. His research interests lie at the intersection of International Relations, cyberwarfare and critical theory. Fabio has published on cyberwar, war simulations, Palestine and gaming/augmented reality. His other areas of interest are cyber-diplomacy and the internet as a human right.

Patrick James Christian is a psychoanalytical anthropologist with a doctorate focused on the psychopathology of ethnic and cultural conflict. He is a retired American Military Special Forces L/Colonel with 24 years in the 1st Special Forces Regiment. He has significant experience researching and engaging communities in conflict in South and Central America, Africa, the Middle East and Asia.

Meike de Goede is a lecturer in African History and Anthropology at Leiden University, Netherlands. She specialises in the political history of Central Africa. She holds a PhD in International Relations from St Andrews University, Scotland. Before joining Leiden University, she worked as a practitioner in development and democratisation in Southern Africa and Central Africa, including several years in the Democratic Republic of the Congo (DRC). Her current research interest focuses on the history of messianism and political resistance in Congo-Brazzaville.

John Heathershaw is Associate Professor in International Relations at the University of Exeter, UK. His research concerns conflict, security and development in Central Asia, particularly Kyrgyzstan and Tajikistan.

Marjaana Jauhola is an Academy of Finland Research Fellow and Senior University Lecturer in Development Studies at the University of Helsinki, Finland. Her primary focus is on the gendered politics of post-disaster and conflict reconstruction, and she is currently writing up her research on the first decade of peace in urban Banda Aceh, Indonesia, using ethnography, short documentarism and life history methods.

Corinna Jentzsch is an Assistant Professor at the Institute of Political Science, Leiden University, in the Netherlands.

Inge Ligtvoet is a PhD candidate at the Institute for History, Leiden University, Netherlands. She is currently writing her dissertation on the ways in which youth in south(east) Nigeria navigate their lives in a context of experiencing long-term socioeconomic uncertainty and political insecurity.

Rose Løvgren is a PhD candidate in the Department of Peace, Risk and Violence at the Danish Institute for International Studies at the University of Copenhagen, Denmark.

Professor Robin Luckham is an Emeritus Fellow of the Institute of Development Studies at the University of Sussex, UK. Since completing his landmark book on the Nigerian military in 1971, he has published widely on various aspects on militarism, violence, disarmament, democracy and peacebuilding. He has held academic positions at Ahmadu Bello University, Nigeria, the University of Ghana, Harvard University and the Australian National University, as well as at Sussex.

Sandra M. McEvoy is an Associate Professor of Political Science and Director of the Political Science and Global Studies programme at Wheelock College, Boston, USA. She has written extensively on the Northern Irish conflict including the gendered motivations for women's participation in political violence; the impact that such participation has on notions of men and masculinity; and the role that perpetrators of political violence can play in long-term conflict resolution strategies.

Henri Myrttinen is Head of Gender and Peacebuilding at International Alert, a London-based non-governmental organisation (NGO). He has been working on gender issues in conflict-affected societies for the past 15 years, and has published extensively on the topic.

Paul Stubbs is a UK-born sociologist who is currently a Senior Research Fellow in the Institute of Economics, Zagreb, Croatia. His main research interests focus on the role of international actors in social policy and social development, social protection and social inclusion, state capture and clientelism, and policy translation. He is an elected member of the National Council for Science and Higher Education in Croatia. He combines research with activism, and was a founding board member of the Centre for Peace Studies, a Croatian non-governmental organisation (NGO).

Sinéad Walsh is an independent researcher specialising in gender, civil society and peacemaking in the former Soviet Union. She was awarded a PhD by Trinity College Dublin in 2016, following a period as a Government of Ireland postgraduate research scholar. Her current work focuses on feminist activism and transnational dialogue in Armenia and Azerbaijan.

Foreword

Robin Luckham

Much research on violence takes place in a way that is removed from the day-to-day experience of those caught up in it, especially so statistical analyses, which reduce motives and events to stylised behavioural patterns. Even ethnographic inquiries find themselves under pressure to organise their methods and findings around theoretical models and research protocols that may ensure rigour, but can filter out the terror and chaos on the ground, what a Tuareg elder interviewed by a contributor to this volume termed *timogoutar*, the 'bad hardness', that overwhelms victims, perpetrators and observers alike.

This excellent book is more than just a series of reflections on how to do research in 'bad', conflict-torn neighbourhoods. It is distinctive in delineating the dilemmas faced by researchers seeking to comprehend both the day-to-day realities and the deep structures of violence. These dilemmas are at root moral and political. Those who investigate violence must come to terms with the harm violence inflicts on bodies, identities, communities and social relationships. They should also reckon with the possibility that social inquiry itself can unleash powerful emotions, disturb fragile compromises and even bring tangible harm to those who participate. In politically charged situations, researchers cannot easily hide under umbrellas of neutrality, nor can they credibly invoke the supposedly higher moralities of peacebuilding or development.

How to navigate these dilemmas is a key question considered by contributors to this book. They highlight questions of identity, gender, positionality and intersectionality, and see them as embedded in power relations, both in violent situations themselves and in the practices of social research. The researchers cannot escape their own identities, and yet, like anyone else in situations of extreme uncertainty and violence, are obliged to renegotiate them as they go along. In a variety of interesting ways, they provide honest, self-critical and reflexive accounts of the research processes in which they were engaged. They pose more questions than they provide answers, but it is this ability to ask questions of themselves as well as of others that may be the most useful lesson they can pass on to students and fellow researchers working in fissile and fast-changing contexts of violence.

Introduction

Althea-Maria Rivas and Brendan Ciarán Browne

There is a growing impetus for graduate students and more seasoned researchers to carry out research in areas affected by conflict and violence. Embedded in these unique places are particular sets of issues that researchers, research participants and communities each face. These particularities present a rich but difficult terrain of inquiry for scholars attempting to navigate complex environments and for the people who reside there, who become involved in the research process. While a modicum of instructional texts has emerged to guide researchers working in conflict incidents around the world, serious attention to the subject of 'doing research in violent settings' remains lacking.

The research process in conflict-affected spaces around the world is rarely reflected in current academic guidelines and ethical frameworks on doing fieldwork. These texts tend to steer researchers towards problem-solving approaches and focus on commonly discussed issues such as consent, confidentiality and 'doing no harm' through narrowly constructed lenses. They also often avoid serious engagement with the realities of conflict research such as negotiating with warlords or working with survivors of sexual violence in ongoing conflict areas. All too often questions of affect, identity, violence and critical self-understanding in such environments are ignored. This book puts these issues at the centre, and posits them as fundamental to comprehensive discussions about researching violence and understanding the potential violence of academic praxis today.

The purpose of this book is to offer a broader lens to conflict research than the common focus on technical questions of methods and ethics. It aims to deconstruct what it means to 'do' research and what research 'does' in conflict-affected or violent contexts to all of those involved in such endeavours – the researcher and research participants and community members.

This short introductory chapter sets the stage for this volume, identifies the chasms in the field that the book seeks to narrow, outlines the key aims and guiding themes of the book, and provides an overview of its contents.

The frame

To interrupt means to break the continuity of a process, a line, a repeated action or an accepted way of thinking. In music, for example, an interruption takes place when a rhythmic or melodic pattern, with a seemingly perfect cadence, moves towards a finale but is then suddenly deflected when the anticipated ending is deferred or replaced by other chords. As a result, the song concludes with an unanticipated and unlikely harmony. Composers use interruption as a tool to illicit attention or give pause. It forces the listener to reconsider ways in which they processed and understood the logic of the chords, and to ponder what this unexpected occurrence, which ends the song with an ironically unfinished finish, really means.

This book aims to interrupt the discourse and praxis of fieldwork in conflict research.

While academic forums that elucidate questions about methods and rigour are important, researchers should not pretend that their experiences researching violence and with violent research can be squeezed into the ethical frameworks of Western universities or addressed through peer dialogues that promote academic indulgence and posturing more than honesty. This volume thus seeks to challenge and move beyond traditional academic-centric conversations about fieldwork often focused on how we can achieve rigour, gain access, collect data and get consent. Instead, it casts a critical lens on the researcher and the research process with the aim of drawing out the broader and more difficult implications of such efforts, and our place as researchers within them.

The overall tone of the volume is critical (and uncomfortably honest), focusing on understanding the self and the practice in the process of doing research in and on conflict and violence. Through both academic chapters and creative reflections, this volume seeks to interrogate as much as highlight the spaces and experiences that are overlooked in traditional methodology texts. We hope to present a more nuanced and grounded view of research that is unapologetic and unafraid to demystify and declare not just the messiness but also the discomfort and doubt that is inherent in the process of research in/on violence, in order to set forth a new set of sensibilities about approaching fieldwork in conflict settings. The book suggests that not only are more conversations needed, but that we must challenge the current discourses about the realities of conducting research in violent spaces. Indeed, it is time to have different conversations that better reflect the diversity and multiple identities of the people involved in conflict research.

All of the chapters in this book tell us something about the entanglements that emerge between research praxis and violence in conflict settings. In the first instance, contributors explore the experiences of researchers while they are researching violence in environments affected by violence. Violence, therefore, refers not only to the context but also to the subject. The nature of the conflict, types of violence, geographic locations, groups involved and conflict timelines vary throughout this edited volume. While several contributors focus on research taking place in situations of ongoing, armed, direct violence, others discuss (post)conflict fieldwork, where the legacy and memory of violence becomes an equally challenging phenomenon. The diverse group of authors in this book all reflect on what it means to do research in warscapes, but challenge the ways in which violence is conceptualised and understood in academic circles.

The second part of the frame suggests that research itself can produce violence. The vast majority of conflict researchers are aware of the 'Do No Harm' and 'Do Good' principles, which underlie ethical frameworks and conflict sensitivity training in most higher education institutions and policy organisations. In that sense, the idea that research could conceivably *do bad* is not a new suggestion. However, this book further complicates how we understand that violent possibility. The plucky and reflective insights of the scholars in this book allow us to gain a nuanced and complex understanding of the potential for violence and the numerous violent manifestations of research that take place with conflict settings, and the iterative and intimate processes through which this occurs.

The themes

The chapters and creative pieces in this book provide fascinating accounts of conducting conflict research. The power of narrative as a medium is well documented, yet it is also important to go beyond a collection of stories about field research. As such there are four key themes that run through the chapters in this volume: diversity, affect, entanglements and intersectionality.

Diversity. The scholars who have contributed to this volume come from a variety of academic disciplines and fields of practice, including international relations, law, military studies, development studies, psychology, sociology, anthropology, and drama and theatre. They are located both within academic institutions and practice-based organisations in Africa, North America and Western and Eastern Europe. Contributors reflect on research undertaken in Europe, Africa, the Near/Middle East and Central and Southeast Asia. The majority of chapters and vignettes draw on a wide range of established critical theories to frame these insights. Chapters from Christian and Broache attempt to push the boundaries of their traditionally conservative disciplines, military studies and law, respectively. Collectively the book interrogates a range of subjects in a variety of localities, and employs diverse methodological tools to speak to the various challenges of researching violence and doing violent research. In this sense, the book highlights the diversity of researchers who are engaged in conflict research and the numerous sites in which this take place.

Affect. The relationship between emotions and fieldwork in conflict- and violence-affected areas is a slowly growing area of scholarship, but has not yet received significant attention. The important 'ethical and emotional challenges the researcher is confronted with before, during and after the presence in the field' (Thomson et al, 2013, p 1) are generally seen as low priority. While peace and conflict studies acknowledge the presence and importance of emotions in conducting fieldwork, it rarely goes beyond emphasising the need for recognition. The current framing of emotion in the literature has meant that little exploration has been done on the 'productive nature of engaging with emotionality' in research (Baillie-Smith and Jenkins, 2012, p 77). Embracing the uncertainty and ambiguity that punctuates fieldwork as productive rather than destructive can lead to new revelations. Reflection on these emotions can help us better understand the actors, organisations and contexts within which we work, challenge hegemonic discourses, and enrich the knowledge that is produced in these spaces.

Thinking through emotionality, therefore, can contribute to both the theorisation of conflict and violence in a range of contexts and the research process itself. Feelings – hope, grief, dignity, pride, despair and love – can become data themselves as 'they often emerge from relational dynamics within particular spaces' (Lee-Treweek, 2000, pp 128–30). Indeed, according to Lecoq (2002, p 273), it is the exploration of one's state of mind during fieldwork that can allow us to understand 'the way fieldworkers, in being their own instruments, practice their research.' Such accounts are rare and yet hold great potential to be sites of discovery. Throughout this book we advocate for a recognition of the centrality of emotion to research, widening of the types of emotions that can be discussed and, perhaps most importantly, consideration of an alternative framing of emotion in the research process as a productive and powerful force. Ultimately the book suggests that emotion and the research process are inextricably linked in conflict settings.

Entanglements. The context of violence produces an intertwining of the researcher, research participants and the environment. As complicated and/or compromising relationships or situations, these entanglements are not only practical but also emotional. They take place in contexts that are characterised by fluidity, unpredictability and power imbalances. Researchers, participants and the environment do not just engage with or observe each other, but rather become entangled in situations that are marked by various degrees of vulnerability and power relationships. Conceptualising the research process through this lens allows us to see it as an intimate space where knowledge production is facilitated by, and often emerges through, these entanglements. The chapters in this book shed light on the intimacy of conflict research and the relationships that take place there. In doing so, they help us to better understand issues such as the long-term effects of research on those involved, the draw to return to the field that so many contributors to this book discuss, and dilemmas over the presentation of findings in academic spaces post-fieldwork.

Intersectionality. Who you are as a researcher influences the research process. Identities are not, of course, immutable or divisible. Therefore it is important to understand the ways in which the intersection of race, gender, sexuality, class and religious affiliation influences how the researcher understands him or herself, is perceived by others and navigates the research environment. It is ironic, then, that little has been said to date about the role of researcher identity in the research process. Even as the diversity of people doing conflict research increases, methodological conversations have not yet come to reflect the realities of all researchers. The patriarchy and eurocentrism of academia manifest themselves in the methods through which researchers are trained, the issues that are highlighted as being important, and the ways in which the researcher is conceptualised. Many researchers are unable to locate themselves in conversations that are too often framed around the experiences of white Western males or neatly constructed frameworks, which fail to elucidate on insider–outsider debates or the multiple sites of privilege and oppression that exist in our world. In response to these omissions, a specific section of the book is dedicated to identity. In addition, several contributors discuss the centrality of gender in particular, in their quest to better understand themselves and the research environment. This is, however, an area where much more remains to be said.

The book

This book joins a growing collection of publications that focus on carrying out research in locations affected by conflict and violence. A key purpose of this book, however, was to go beyond summarising experiences and challenges. Authors were required to cast a critical and reflective lens on themselves and the research process, and to interrogate what research does. The chapters highlight the interconnectedness of the researcher, research participants and the environment, and take as a departure point the position that objectivity, neutrality and distance are rarely possible – or desirable – for conflict researchers. Researchers were thus freed from the burden of having to mould their experiences into preconceived frameworks based on traditional academic research models. Authors were able to share honest and sometimes difficult reflections on topics that have received less attention in both academic and practice circles, such as the intensity and variety of emotions that occur in fieldwork, how often decisions are guided by uncertainty rather than knowledge, and the necessity of humility in the research. In addition, the editors invited contributors to write vignettes, placed at the end of every section, in order to offer researchers a different medium through which to share their experiences. This creative space allowed the sharing of ideas that are perhaps less powerfully communicated in formal academic writing, but are no less important.

The key themes identified earlier – diversity, affect, entanglements and intersectionality – cross cut the various chapters. The book is divided into five sections: violence, uncertainty, identity, technology and methods, which speaks to the specific focus of each chapter. Each section reflects the specific topical focus of the chapters included. Readers will find rich accounts of researcher experiences in a diverse range of conflict spaces.

Section I, entitled *Violence*, explores the ways in which violence – whether direct, structural or cultural – influences the subjectivities of the researcher and research participants. Through an exploration of her fieldwork in Rwanda, Rose Løvgren argues that interactions between researchers and participants in violent research settings can cause interviewees to experience harm through a loss of control in a setting where control means life or death. She further explores the ethical and political meanings of her own doubts and insecurities with regards to these encounters. The chapter highlights the ways in which insecurity in the aftermath of a research encounter structured the author's gendered and sexed positionality in the field.

Working within the disciplines of military studies and psychology, Patrick James Christian presents a different view from the field. Drawing on experiences in Somalia, Yemen, Darfur (Sudan), Niger, Colombia, Iraq and Afghanistan, he argues for a deeper appreciation of the importance of qualitative field research in studies involving violent communal conflict and for an understanding of how transference and countertransference work to influence data collection and analysis. A vignette in the form of a play by Laurel Borisenko finishes off the section. This creative reflection provides a poignant description of the tensions and complex questions that arise from conducting research in conflict settings that can put both the researcher and respondents in a place of insecurity and violence.

Section II, *Uncertainty*, highlights the doubt and ambiguity that often underlies the ways researchers and research participants navigate the research process, their relationships with each other and their own positionality. Paul Stubbs explores challenges inherent in activist research in conflict and (post)conflict environments, focusing on Croatia and the wider post-Yugoslav space. He reflects on over two decades of experience in the region and how his approach has changed over time as his understanding of the context and people have developed. Framed in terms of 'ambivalence', 'positionality' and 'reflexivity', the chapter emphasises the importance of multi-voiced ethnography, a conscious postcolonial positioning and a stance of deep humility as preconditions for activist research open up new arenas of possibility, struggle and change.

Corinna Jentzsch reflects on the unintended consequences of fieldwork in polarised societies, which may affect the autonomy of both the researcher and the researched. The chapter builds on fieldwork conducted in rural Mozambique. Through an exploration of the manifestations of power and myths of neutrality during fieldwork, she shows that conflict research needs to be understood as a form of intervention in local affairs.

The final part of this section comes from one of a few authors in the book located in the practice field. In his concise vignette, 'Packing for Kabul', Henri Myrttinen explores feelings of apprehension and fear linked to his visit to the Afghan capital, but also the privileges that come with being a male, Western researcher. The vignette also highlights the need for the non-governmental organisation (NGO) community to take the effects of conflict research more seriously.

The chapters in Section III, *Identity and power*, provide insight into the ways in which race, gender, ethnicity, sexuality and religion enter into the research process and knowledge production. The authors highlight how intersectionality, positionality and power interact to produce particular discourses, shape relationships and challenge the researchers' understanding of themselves. Sandra McEvoy examines her experiences as a lesbian researcher from the US conducting fieldwork in (post)conflict Northern Ireland. The chapter outlines the author's fears that her sexuality would hamper her ability to access Protestant paramilitary networks, and her concerns that her diasporic connection to communities in Northern Ireland might compromise scholarly analysis. The chapter demonstrates the potential of feminist research methodology and the role that identity can play in the process of meaning making.

Fathima Azmiya Badurdeen probes into an array of debates centred on the researcher's religious identity, and debates that arose while conducting research in Kenya on the radicalisation and recruitment of youth for the al-Shabaab terrorist organisation. She discusses the complexity of locating herself as either an insider or an outsider (or even being in-between) when doing intragroup research. She also unpacks the linkage between religion, identity and positionality in research related to violent radicalisation. Finally, a vignette by Althea-Maria Rivas highlights the silences around different subjectivities, specifically race and gender, in academic discussions about conflict research, and examines the complex and intense ways in which issues of identity emerge in the process of field research. The vignette also challenges the power structures within the academy, which comfortably reproduce and perhaps even depend on these silences.

An edited volume that suggests the need for new conversations on conflict research cannot ignore the growing role of technology in such endeavours. Section IV, *Technology and social media*, explores the potential for technology and social media to both produce knowledge and contribute to violence and insecurity in conflict research. Fabio Cristiano's chapter draws on the author's research on Palestinian cyberwar to suggest the need to expand our understanding of embodied violent experiences beyond the limits of corporeality. This broader conceptualisation of violence is reconciled with its implications for the study of war in cyberspace.

Through a detailed account of their research experiences in Nigeria and Congo-Brazzaville, Mieke de Goede and Inge Ligtvoet demonstrate that while information and communication technologies (ICTs) have become important tools for research, they also create new dilemmas for the researcher. Thus new subjective fields of insecurity emerge for the researcher that can produce emotional responses and inform decision-making processes, such as an inclination for deeper engagement or disengagement. The section ends with a vignette by Marijaana Jauhola, that provides a reflection on visual ethnographic and life-historical research in the city of Banda Aceh, Indonesia. It focuses on the gendered everyday of (post)conflict urban life and an ethnographic encounter with an elderly ex-combatant. The vignette suggests that ethnography, rather than providing a tool for the researcher to represent 'the other', can facilitate the co-creation of reality and its limits.

The book concludes with Section V, *Methods*. Brendan Ciarán Browne shares excerpts from his own research diary to suggest that diaries can be useful repositories for the practice of critical reflexive thinking. Based on research conducted in the West Bank, Occupied Palestinian Territories, the chapter suggests that in the absence of commonly available, familiar support networks, the research diary acts as a cathartic tool to provide the mental and emotional space to document the fears and anxieties of the individual researcher in a conflict setting. Michael Broache draws on his experiences interviewing members of armed groups involved in atrocities in the Democratic Republic of Congo to explore ethical dilemmas arising from research involving perpetrators of atrocities, specifically the possibility that such research may aid perpetrators and abet future atrocities.

In the final chapter of the book, Sinéad Walsh shows how empathetic research relations impacted the methodological design for a study of women's NGOs and peacebuilding in Armenia and Azerbaijan. Drawing on feminist methodologies, the chapter argues for reflexivity as a way of navigating relationships responsibly and of analysing and representing information ethically after one leaves the field. An ethnographic vignette by John Heathershaw concludes the book. This detailed narrative discusses his experiences conducting research in Kyrgyzstan, and shares reflections on the risks and limits of fieldwork and the privileges and partialities of the part-time political ethnographer.

What may be considered the chosen fields of enquiry throughout the volume are areas where violence has become the everyday lived reality for those who call them home. Our presence in them has been a luxury and it has been our desire to convey this privilege sensitively, through honest, empathetic reflections. This is not a collection written by scholars whose ultimate aim is to engage in an act of academic naval-gazing. While recognising that such indulgence is not unheard of in academic circles, such criticism, despite being commonplace, can also be lazy and poorly conceived (see Wacquant, 1989, 2011). At worst it can serve to marginalise those who choose to take stock of their capacity for managing, at times difficult research experiences as a means to normalise discussions that refuse to take on hard topics. Rather, through a shared desire and commitment to gaining a deeper understanding of the impact that researching violence can have on the researcher and others involved in the research process, and the violent potential of research itself, we have put together a volume that reminds those who seek to conduct research on or in violent settings to be acutely cognoscente of the self and surroundings.

This edited collection reflects a desire to shine light on the, at times, dark experiences, uncertainties and mistakes of those for whom researching violence or conducting violent research has become their contribution to better understanding the social world. It is our call to transform 'apathy into movement' (Jung, 1938) by encouraging the stimulation of a meaningful discourse that transcends disciplines on the potentially pernicious impact that such research can have on the researcher. The literature that exists on conducting fieldwork in violent contexts, or about violence, is swollen with an emphasis on methodological considerations around issues such as research design, overcoming institutional hurdles and managing ethical research governance. Our contribution to the field is not to downplay or call into question the importance of such a literature that has been, broadly speaking, useful in providing a checklist of 'dos and don'ts' for the erstwhile fieldworker (see, for example, as cited in this volume, Sluka, 1990; Kovats-Bernat, 2002; Sriram et al, 2009). Rather than muddying the waters by propagating yet further models of best practice, we have focused on complicating the myriad ways in which researching violence can impact the individual researcher, those we engage with in the process of doing research and the environment itself, conversations that have received far less by way of critical reflection.

References

Baillie Smith, M. and Jenkins, K. (2012) 'Special Issue editorial and introduction: Emotional methodologies: The emotional spaces of international development', *Space and Society*, vol 5, no 2, pp 75–7.

Jung, C.G. (1938) 'Psychological aspects of the mother archetype', *Collected Works*, vol 9, p 149.

Kovats-Bernat, C. (2002) 'Negotiating dangerous fields: Pragmatic strategies for fieldwork amid violence and terror', *American Anthropologist*, vol 104, no 1, pp 208–22.

Lecoq, B. (2002) 'Fieldwork ain't always fun – Public and hidden discourse on fieldwork', *History in Africa, A Journal of Method*, vol 29, pp 273–82.

Lee-Treweek, L. (2000) 'The insight of emotional danger', in G. Lee-Treweek and S. Linkogle (eds) *Danger in the field: Risk and ethics in social research*, London: Routledge, pp 114–28.

Sluka, J.A. (1990) 'Participant observation in violent social contexts', *Human Organisation*, vol 49, no 20, pp 114–26.

Sriram, C.L., King, J.C., Mertus, J.A., Martin-Ortega, O. and Herman, J. (eds) (2009) *Surviving field research: Working in violent and difficult situations*, Abingdon: Routledge.

Thomson, S., Ansoms, A. and Murison, J. (2013) 'Introduction', in S. Thomson, A. Ansoms and J. Murison (eds) *Emotional and ethical challenges for field research in Africa: The story behind the findings*, Basingstoke: Palgrave Macmillan, pp 1–11.

Wacquant, L.J. (1989) 'Towards a reflexive sociology: A workshop with Pierre Bourdieu', *Sociological Theory*, vol 7, no 1, pp 26–63.

Wacquant, L.J. (2011) 'Habitus as topic and tool: Reflections on becoming a prizefighter', *Qualitative Research in Psychology*, vol 8, no 1, pp 81–92.

Section I
Violence

1

Conducting unleashing interviews where control means life or death

Rose Løvgren

Introduction

On using interviews to research violence, Cynthia Enloe has argued that '[i]t takes feminist listening ... to *take on board* interviewees' contradictions, confusions and anxieties' (Enloe, 2011, p 142; emphasis added). This chapter sets out to explore the dynamics of 'taking on board' the emotions of interviewees in settings marked by violence. Within feminist international relations, ethnography and similar approaches to studying violence, it is often argued that engagement with the field should first and foremost be empathetic (see, for example, Dominguez, 2000; Fontana and Frey, 2005; Cowburn, 2013; Johnston, 2015). However, we spend less effort considering what processes empathetic engagement may open up within the field or what aftermath follows from it.

The interviews I have carried out as part of my research about violence in Rwanda have often engaged intimate and traumatic aspects of my respondents' lives, which, due to their political and social sensitivity, they had rarely delved into in conversations with others. When research interviews engage such issues, interviewees may come to experience the disclosure as prompting new understandings of past events (Birch and Miller, 2000; Hollway and Jefferson, 2000; Rubow, 2003; Holmes, 2013). Thus, 'this sort of qualitative interview setting can be seen to parallel the therapeutic encounter' (Birch and Miller, 2000, p 190). While there are differences in the aims and structure of research interviews and therapeutic encounters (Kvale, 1996; de Laine, 2000; Seidman, 2013), my interviewees often told me that the interview felt therapeutic simply because telling their story, even without therapeutic feedback from my side, gave them an outlet in a situation where such outlets are few. Relief, however, was often followed by anxiety about the consequences of having shared too much information. Feeling that he had exposed himself, an interviewee subsequently called my assistant and asked accusingly: "What kind of girl did you bring into my office?"

In discussing such mixed reactions to the research interview, I present two arguments, one concerning the ethical aspects of researching violence, and another wherein I argue that the emotional ambivalence my research encountered speaks to an analytical point about political subjectivity and violence. That is, the violence my research engages worked to make a number of my respondents choose a strategy I here term 'subduing their sense of self' in order to survive it. By subduing their sense of self, I refer to what my respondents described as a choice of obeying the orders they were given, as well as 'accepting'[1] their violent conditions by controlling their emotional responses of, for example, humiliation, sorrow or anger. The research interview gave them an opportunity to use me as an audience to re-affirm their sense of self, but not without again causing anxiety about how this self-affirmation could threaten their survival. Self-affirmation, moreover, was often accompanied by an expressed desire for my response to the narrative presented. With a focus on the unleashing aspects of interviews about violence, I argue that my gendered and sexed positionality among my respondents was structured, not only by my embodied presence, but also by the emotional connection experienced by some of my interviewees in our interviews.

Background

My original research focus in Rwanda was the rehabilitation centre for 'delinquent' (MYICT, 2012) young men placed on Iwawa Island in Lake Kivu, where around 2,000 men at a time have been regularly detained for periods of one to three years since early 2010. Delinquency refers, for example, to drug and alcohol abuse, street vending and street loitering. Between 2013 and 2014 I did three months of research about the centre, which was mainly based on semi-structured interviews with men who had graduated from Iwawa. The centre is run by military authorities and access is limited due, in part, to their efforts to keep its activities minimally exposed. Since 2013, I have spent close to three years living and working in Rwanda, and from 2015–16, I attempted to follow up on my research concerning Iwawa. In April 2016, after having tried for 18 months to get a renewed research permit, I was, instead, deported from Rwanda with reference to how my application was 'illegal'. Violence thus features in my research in a number of ways. Rehabilitation includes psychotherapy, civic education and vocational skills training, but was, in my interviews, also commonly portrayed as a violent process. Beatings, ceremonial humiliations and a demanding physical military regiment, on an island with limited nutrition and healthcare facilities, are among the factors that threaten and cost the lives of many young men on Iwawa. In its military hierarchical organisation, trainees are, moreover, trained in inflicting violence on those below them in the chain of command.

More broadly, violence is heavily employed in the control of information in Rwanda. As a foreign national, I experienced this during my deportation, where the possibility of violence was repeatedly implied. Being deported, however, is a mild fate compared to the many Rwandan journalists, researchers, artists and other members of the public who have suffered long prison sentences, intimidation and even death by the hand of different representatives of the government for offences as small as encouraging a delay in the implementation of government policy (Purdeková, 2011; Straus and Waldorf, 2011; Chakravarty, 2012; Sundaram, 2015).

In this way, control of information in Rwanda is clearly linked to survival. Existing literature on the therapeutic dimensions to qualitative interviews has engaged the ethical concern that they may work to 'unleash' (Birch and Miller, 2000, p 195) and change the interviewees' emotional state and sense of self in a way that researchers do not necessarily have the resources to handle (see also de Laine, 2000; Connolly and Reilly, 2007; Holmes, 2013; Seidman, 2013). Arguably, there is even more at stake when the research interview works to unleash information in a violent setting, where this may lead to very concrete and tangible consequences such as arrest, physical punishments and death. In this chapter, I discuss the additional ethical challenge this poses for researchers of violence, as well as my ethical concerns about interviews that unleash emotional reactions in a context where controlling one's emotions has often been explained to me as a question of life or death.

In 2013–14, I worked with a research assistant who acted as my interpreter during most of the interviews. At the time, I spoke little Kinyarwanda, which is the national language of Rwanda, and for around 90 per cent of the country's population the only language they speak (Tollefson, 2013). In some places we used cooperatives for Iwawa graduates in order to get in touch with them, while in others we simply approached the groups of young men hanging out on the streets and asked them if they knew any Iwawa graduates who might be willing to talk to us. Using these tactics we found 50 graduates, and some of their relatives, living inside or in the areas near three of

Rwanda's larger cities. Some interviews took place in people's homes, but often our respondents had no stable place to live, and we instead sat in bars or other places in the cities where we could have the best possible degree of seclusion. Rehabilitation is both politically, socially and personally a sensitive subject, so whenever we were hanging out in public spaces, we never broached the subject. This framing of the interview situation, I believe, played a part in making the interviews work like small pockets where sensitive issues were shared with great intensity, because of their delimitation in time and space.

Ambivalence of relief and threat

A Rwandan friend of mine once told me that Rwandans keep their secrets locked up so tightly and for so long that when they do talk about them it is like they are vomiting. In 2013, I conducted an interview with a mother of one of the graduates from Iwawa, whom I here call Josephine,[2] in her house. My assistant explained to Josephine in Kinyarwanda what the interview was going to be about, its purpose, how long it would take, and assured her that she could stop the interview when she wanted to move on to other things. From her son's wife, we had previously been told that Josephine was responsible for sending her son to Iwawa, and she probably knew this since she had seen us meet and talk to her. Our presence in her compound and the topic of the interview seemed to constitute an accusation in itself for Josephine, and I perceived her as being very defensive from the outset of our meeting. In her narrative, she had been fighting with her son about a financial issue, and the fight had escalated to the point where she had him arrested by the local police force. It is not uncommon to involve the police in domestic disputes in Rwanda (see also Kagaba, 2016), and Josephine is by no means the only parent among my respondents who caused her son to go to Iwawa.

Josephine had lost control of the process, however, when the police decided not to release her son, again, at her request, but to send him to Iwawa. She explained that she had felt an enormous amount of guilt and sorrow about her involvement. She had at first anguished about where her son was sent, as she had not been informed about it. When she learned that he was on Iwawa, she had spent many sleepless nights fearing for his life, she told us. She spoke quickly and urgently, giving me the impression that she was trying to relieve herself of the story as fast as possible. She sat with her side to me and was mostly explaining things to my assistant. When she turned and faced me for the first time since we sat down, it was to ask me, "Isn't it enough now?"

Before I could respond to the question she immediately continued talking, adding other perspectives to what she had just said. Feeling dumbfounded, curious and wanting to give her space to talk about the issues that were spilling out of her, I said nothing and waited for her to pause. I then asked what was thought to be an innocent question to understand the context of what she was talking about. She started talking again, including many details in her story, especially about her emotional state. Then she turned to me again in the same way, asking me exhaustedly if it was not enough now, and again she continued straight into more aspects of the story without waiting for me to answer.

A few months after, I was discussing the interview with a colleague who, in response to Josephine's plea, jokingly accused me of being too ruthless to release her. At the time, I had felt very passive, and receptive, yet also aware that she was obviously communicating to me that I was hurting her in some way, and unsure of what my role was in producing the ambivalent emotions that arose as we talked. At the beginning of the interview, I felt angry with her, having heard only her son's wife's version of how he had ended up at Iwawa. Not a hot, fiery anger, but a general sense of frustration over the many cases of parental involvement in a process that costs young men their lives. This anger dispersed, however, almost immediately after Josephine began to talk. She had such an unmediated expression of regret, shame and pain, and I felt intense sympathy for her. When I did not stand up to end the interview, although she almost begged me to stop, it was because I had the impression that she also wanted space and time to finish her story.

Undoubtedly, part of what produced the ambivalent emotions in our interview was the unequal power dynamic between us. As discussed elsewhere, interviews about an interviewee's wrongdoing may easily come to resemble religious or criminal confessions (Kvale, 2006; Tanggaard, 2008; MacLean, 2013). Foucault (1990) has argued against what he terms a modern tendency to view confessional tales as liberating conveyors of truth. He explains that the inequality of the confessional relation itself produces, rather than simply communicates, the content of the narrative. The context of power inequality matters, and while objections during interviews can be interpreted as a way for the interviewee to challenge or draw attention to the authority of the researcher (Tanggaard, 2008; Watson, 2009), I here want to explore another aspect of how power inequality has played out in my interviews.

Unleashing interviews can be experienced as strongly relieving when the topic is violence and one's own role in producing it. For those who live in a setting marked by violence, however, there is something scary about the loss of control this process entails. Rwandans have often been described as a people who value composure and control of emotional expressions – as 'stoical citizens' (Gakuba, 2016; see also Rusagara et al, 2009; Uwanziga, 2015). More generally, valuing composure relates to the form of violence surrounded by and productive of secrecy. Knowledge and communication about the violence in Iwawa rehabilitation, I argue, function as 'public secrets' (Bellman, 1984, p 3) – the content is widely known, but still treated as explosive if revealed. Such secrets function not solely by being kept, but by being open to exposure (Bellman, 1984; Taussig, 1999; Højbjerg, 2003). It is the lingering possibility of sharing sensitive information that takes part in making it sensitive. As I experienced in my interview with Josephine, she felt a sense of relief in, on the one hand, having a stranger listen to a story that she could not easily share with those around her (see also Gammeltoft, 2003; Simmel, 2010), while on the other, I believe she felt exposed and that she was not comfortable being that exposed with me.

On the ethics of handling sensitive information produced by research interviews that resemble therapeutic conversations, Marlene de Laine writes: 'The problem could then become "is one to use the information or forget it altogether?"' (de Laine, 2000, p 118). There is, however, an additional ethical aspect to this kind of research interview, namely, whether the information is used or not, it may be experienced as threatening for interviewees to have shared it. In interviews with Iwawa graduates, they have at times changed their mind after sharing sensitive information with me:

Rose: 'You told me you experienced some of the other trainees commit suicide?'

Rafiki: 'Actually no.... I did not.... Some swam out in the lake in order to commit suicide, but they changed their minds and came back.'

Rafiki's retraction does not create the dilemma described by de Laine as I do not need to quote him for something he did not mean to say, or that I simply misunderstood. My claim that suicides happen on Iwawa is based on stories from many other Iwawa graduates, who did not express regret or retract their statements, but on the contrary, emphasised that they wanted me to do something with the information by bringing it before a relevant audience.

What concerns me more is the unsettled emotional situation in which I left Josephine, Rafiki and those of other interviewees who changed their minds. As soon as I experienced interviewees regretting what they just told me, I would change the subject and go into less controversial themes. My assistant, too, was very sensitive to changes in the interview atmosphere, and eager to partake in steering the conversation to where he felt that our interviewee was more at ease. We would end interviews by giving interviewees time to ask me questions, correcting something they said, and expanding on or emphasising something they told us. These practical measures, however, do not solve the problem of mistrust and anxiety about my respondents' loss of control over information. In this way, my function of sometimes being considered a stranger to whom much may be divulged also made me an object of suspicion in the aftermath of an interview that unleashed more than my interviewee might have planned. Moreover, changes of mind, during or in the aftermath of interviews, also relate to the violence of the research act. As violence is reflected in my participant observations and interviews, it works to make my respondents subdue their sense of self as a strategy for surviving it. The research encounter disturbs this tactic for survival, and the emotional ambivalence of relief and threat occurring in my interviews may be interpreted as a reaction to this disturbance.

Using the research interview to regain a sense of self

In Homer's *Odyssey*, the main character Odysseus passes by the island of Polymorphous, the Cyclops. Knowing that he will only survive his stay on the island by denying his own name, Odysseus introduces himself to Polymorphous as Udeis, meaning 'no one' in Ancient Greek (Homer, 2005). Using this tactic, he paradoxically saves his life by negating himself. In Theodor Adorno and Max Horkheimer's interpretation: 'the subject Odysseus denies his own identity, which makes him a subject, and keeps himself alive by imitating the amorphous.... But his self-assertion – as in all epics, as in civilization in general – is self-denial' (Horkheimer and Adorno, 2001, pp 67–8).

On Iwawa, my respondents have often described using a strategy for survival that shares this aspect of hiding away their sense of self. That is, they chose to accept to carry out all orders, to accept all kinds of humiliating ceremonial punishments, and especially to control their emotional response to these situations in what they describe as deliberate manoeuvres to survive. In an interview with Musa, he first told me that he had tried hard to be allowed a trial to defend himself against the accusations that sent him to Iwawa. Since Iwawa is a place for rehabilitation and not a prison, however, this was not possible.

Musa went to Iwawa convinced of his own innocence and with a strong feeling of being wronged. While on Iwawa, however, he told me that he could not allow himself to indulge in such considerations.

The topic came up as we were discussing nutrition at Iwawa. Hearing countless stories of starvation on the island, I had been surprised when I attended a graduation ceremony on the island and saw a number of obviously well-fed men weight lifting to entertain us guests. Musa argued that the difference between starving and being able to grow muscles related to controlling one's mindset. The trainees who starved on Iwawa, he said, "don't accept, and when you don't accept the life you are living, you grow thin. If you are there [on Iwawa] and when you accept the life you are living, you live in peace." In this way, acceptance as a strategy for survival is explained both as willingness to comply with orders and as placing yourself in a state of mind where you do not allow yourself to fully feel your emotional response to a given situation.

Having used a strategy of self-denial to survive on the Cyclops's island, Odysseus nevertheless brings himself and his crew into a lot of danger by calling out his real name to Polymorphous as they are leaving the island. This act of self-affirmation brings on him the curse that causes his journey home to last more than 10 years. Here again, a parallel may be drawn between Odysseus's self-affirmation and that undertaken by some of my interviewees. Violence on Iwawa causes many men to subdue their sense of self, and the interview situation is an opportunity to reaffirm it. In itself, retelling the course of events means reclaiming a story as one's own. In the retelling, an interviewee is no longer passive, no longer the receiver of orders, but someone who produces order through the narrative. As argued by Jackson:

> ... storytelling reworks and remodels subject-object relations in ways that subtly alter the balance between actor and acted upon, thus allowing us to feel that we actively participate in a world that for a moment seemed to discount, demean and disempower us. (Jackson, 2002, p 16)

When my respondents, through our interviews, unleash their sense of self by producing a narrative that frames them as active rather than passive, they are nonetheless often still in a dangerous situation. In a manner similar to Odysseus, they may then be understood to affirm their sense of self before having left the liminal and life-threatening zone. Some of my respondents had moved on after graduation to better situations, but the majority of them were back on the streets, in situations similar to what had got them arrested in the first place.

Researching violence, we are often engaging people who are continuously in very insecure situations. When people use some degree of self-denial to survive, the research interview may be experienced both as relieving and threatening. In both cases, it may create intense desires for those in power positions during the process, such as the researcher, to react and take an active part in forming the interviewee's self-affirmation. That is, while I get the impression that my interviewees at times share with me so intensely because of my status as a stranger or 'non-person' (Gammeltoft, 2003, p 277; author's translation) in their daily lives, it is, in the interview situation, highly significant that I *am* a person with personal reactions to their narratives. Especially in a context marked by secrecy where my assistant and/or I may be the only audience to the story, I felt a claim on my reaction and judgement from my interviewee.

In an interview with Daniel, he told me that he had accepted all orders and that he had often been responsible for beating up the trainees below him in the Iwawa hierarchy. At the same time, he also kept coming back to the ways he had influenced these practices. Following up on his characterisation of violence in the Iwawa hierarchy, he added:

> 'But you see, I am some sort of a humanitarian, eh? I have some love for humanity, and I did many things to, to, to change the procedures there.'

The desire to be understood and the desire for me to take an active part in affirming my respondents' sense of self, I argue, animated much of how my gendered and sexed positionality was established in the field.

Desire and love in the unleashing interview

Discussions of gendered and sexed positionality in research often centre on the threat posed to female researchers by expressions of desire in the field (see, for example, Nordstrom and Robben, 1995; Pollard, 2009; Kloß, 2016). While these discussions are highly important, there is often more being communicated in the expressions of desire that occur during research. My relation with one of my respondents illustrates how the emotional connection felt during an unleashing interview framed how he responded to my gendered and sexed positionality.

Daniel, who was very eager to use our interviews to establish a narrative of his rehabilitation process that presented him as having actively changed how violence was performed on Iwawa, was also eager for me to understand him. He would at times get very frustrated and impatient with my clarifying questions:

Rose: 'Did they explain to you why you were being arrested?'
Daniel: 'No! They do … haha…. I don't know, I don't know, I don't know, how can I explain it to you?'

Daniel's 'no' came with such urgency I can hardly do justice to it on paper. Our transcribed interviews are full of pleas for me to understand him, to understand how he suffered, and to understand how he ended up committing the violence he committed; more than anything, for me to understand what kind of person he is – that he is, at his core, a humanitarian. After we finished our second interview, he explained to me that we had to meet again. He had a lot more stories that I should hear in order for me to understand Rwandan politics. He also wanted to see me again, he told me, because he loved me and thought we should be together.

I was again surprised at his strong emotional reaction to the interviews, as I had been with Josephine's strong reaction. I had felt passive and receptive and thought that there was little basis for Daniel to declare that he understood what kind of person I was and that we would both be better off together. I told him that I was in a relationship and that I did not want us to be together. When we later talked, and Daniel was giving me the impression that he was going to wait until I was single and we could be together, I continued to tell him that even if I should become single we would not be together, because I was not in love with him. At that time, I remember him telling me something like: "You have just decided that you hate me, and I don't stand a chance."

Daniel and I spoke with each other in English, and many Rwandans translate the Kinyarwanda word *kwanga* with both 'to refuse' and 'to hate'. I specified to Daniel that I did refuse to be his girlfriend, but that when he used the English word 'hate', it carried more of the connotation of *kuzira* – to loath, to hate, to consider abominable – which I did not at all. In the situation it felt important to say, to take his fear that I might hate him seriously, in light of the many exposing stories he had shared about his own violent actions. Therefore, the relation between us filled me with doubt and uncertainty about what my role was in it and how I should proceed. Our dynamic never felt threatening to me and we have never been in a situation where I feared that he would not respect my personal boundaries. Daniel has commented once on the sexual aspect of his attraction (telling me that white and brown chocolate is a delicious combination), but his emphasis has mostly been on our emotional connection. Thus, what I have struggled with is how to react to his expressed need for emotional acknowledgement. Rethinking my confusion now, about a year after Daniel accused me of hating him, I think first, that Daniel's declaration of love also had something to do with the unleashing aspects of our interviews. Second, I question whether I was really all that passive, and recognise that my fascination with him as a storyteller must have come across as its own kind of desire.

Thinking about qualitative interviews as unleashing, I venture the interpretation that part of what happened in our research encounter was that it became an opportunity for Daniel to talk about violence that impacted him deeply, and to re-make and re-present his own role in this violence. Subduing his sense of self with regards to his actions on Iwawa for more than a year and then re-affirming it in front of me, I propose, made Daniel want me to affirm it too. Love can be seen as a clear way of saying yes to and affirming another person (see also Sternberg and Weis, 2006). In this view, his declarations of love have something in common with the phone call asking, "What kind of girl did you bring into my office?" That is, in both of these situations, our research encounter left my respondents feeling vulnerable, and they both reached out to me to keep track of how I received their information and to ask what aftermath would follow from it. Framed in this way, desire may also be related to the power inequality of the interview situation. The confessional relation that easily arises in interviews about violence plays a part in producing a desire for being absolved and affirmed.

As for my role in our relationship, I have always been intensely interested in what Daniel had to say. He is a reflective person who is generous with words, analytically perceptive, and has a way of narrating that is often poetic and beautiful. As discussed elsewhere, ethnographic field research involves making relations, which again produces emotional investment in the field (Dominguez, 2000; de Pina-Cabral, 2013; Besteman, 2015). Unleashing interviews work as an involvement both in very intimate aspects of the emotional lives of interviewees and in their making of order and self-affirmation (Birch and Miller, 2000; Rubow, 2003). I felt care and concern for Daniel while listening to his stories, and felt at the time that I did little to provoke what seemed like grand declarations of love; I have since then come to think about how intensely my attention was directed towards him.

In her discussion of emotional investment during field research, Catherine Besteman develops a concept she terms 'ethnographic love', comprising of 'an openness to self-transformation and to the changes in intersubjectivity that happen over time. It insists on moral reflexivity, a critical moral awareness that shapes and defines the ethnographic encounter' (Besteman, 2015, p 33). What does it mean to have a critical moral awareness in the unleashing interview? For one thing, it means considering how love and empathy may open up processes experienced as deeply intrusive and disturbing by interviewees. As I have sought to show in this chapter, the very relief experienced by my interviewees as a response to my attempts at showing them acknowledgement, and giving space for them to talk openly about traumatising experiences, carries a threat with it.

The intensity of Daniel's declaration of love, and his repeated emphasis on how important it was that I understood him correctly and loved his true character, suggests to me that these emotions were also intertwined with strong feelings of anxiety about the aftermath of unleashing interviews that left him feeling exposed and vulnerable. This is not to say that Daniel's emotions can be reduced to an issue resembling what psychologists describe as 'erotic transference' (Chiesa, 1999, p 125) – when patients fall in love with their therapist. What I have described here is simply my interpretation of one part of the story. My reason for emphasising this part is that it speaks to a larger story; a story about how unleashing research encounters take part in producing desire in the field, and about how the intensity with which desire is expressed may be related to feelings of guilt, threat and uncertainty in the aftermath of research engagement.

Conclusion

More than providing answers about how to proceed in interviews about violence, I have in this chapter raised my doubts and uncertainties in conducting them. Such doubts and uncertainties in the field, I argue, are not only a result of my being a young researcher working outside of the context I was born in, but speak to an aspect of what violence does. Analysing interviews with a focus on their unleashing effects, I have made an argument in favour of additional ethical consideration and concerning political subjectivity and violence. When I argue in favour of additional ethical consideration, I do not offer a list of dos and don'ts that will guide future researchers through interviews about violence without causing harm in the field. Instead, I offer the concerns

I have raised here as inspiration for the continuous reflective process that is ethical navigation in the field (see also Fujii, 2012).

The situations and experiences that caused my ethical concern moreover inform my argument about political subjectivity and violence. My respondents' ambivalent emotional expressions of relief and threat when talking openly about violence, I have argued, relates to how violence in many cases makes subjects subdue their sense of self as a survival strategy. In an interview that unleashes information, emotions and the interviewee's sense of self, relief may be understood as related to self-affirmation. But this very relief carries threat within it in contexts where self-preservation is linked with a form of self-denial.

Reversely, framing political subjectivity in this way informs my ethical concern about the aftermath of unleashing interviews and unleashing research encounters in general. In other words, I have learned more about what is at stake ethically in my research encounters in Rwanda by understanding more about political subjectivity in this setting so thoroughly permeated by violence. These ethical and analytical considerations motivated my argument about desire in the field. The desire directed at me as a woman in the field related not only to my embodied positionality, but also to the role I played as the interviewer in my interviewee's self-affirmation and to the power inequality of the research encounter.

These are examples of how our empathetic engagements with the field are not always harmless. Enloe's concept of 'taking on board' the emotions of interviewees, mentioned at the beginning of this chapter, may therefore be guided by the critical moral awareness championed by Besteman in her account of 'ethnographic love'. Specifically, conducting unleashing interviews requires moral awareness about the possible experience of harm and intrusion caused by empathetic engagement through loss of control in a violent setting where control means life or death.

Notes

[1] The Rwandan verb *kwihangana*, which was the word used most often by my respondents, may be translated as 'to bear with', 'to accept' and/or 'to be patient'.

[2] I have changed the names of all my respondents, and in what follows I refer to them by their pseudonyms.

References

Bellman, B.L. (1984) *The language of secrecy: Symbols and metaphors in Poro ritual*, New Brunswick, NJ: Rutgers University Press.

Besteman, C. (2015) 'On ethnographic love', in R. Sanjek (ed) *Mutuality: Anthropology's changing terms of engagement*, Philadelphia, PA: University of Pennsylvania Press, pp 259–84.

Birch, M. and Miller, T. (2000) 'Inviting intimacy: The interview as therapeutic opportunity', *International Journal of Social Research Methodology*, vol 3, no 3, pp 189–202.

Chakravarty, A. (2012) '"Partially trusting" field relationships: Opportunities and constraints of fieldwork in Rwanda's postconflict setting', *Field Methods,* vol 24, no 3, pp 251–71.

Chiesa, M. (1999) 'Erotic transference in clinical practice', in D. Mann (ed) *Erotic transference and countertransference: Clinical practice in psychotherapy*, New York: Routledge, pp 115–25.

Connolly, K. and Reilly, R. C. (2007) 'Emergent issues when researching trauma: A confessional tale', *Qualitative Inquiry*, vol 13, no 4, pp 522–40.

Cowburn, M. (2013) 'Men researching violent men: Epistemologies, ethics and emotions in qualitative research', in B. Pini and B. Pease (eds) *Men, masculinities and methodologies*, London: Palgrave Macmillan, pp 183–96.

de Laine, M. (2000) *Fieldwork, participation and practice: Ethics and dilemmas in qualitative research*, Thousand Oaks, CA: Sage Publications.

de Pina-Cabral, J. (2013) 'The two faces of mutuality: Contemporary themes in anthropology', *Anthropological Quarterly*, vol 86, no 1, pp 687–710.

Dominguez, V.R. (2000) 'For a politics of love and rescue', *Cultural Anthropology*, vol 15, no 3, pp 361–93.

Enloe, C. (2011) 'When feminists explore masculinities in IR. An engagement by Cynthia Enloe', in J.A. Tickner and L. Sjoberg (eds) *Feminism and international relations: Conversations about the past, present, and future*, New York: Routledge, pp 141–5.

Fontana, A. and Frey, J. (2005) 'The interview. From neutral stance to political involvement', in N.K. Denzin and Y.S. Lincoln (eds) *The Sage handbook of qualitative research* (3rd edn), Thousand Oaks, CA: Sage Publications, pp 695–728.

Foucault, M. (1990) *The history of sexuality: Volume 1: An introduction* (4th edn), Harmondsworth: Penguin Books.

Fujii, L.A. (2012) 'Research ethics 101: Dilemmas and responsibilities', *Political Science & Politics*, vol 45, no 4, pp 717–23.

Gakuba, J.D. (2016) 'Our destiny: Ubutore will transform Rwanda forever', *New Times*, 14 January (www.newtimes.co.rw/section/article/2016-01-14/196092/).

Gammeltoft, T. (2003) 'Intimiteten: Forholdet til den anden', in K. Hastrup (ed) *Ind i verden: En grundbog i antropologisk metode*, Copenhagen: Hans Reitzel, pp 273–96.

Højbjerg, C. (2003) 'Hemmeligheden: Det etiske dilemma', in K. Hastrup (ed) *Ind i verden: En grundbog i antropologisk metode*, Copenhagen: Hans Reitzel, pp 297–324.

Hollway, W. and Jefferson, T. (2000) *Doing qualitative research differently: Free association, narrative and the interview method*, Thousand Oaks, CA: Sage Publications.

Holmes, J. (2013) 'A comparison of clinical psychoanalysis and research interviews', *Human Relations*, vol 66, no 9, pp 1183–99.

Homer (2005) *The Odyssey* (1st Pocket Books edn Enriched Classic) (translated by A. Gafton, G. Most and J. Zetzel), New York: Pocket Books.

Horkheimer, M. and Adorno, T.W. (2001) *Dialectic of enlightenment*, New York: Continuum.

Jackson, M. (2002) *The politics of storytelling: Violence, transgression, and intersubjectivity*, Copenhagen: Museum Tusculanum Press.

Johnston, M.S. (2015) 'Men can change: Transformation, agency, ethics and closure during critical dialogue in interviews', *Qualitative Research*, vol 16, no 2, pp 131–50.

Kagaba, M. (2016) 'Understanding gender equality in Rwanda. The experiences of people living in rural communities', PhD, Gothenburg, Sweden: University of Gothenburg.

Kloß, S.T. (2016) 'Sexual(ized) harassment and ethnographic fieldwork: A silenced aspect of social research', *Ethnography*, pp 1–19.

Kvale, S. (1996) *Interviews: An introduction to qualitative research interviewing*, Thousand Oaks, CA: Sage Publications.

Kvale, S. (2006) 'Dominance through interviews and dialogues', *Qualitative Inquiry*, vol 12, no 3, pp 480–500.

MacLean, L.M. (2013) 'The power of the interviewer', in L. Mosley (ed) *Interview research in political science*, Ithaca, NY: Cornell University Press, pp 67–83.

MYICT (Ministry of Youth and ICT) (2012) 'IRVSDC – Iwawa Rehabilitation Centre' (www.myict.gov.rw/agencies/irvsdc-iwawa-rehabilitation-centre/).

Nordstrom, C. and Robben, A.C.G.M. (eds) (1995) *Fieldwork under fire: Contemporary studies of violence and survival*, Berkeley, CA: University of California Press.

Pollard, A. (2009) 'Field of screams: Difficulty and ethnographic fieldwork', Anthropology Matters, vol 11, no 2.

Purdeková, A. (2011) '"Even if I am not here, there are so many eyes": Surveillance and state reach in Rwanda', The Journal of Modern African Studies, vol 49, no 3, pp 475–97.

Rubow, C. (2003) 'Samtalen: Interviewet som deltagerobservation', in K. Hastrup (ed) Ind i verden: En grundbog i antropologisk metode, Copenhagen: Hans Reitzel, pp 227–46.

Rusagara, F.K., Mwaura, G. and Nyirimanzi, G. (2009) Resilience of a nation: A history of the military in Rwanda, Kigali: Fountain Publishers Rwanda.

Seidman, I. (2013) Interviewing as qualitative research: A guide for researchers in education and the social sciences (4th edn), New York: Teachers College Press.

Simmel, G. (2010) On individuality and social forms: Selected writings (edited by D.N. Levine), Chicago, IL: University of Chicago Press.

Sternberg, R.J. and Weis, K. (eds) (2006) The new psychology of love, New Haven, CT: Yale University Press.

Straus, S. and Waldorf, L. (eds) (2011) Remaking Rwanda state building and human rights after mass violence, Madison, WI: The University of Wisconsin Press.

Sundaram, A. (2015) Bad news: Last journalists in a dictatorship, New York: Doubleday.

Tanggaard, L. (2008) 'Objections in research interviewing', International Journal of Qualitative Methods, vol 7, no 3, pp 15–29.

Taussig, M.T. (1999) Defacement: Public secrecy and the labor of the negative, Stanford, CA: Stanford University Press.

Tollefson, J.W. (ed) (2013) Language policies in education: Critical issues (2nd edn), New York: Routledge.

Uwanziga, J.N. (2015) Manners in Rwanda: Basic knowledge on Rwandan culture, customs, and Kinyarwanda language, Portland, OR: Inkwater Press.

Watson, C. (2009) 'The "impossible vanity": Uses and abuses of empathy in qualitative inquiry', Qualitative Research, vol 9, no 1, pp 105–17.

2

Qualitative research in the shadow of violent conflict

Patrick James Christian

Introduction

> He who learns must suffer. (Aeschylus Agamemnon, *The Oresteia*, 458 BCE)

This chapter explores the physical, psychological and emotional challenges of qualitative research into the underlying drivers of violent communal conflict and covert inhibitors of successful resolution. Such research settings are usually found in the under-governed spaces of failed or failing states, and involve what Hobbs (2006, p 57) calls 'dangerous fieldwork'. The qualitative nature of these drivers of conflict and inhibitors to resolution requires the field researcher's immediate presence within the conflict zone, as the phenomenological inquiries and specific contexts of trauma and loss cannot be subcontracted to incidentally present observers, or victim-perpetrator participants to the conflict. The ongoing intra-state conflicts in Syria-Iraq, Libya, Yemen, Sudan, Somalia, Mali-Niger and Nigeria, for instance, illustrate the need for increasing levels of qualitative investigative research into these conflict drivers and resolution inhibitors. Over the past 15 years I have worked in most of these conflict zones as a uniformed military officer and researcher tasked with analysing and ultimately resolving intractable communal violence.

My first field experience researching genocidal communal violence was at the destroyed village of Ambarou in West Darfur, Sudan, in the summer of 2004. The village had reportedly come under attack, and my African Union ceasefire mediation team was tasked with assessing the report and mediating with the conflict parties. From our base in the abandoned town of Tine, in the South Libyan desert, we drove across open terrain for a day, only to find the village in smouldering ruins (see *Special Warfare*, 2006). As I walked among the burned-out houses and partial human remains, I felt an indescribable chill on my face and neck, and realised I was no longer perspiring from the heat. I felt as if I had become unconnected to everything and everyone around me. When I looked at my African Union colleagues, their faces were blank, eyes staring at the carnage surrounding us.

At one point, I came across a small figure charred in ashes with his or her hands still manacled to a wooden post. The dull stainless steel of the old-fashioned handcuffs still glittered in the bright sun, and whispered to us of the unspeakable things that our fellow humans had only recently been doing in the secrecy of the desert. I could not begin to imagine the sheer suffering that accompanied the death of that child and how I would have borne it at such a young age. We were well beyond the possibilities for restorative justice for either the victims or the perpetrators. It seemed as if we were just witnesses in a play where our humanity, love and compassion were as out of place as our ignorance.

In 25 years of experience as a government officer deploying to zones of communal conflict, I have found that most of our interventionist academic preparation had been of little value. First, we failed to account for differences in psychological organisation, sociological construction, emotional conjugation and cognitive imprinting based on geography, geology, climate or historical narrative (Stein, 1984). Second, encouraged by political science and international relations theory, we found ourselves reducing entire large group identities to the status of individual actors operating with independent agency. Thereafter, we were easily able to assign motive and intent in violent conflict to rational utilitarian goals of the sort elucidated by political scientists operating from distant frames of alien reference.

On arriving in the conflict zones, however, we learned that what really matters are the psychosocial constructions of trauma, terror, starvation, alienation, shame, rage, hopelessness and grief as experienced by the surviving population. We learn that compassion is not sympathy, but rather the deeply emotional sharing of physical and psychological pain that we are often unprepared, or even unwilling, to participate in (Burton, 1987). We find that human dignity cannot survive in the massive refugee camps where the movement of dysentery-laden bowels is equally as public and victimising as one's inability to save beloved children from starvation, thirst or hopelessness. Most importantly, we found that the quantitative research that drove our plans and programming were based on the logic of rational actor theories of political science and international relations in complete defiance of the realities we now faced in these open conflict zones.

The emotional and cognitive stability of the field researcher in violent conflict zones is of increased importance. Institutional review boards invariably question the would-be researcher's capacity to endure exposure to suffering and violence. Equally important is the research informants' emotional, cognitive and psychological coherence (or lack thereof) and related capacity to articulate their lived experience even as they are unable to disengage from the conflict that is killing them. These complex issues can destabilise the research activity and call into question their subsequent analysis and findings. In extreme environments where families and villages are engaged in violent communal conflict, the subject of the research (the community) is likely to be suffering from psychosocial incoherence. The nature of this psychosocial incoherence involves sociological disintegration, psychological devolvement, and emotional totalisation of overwhelming traumatic experiences from violent losses suffered by the research informants. The visible emanation of their incoherence is often expressed in alternating emotional episodes of rage, hopelessness and depression that are accompanied by physical episodes of drug or alcohol anesthetisation, sexual promiscuity or self-inflicted injuries (Kalsched, 1996).

Together, researcher stability and research subject coherence constitutes the focus of this chapter that is organised into sections that discuss the challenges of communicating through extreme emotion; considerations of research participants' conditions of trauma, transference and ethical entanglements; non-overlapping translation of cultural contexts; and the effects of informant trauma on memory distortion. While several of the sections make for emotionally difficult reading, the value of this discussion is in the support of increased qualitative research in conflict zones around the world.

Communicating through shame and rage

Abdul Salam was a Muslim man, native to the Kandahar province of Afghanistan. On 4 November 2008, he was approached by a female field researcher who attempted to interview him about the rising prices of gasoline. He was probably selected because he was carrying a container of benzene (gasoline). While the actual exchange between the female researcher and the Muslim man is unknown, the subsequent events are quite well known. Abdul Salam tossed the contents of his jug of benzene onto the female researcher and set her on fire. In the events that quickly played out, the female researcher, Paula Lloyd, was thrown into a water source to extinguish the flames that covered her body and rushed through escalating levels of medical treatment that ended two months later when she finally died from her injuries. Abdul Salam was immediately captured by Afghan authorities, but an enraged colleague of Lloyd's summarily shot him in the head in a sensationalised and politicised international incident (Gezari, 2013). I recount this story to centre the discussion on the inherent danger of communicating to fellow human beings who are immersed in the throes of shame and rage of violent conflict.

The cycles of violence and rage in some zones of conflict can be overwhelming, literally beyond one's ability to communicate. The cycles of loss, mourning and revenge lurch from one side to the other on fields of battle that overlay homes and villages of the subjects of qualitative research. The emotional dialogue supersedes that of the intellectual in terms of volume and velocity as intra-family relationships become distorted through loss, unbearable pain and betrayal. These emotional states of being for the participants, victims and witnesses are not momentary; they linger long after the visible violence has ended or moved on, sustained by the trauma of war. Understanding the emotional states of being for those who remain is a necessary precondition for effective communication during qualitative field research.

The traumatised person cannot be avoided or overlooked. The trauma of violence does not happen only to some, or only to women and children. All are victimised, whether they are perpetrators, victims or even witnesses. All will speak through the distorting lens of trauma that the researcher must make sense of in order to investigate. The cycles of trauma have stable conditions and effects across cultures. Beginning with the shame of victimisation, for instance, such emotions and the responses they trigger can be understood and tracked in communal behaviour. Specific psychological actions occur with the onset of victimisation producing shame of rejection, displacement and loss. Shame and humiliation in turn are igniters of anger, rage and hate that fuel a 'logic-of-violence'.

Trauma, transference and ethical entanglements

Violence possesses an emotional logic that predictably affects an individual's psychological reality in the form of trauma, transference and ethical instability. The first part of this logical sequencing involves direct overwhelming emotional conjugations of an affected individual from visible and audible external conflict events. A father, for instance, in a bombed-out neighbourhood in Sana'a, Yemen, searches the rubble of his home for his wife and daughter. He is driven by cultural demands to restore dignity to the dead through their cleansing and burial. He finds his loved ones in small parts and tenderly prises the pieces out from the dusty concrete and rebar, barely able to see and breathe through tears and saliva. Each time his slick hands slip, or a piece of loved remains is jostled against the rubble, another small wave of psychic pain crests, creating neurological impulse storms that precede the failing boundaries of reality and reason. These visible emanations of the emotional conjugations of overwhelming grief and guilt are the most obvious signs of a disintegrating family identity and irresolvable survivor guilt for having abandoned life and love in the ruined remains of a home.

The father's damaged reality exists in an altered state because phenomenological symbolic objects of cognitive, psychological and emotional suffering distort his sociological structure. These symbolic objects are his mental ideations of terror, betrayal, victimisation, alienation, shame and rage, powerful enough to unravel the sociocentric psychological organisation of his remaining family. In an extended duration, the effects of these symbolic objects tend to overwhelm the emotional conjugation of families and even entire villages. In combination, these objects activate neurobiological responses of flight, inescapable shock or fight, which creates perpetrators out of victims in an endless cycle of violence that no one quite comprehends outside of the victims and perpetrators themselves (d'Anniballe, 2016).

This suggests, then, the other part of the logical sequence of violence, the disintegration of intimate sociocentric community. Multiple repetitions of the example above violate and deny the available and possible interactions between families affected by the fighting, leaving them engaged in a dyad of psychosocial destruction. This dyad involves adversary symbiosis characterised by trait dissociation (Stein, 1982) and a logical progression of alienation, shame and rage (Scheff and Retzinger, 1991). The former represents a group psychological struggle with failing boundaries of self-identity combined with cognitive dissonance of perpetrator actions that are projected onto their 'enemy other'. The latter side of the dyad harbours intense emotions conjugated from victimisation of shame and rage created by perceived betrayal and alienation. The conclusion of both parts of the dyad results in the subsequent (and continuous) denouement of justice that each serves on the other as a temporary cleansing of emotional vengeance.

In the middle stands the conflict field researcher attempting to comprehend cause and effect and apply rapidly diminishing valuations of academic theory. The reality of human suffering up close, however, has a certain feel, a different smell that cannot be adequately explained in words or conveyed in pictures. The raw pain, physical, emotional and spiritual, of another human being has the power to traumatise both researcher and observer in an emotional entanglement called counter-transference and secondary trauma (Pearlman and Saakvitne, 1995). To the field researcher, this dyad of victimisation and revenge appears as a nearly paralysing state of open insanity between communities connected by history, land and love.

The endless betrayal of victim and perpetrator changes hands between villages and tribes until entire families and clans operate in a confused state of traumatic agony from which they perceive no escape outside of psychic annihilation and existential disintegration. Families caught in violent communal conflict do act in a rational manner, but in accordance with a damaged or traumatised reality that is not initially visible to the researcher or interventionist (Herman, 1992). Their rationality is based on a phenomenological reality of extended violent loss and abandonment that is difficult to understand until one has sufficiently descended into the shared and physical and emotional pain of their research informants.

The interview excerpt below with Saeed Ahmed, an Amenokal (tribal leader) of the Kel Tamashek (Tuareg) of the Agadez and Tahoua regions of northern Niger, illustrates the ever-exchanging roles of victimisation and perpetration based on the logical sequencing of traumatic conditions:

> 'With amaghr [war] and iban-aman [famine] always comes tatreet [disease] twarna or tiwarnawen is one sickness or many sickness ... and when it leaves, we have lost our wives and children to emutyen [bad change]. My brother he went mad when his children died from hunger ... he attacked the government camp with only a stick and they killed him ... we have found timogoutar, the bad hardness that does not let us do anything to end it.'

I interviewed Saeed Ahmed in a small village house in the rural commune of Ingall, about 60 kilometres west of the ancient city of Agadez near the base of the Aïr Mountains. The elderly Amenokal rocked back and forth as he recounted the death of each thin child and subsequent burial, wet tear tracks marking his dusty, wrinkled face. Like all conflict stories, the example recounted here conforms to a logical sequence of violence: first, an alienating injustice, then a descent into shamed suffering, followed by a psychologically restoring denouement. For Saeed, the injustice or betrayal of his brother was the war and famine; his suffering was the loss of children to starvation; and his attempt at a restoring denouement with a stick was quickly ended by the betrayer government's bullets. For Saeed and his remaining family, this failed denouement was a further descent into a place the Tuareg call *timogoutar*, which psychologically translates into inescapable shock, or the inability to engage in fight or flight.

If the researcher is successful in penetrating painful lived experiences such as Saeed Ahmed and his brother's, he/she will begin to visualise (and possibly empathise) the meaning intentionality of the relationship between the betrayer and the betrayed. He/she will perceive the intensely psychological and emotional nature of the violence, where victims clash over systems of honour, and where attacking with a stick instead of a gun constituted a verbal protest rather than a physical threat requiring bullets and further death.

The researcher's physical and psychological (through phenomenological inquiry) collocation to victim and perpetrator heightens the possibilities for transference and counter-transference in such compelling conflict, especially during periods of emotional and physical exhaustion (Marshall and Marshall, 1988). The elevated levels of transference and exhaustion, in turn, establish the conditions for a triad relationship between researcher-bystander, victim and perpetrator. This triad relationship in conflict zones creates ethical challenges to 'research relationships', specifically with regard to responsible data collection and analysis (Doucet and Mauthner, 2002, p 124). In such cases, the researcher possesses an incidental role as primary witness to the continuously traded roles of informant-victim and informant-perpetrator, a role-sharing process that is inherent in extended communal conflict and other, 'violent systems' (Ofer, 1994, p 15).

This triad relationship based on the researcher's incidental role as witness establishes the possibility of an unintended participatory (researcher) role in the conflict story based on a failure of heroic archetypes. None of those present at the scene of violent conflict can claim public status to heroism; not the victim in a context of heroic suffering, for they have gained nothing with the loss of their ability to create and sustain existential identity and its metaphysical conjugate, generational memory (Attias-Donfur and Wolff, 2003). Not the perpetrator, unable as they are to justify the necessity of their genocidal deeds outside of their own inner circle of cultural brethren (Adelman, 1997). And finally, not the researcher-as-witness as he/she bears witness not merely to another's extinction, but to their own indifference or impotence to meet the demands of their culture's archaic typology of heroism.

As a conflict researcher, I have experienced the reappearance in immediate waking memory of images of disfigured faces and bloated bodies in unexpected instances long after my return to the safety of home and rationality of the academic classroom. Such waking memory comes laden with emotional texture that is accompanied by a rush of sound and a physical flush of the face as involuntary tears shock ongoing collegial discussions about civil conflict into shamed silence. Beyond the involuntary physical displays of ravaged emotion, this embarrassment presents ideations of guilt and shame from one's personal collocation with victimisation and perpetration by and between their research informants (van der Kolk, 1988).

The non-overlapping contexts of victims and researchers

Intractable communal conflicts involve communities whose cognitive structure, psychological organisation and emotional conjugation are deeply affected by geographical, geological and climatological contexts of human reality. These deeply affected contexts establish communication barriers between bounded cultural communities that psychologist Donald Spence calls 'non-overlapping translation' (1982, p 83). Non-overlapping translation is a communications failure, where a barrier to effective understanding exists despite the proximate location of those purportedly in direct communication.

This communication failure between researcher and informant can deepen and intensify barriers to successful phenomenological inquiry and healthy emotional exchange, which, in conflict settings, can complicate traumatic experience and destabilise data collection and analysis (Bhugra and Becker, 2005). Most of my field research in violent conflict zones has been within communities in North Africa whose contexts of reality were so far removed from my own that theirs and mine did not overlap in terms of meaning and understanding. This section tries to illuminate how psychological imprinting from extreme contexts of geography, geology and climate can create such non-overlapping translation. Within this explanation are descriptions of how conceptions of modern individual agency can be overwhelmed by environmental contexts, while traumatic conditions of adaptive failure can serve as inhibitors to effective conflict analysis and resolution.

One of the largest conflict zones in the world is the Sahara desert and its Sahel transition zone, encompassing the conflict communities of West Sudan in Darfur (Fur, Zaghawa, Masalit, Rizeigat), northern Chad, Niger and Mali (Tubu, Hausa, Fulani, Kel Tamashek or Tuareg, Maghreb Berber), and Western Sahara (Saharawi). All of these communities possess physical contexts of reality that can defy etic understanding without extensive investment in research time and effort (Stein, 2008).

The Sahara desert and the Sahel transition zone is the largest continuous geologic space on earth. It is a space that defies cognitive conception and denies the possibilities of egocentric individual agency so characteristic of developed Western societies. Geographical horizons in the desert create interior ideations of perpetual movement that powers psychological imperatives of nomadism through what Mohammed Bamyeh (1999, p 3) describes as an 'ideology of the horizon.' Geological formations of dunes, massifs and salt pans harbour mesmerising beauty that illustrates eons of historical narratives necessary to the continuation of communal self-love and existential identity. Finally, climatological patterns of wind, rain and sun establish sociological structures in perfect harmony with the possibilities of human collective survival and archaic types of heroes and saviours. From 2013–14, I researched the *touchetts* (communities) of the Kel Tamashek in the central Sahel of northern Niger and Mali. As we travelled ancient trade routes northward through Agadez in the Valley of Azawa towards the South Libyan desert, the horizons receded in perfect step, establishing the illusion of motionlessness, even timelessness. In the northern Sahel, giant, rolling dunes as high as apartment complexes compete for space against even larger massifs of ancient rock that are larger than modern cities. The sheer domination of natural terrain combined with the majesty of antiquity relegates speech and time into unnecessary, even alien, activities. In the desert, one sees, breathes and moves. Speaking and keeping time are of little practical utility.

During an interview with members of a semi-nomadic family near Libya's southern border with Niger, a father pointed to the vapour trail of a passenger jet nearly invisible to my naked eye and said – *jinn*, or spirit. I said nothing in response, thinking which was more likely the believable story, that the white line in the sky was spirits, or an aluminium tube with wings full of humans and luggage that was flying many kilometres above the earth? As we set out to follow this father to his family's village somewhere north of us, I had to stop myself from asking where we were going or how long the trip would take. The question was meaningless. In the company of the Kel Tamashek, routine communication becomes meaningless. For instance, asking someone to meet me next Wednesday at four o'clock in the afternoon at the 10th dune due northeast from the base of a certain massif formation in the Aïr mountains would be an exercise in irrationality. As we moved along an ancient but unseen trail, a *shamal*, or north windstorm, began to form in the east and head toward our caravan. Slowly the horizon in that direction became obscured and taught me yet another lesson in the context of life in the desert (see Christian, 2015).

A *shamal* is a living entity in the desert, constituting a wall of sand that is suspended in air higher than 400 metres with winds capable of blowing a man and his camel for several kilometres across the land. As the *shamal* passes over the ground, cars and even small structures can be nearly completely covered in fallen sand. There is no escape, nowhere to run to unless within the safety of the massifs where one can hide an entire village in the recesses of its crags. This is the essence of a shift in the context of reality, the forced acceptance of natural events and power of the natural world over the capacity of human individual agency.

In the desert during the *shamal*, there are no storm shelters constructed through individual agency. There is only acceptance of what is and what will be. Anticipation of saving intervention becomes the irrational ideation. The possibilities of outside rescue, external justice or social safety nets are as unlikely as the possibility that I could explain modern winged flight and jet engine propulsion to an old man convinced that the passenger plane is simply a beautiful *jinn* spirit heralding some action or thought of the creator. Here in the geographically, geologically and climatologically remote landscapes of the Sahara and Sahel, the developed modern/urban reality simply does not overlap with the ancient reality of the desert, the mountain or the ever-shifting horizon.

Recording the structure and texture of traumatic memory

In qualitative field research, both informant and investigator interpret events, creating meaning that translates into cause, effect and conditions that are necessary for purposeful thought. The informant's created meaning turns his or her events into emic historical narrative, while the investigator's created meaning turns his or her events into etic research analysis. The investigator does this from his or her external position as a neutral observer, partially or fully removed from the conflict events, using phenomenological inquiry to record the lived experiences of his or her informant. The informant does this at the moment of the event; where the event drives the creation of the meaning for each participant and for a group of participants as they collectively experience the structure and the texture of the conflict event simultaneously.

For the purposes of this chapter, think of the structure of the event as the factual occurrence devoid of meaning, cause, effect and conditions. Think of the texture of the event as the psychological and emotional impact of created meaning, which is constructed and attributed to the event as cause, effect and conditions as they relate to the person and loved ones of the meaning making. The structure of how a participant's terror might be experienced consists of received visual, audible, tactile and olfactory stimuli combined with internal cognitive functions of memory and self-awareness. The texture of a participant's experience in terror overlays emotionally charged mental objects such as terror, shame, rage and betrayal on to the structure, that in turn become covert drivers of communal violent conflict.

The participant informants I interviewed in my fieldwork record their phenomenological experiences of terror, hopelessness, abandonment and betrayal within their internal reality with a greater clarity and complexity than most researchers initially comprehend. Returning again to my research in the central Sahel region, the affected populations experience a drought that dries wells, the lack of water for dying animals, the bloated bellies of hungry children, the carcasses of once treasured animals whose lives and nourishment were a central object of sociological existence or the mental instability of family members driven to madness because of thirst and famine. These memories of physicality constitute the structure of the experience. The structure of the stories focus on cognitive memory of events that were experienced and processed by the brain's prefrontal cortex and the hippocampus' organisation of spatial memory and transition from short to long-term memory (Winson, 1985). This recorded structure of their experience is the externalised record of the visible part of their actual lived experience that in turn serves as overt drivers of intractable conflict.

What is missing from this factual accounting is the textural experience that completes the researcher's understanding of the lived experience of victimisation, betrayal, shame and rage. The texture of the story is recorded within the brain's amygdale, which processes and stores memory of emotional reactions, social behaviour and sense of smell. A painful inability to swallow or urinate conjugates to intimate fear of bodily failure and childhood memories of decay. The peculiar smell of starvation that emanates from the bodies of loved children conjugates to alienating shame for failing to provide food, water and medical aid. The terrifying inability to recognise the mounds of putrefying flesh, covered with blue-black flies that could be a goat, or possibly your child, conjugates to rage borne of shame and un-integrated grief. The pure guilt of the parent unable to feed a dying child can conjugate to self-hatred and debilitating depression.

These are glimpses of the emotional texture of the violence of the lived experience of what the Kel Tamashek thinks of as *timogoutar*, that place of 'the bad hardness'. The verbs and nouns of feel, smell, guilt, terror, loneliness and emptiness describe the intentionality of the interviewee's experience. The direct object expressions such as the 'smell of starvation' or 'pure guilt of the parent' articulate the presentation of structure and its link to the texture of the experience. The surviving parent I'm interviewing feels pain and anguish; she experiences terror, loneliness and emptiness; suffers from guilt from the look of her children, the feel of their extended bellies and the smell of dying bodies from her first-person perspective. She reacts not to the external events, but rather to what the external events mean, how they appear, what they portend – as they are conjugated into raw emotion that covertly drives the conflict into intractability.

In the data collection and analysis of violent conflict, the structure of the experience is often the most frequently described portion of the event, usually to the exclusion of the texture. This is because the structure constitutes the research investigator's visual-factual representative account of actors involved and the activities as they seemed to occur that invoked or created the conditions for the experience. The most visible part of the event, the structure, most directly informs the research data collection and analysis because it is the least invasive to the participant and therefore easiest to acquire. Left unrelated is the completion of the meaning experience. The phenomenological texture is avoided, painfully invasive as the description of such re-enactments must be, in contexts where suffering and dying are an integral part of the landscape.

The divergence between structure and texture can be illustrated by the simple recounting of a midnight raid of an opposing militia on the village of an 'enemy other'. The survivors' internal, mental remembrance of bullets that puncture the walls of a fragile abode; the roaring mix of riders on horses and vehicles with machine guns; or the audible expulsion of empty bullet-casing cartridges as they spatter the ground around the entry of the village. These remembrances constitute their verbalised structure of an experience in terror, which constitutes the research data collection and subsequent analysis. Only through emotionally charged episodes of phenomenological inquiry, however, is the underlying emotional texture of the event recorded. This is the heart of the meaning intentionality of the experience. These deeper emotional remembrances involve a terrifying, deafening crescendo of noise that pulls a father awake during the raid. The victims might remember the smell of cordite mixed with the tactile feel on hands and legs of something wet and warm smelling of coppery cinder, resulting in a sudden cognition that the wetness is blood that is not his and must therefore be from his child. The father might remember the explosive startle as holes explode in the walls above the bed, raining wood and mud brick down on the bedclothes already soaked with wet, warm fluids and the new smell of excrement. These deeper, more emotional remembrances constitute a glimpse of the texture of an experience in terror and the subsequent breaking of psychological reality (see Christian, 2013). These remembrances, if the researcher is able to elicit them, constitute the rest of the data collection and the lived experience of the collective memory of terror. These mental objects of emotional conjugation that function as covert drivers of violent action are often the missing piece of data collection and analysis in communal conflict.

Conclusion

The international threat of interstate nuclear conflict has receded only to reveal an even more complex security challenge; that of the failed or failing state beset by intractable, violent communal conflict. Left untended, these intractable conflicts spread their twisted virus-like ideologies into even the securest of developed nations. Fifteen years of large-scale conflict engagement in Afghanistan and Iraq have demonstrated that kinetic firepower cannot resolve intractable communal intrastate conflicts on their own. Qualitative research into the underlying overt and covert drivers of violent communal conflict has become a critical pathway necessary to plan for and engage communities in conflict.

Effective qualitative field research as a blended part of security, governance and development reform serves as the knowledge basis for several critical security objectives. First among these objectives is the identification and explanation of covert and overt drivers of violence and inhibitors of resolution. Examples of these inhibitors have been shown in the preceding sections. Even after overt and covert conflict drivers are explained, further qualitative research is required to rehabilitate indigenous structures of law, justice, conflict resolution, physical and mental health, and economic identity expression. Finally, qualitative field research lays the foundation for the repair of damaged group psychological organisation and the assuagement of emotional damage to individual and family relationships.

The growing threat that intrastate communal conflicts pose to failed and failing states requires the development of ontology and the accompanying epistemology of collective human psychosocial-emotional states as they relate to violent communal conflict and resolution. Current single-discipline fields of sociology, psychology, political science and anthropology have all proven themselves to be anaemic and insufficient theoretical platforms for the resolution of violent communal conflict. Newer, emerging fields of ethno-psychology and psychoanalytical anthropology hold promise, but lack a sufficiently broad multidisciplinary inquiry.

Equally essential is the construction of an ethical framework for guiding qualitative field research into ongoing communal violence that accepts the imperative to provide data and analysis to the intervention efforts of humanitarian, diplomatic and security reform organisations, and that addresses issues of research subject transference as well as researcher counter-transference and secondary traumatisation. Such an ethical framework would need to provide research data collection and analysis guidelines for field research in vast communal conflicts that involve ongoing suffering as well as the threat and consequences of genocide.

Finally, due to the unique nature of the conflict zone research setting, specialised theory and practice courses in qualitative research need to be developed for potential field researchers, designed to help them stabilise their own psychological organisation amidst the devolution of large group identities, genocidal warfare and human suffering far beyond what is acceptable in their own home culture. These new theory and practice courses must include grappling with the philosophical ontology of respect, dignity and the cross-cultural relativity of poverty and suffering.

References

Adelman, H. (1997) *Membership and dismemberment: The body politic and genocide in Rwanda*, 2nd draft, Centre for Multiethnic and Transnational Studies, University of Southern California, Toronto, Canada: York University, pp 1–28.

Attias-Donfur, C. and Wolff, F.-C. (2003) *Generational memory and family relationships*, Paris: CNAV.

Bamyeh, M.A. (1999) *The social origins of Islam: Mind, economy, discourse*, Minneapolis, MS: University of Minnesota Press.

Bhugra, D. and Becker, M.A. (2005) 'Migration, cultural bereavement and cultural identity', *World Psychiatry*, vol 4, no 1, pp 18–24.

Burton, J.W. (1987) *Resolving deep rooted conflict: A handbook*, Lanham, MD: University Press of America.

Christian, P.J. (2013) 'Darfur – Ground Zero for Africa's crises of identity: A psychohistoriography of tribes in conflict', *African Security*, vol 6, no 1, pp 1–38.

Christian, P.J. (2015) 'Between warrior and helplessness in the Valley of Azawa – The struggle of the Kel Tamashek in the war of the Sahel', ProQuest Dissertation Press.

d'Anniballe, J.P. (2016) *Understanding the neurobiology of trauma: Implications for working effectively with adults and adolescents*, 7 March, Vermont Center for Crime Victim Services (www.ccvs.state.vt.us/content/understanding-neurobiology-trauma-implications-working-effectively-adults-and-adolescents).

Doucet, A. and Mauthner, N. (2002) 'Knowing responsibly: Linking ethics, research practice and epistemology', in M. Mauthner, M. Birch, J. Jessop and T. Miller (eds) *Ethics in qualitative research*, London: Sage, pp 123–45.

Gezari, V.M. (2013) *The tender soldier: A true story of war and sacrifice*, New York: Simon & Schuster.

Herman, J.L. (1992) *Trauma and recovery*, New York: Basic Books.

Hobbs, D. (2006) 'Dangerous field work', in V. Jupp (ed), *The Sage dictionary of social research methods*, London: Sage Publications, p 57.

Kalsched, D. (1996) *The inner world of trauma: Archetypal defenses of the personal spirit*, London: Routledge.

Marshall, R.J. and Marshall, S.V. (1988) *The transference-countertransference matrix: The emotional-cognitive dialogue in psychotherapy, psychoanalysis, and supervision*, New York: Columbia University Press.

Ofer, Z. (1994) 'Rethinking "Don't Blame the Victim": The psychology of victimhood', *Journal of Couple Therapy*, vol 4, no 3/4, pp 15–36.

Pearlman, L.A. and Saakvitne, K.W. (1995) *Trauma and the therapist: Countertransference and vicarious traumatization in psychotherapy with incest survivors*, New York: W.W. Norton & Co.

Scheff, T.J. and Retzinger, S.M. (1991) *Emotions and violence: Shame and rage in destructive conflicts*, Lexington, MA: D.C. Heath & Company.

Special Warfare (2006) 'Brokering peace in Sudan', vol 19, no 2, pp 6–13 (www.dvidshub.net/publication/issues/8264).

Spence, D.P. (1982) *Narrative truth and historical truth; Meaning and interpretations in psychoanalysis*, New York: W.W. Norton & Co.

Stein, H.F. (1982) 'Adversary symbiosis and complementary group disassociation: An analysis of the US//USSR conflict', *International Journal of Intercultural Relations*, vol 6, no 1, pp 55–83.

Stein, H.F. (1984) 'The scope of psycho-geography: The psychoanalytic study of spatial representation', *Journal of Psychoanalytic Anthropology*, vol 7, pp 23–73.

Stein, H.F. (2008) *Developmental time, cultural space: Studies in psychogeography*, Oklahoma City, OK: University of Oklahoma Press.

van der Kolk, B.A. (1988) 'The biological response to psychic trauma', in F.M. Ochberg (ed) *Post-traumatic therapy and victims of violence*, New York: Brunner/Mazel, pp 25–38.

Winson, J. (1985) *Brain and psyche: The biology of the unconscious*, New York: Anchor Press.

Vignette 1: The play I could not publish

Laurel Borisenko

Conducting research in a context of violence was such a powerful experience that in addition to writing up my results, I wanted to explore in a more creative way questions such as the security of respondents and researchers and the impact of censorship on research. Thus I decided to write a reader's theatre piece, to give voice to the actors in my personal research drama. My intention was to include the entire play as a chapter in this book, but when checking with local sources, I was warned against doing so as it would put those in the country at risk. So below I offer an abbreviated and redacted version of this play.

Excerpt from reader's theatre play: 'Talking drums'

Readers

Researcher: A young Western woman coming for the first time to conduct research in a context of violence. She is smart, enthusiastic, and naive.

Narrator: Middle-aged man from this country; he has the solid feel and voice that comes from years of experience handling difficult situations.

Artist: An attractive young woman from this country, with passionate fiery eyes, wanting to speak out, but still nervous.

Scene 1: Arrival

[Sounds of a balafone begin off-stage. Three readers enter together, the researcher holding a clipboard, the narrator, purposeful, and the artist swaying to the music. The music fades as they sit on chairs]

Narrator: Even after being in ███████ four times over 10 years, she hadn't quite grasped how threatened the government was by artists. She didn't realise that her research would be seen as subversive, simply because she was interested in the impact of the arts. But before she could actually confirm ██████████ would be one of her research sites, she had to go there on faith and hope that she could pull something erudite out of the hat.

[Artist beats a djembe drum; researcher bounces around]

Researcher: So there I was, on the bus from to ████████ squeezed in between ██████████████ and ████████████████, sharing food, bopping to non-stop music, and I mean non-stop for 20 hours. The bus wove its way through green hills and stopped at ████████████ I used a dirty bathroom at the back of a dark café, passing men playing checkers on cardboard using bottle caps. I got back on the bus. It kept winding and finally arrived in ████████ just as night was falling.

[One loud drum beat]

Researcher: [Pulls papers from pocket] I came to ████████ with three email contacts in my jean pockets. I arrived in ██████████ an atmosphere of high insecurity. I was warned to be very careful who I spoke with and where, as there were ████████ security agents everywhere. You couldn't talk in public places, even taxis. But I did meet people, often through serendipity. I watched a play on ████████████ and after the play I grabbed one of the actors and introduced myself. Despite the atmosphere of insecurity, she invited me back to █████████████ Her friend ██████████ joined us and became my most trusted confidante and cultural guide.

Artist: [Stands, then walks around with a jaunty step] I invited this muzungu, this white woman, back to my place. Why not – she was friendly. And besides, you never know who will be a good connection. I started talking about what happened to me, then it was like I couldn't stop. I told her about the fear of talking in public, not knowing who might betray you, and about the time I was arrested.

Researcher: Talking to these artists put flesh on abstract concepts like freedom of speech, human rights and resilience. They were no longer just words, but human beings with faces and voices and stories. Here is what I heard during interviews:

Artist [Using different voices for each line]: 'It would be easier if you could see blood running in the streets but ███ are not that kind of people.'

'We had to disguise the performances. ███ would pretend to use a wedding, then we would put on the play.'

'I am afraid to speak out because I am afraid ███ will be killed. And I don't want to die.'

'I have the right to tell my story in any way I need. You can kill ██████ all you want but ███ will never die.'

Scene 2: Focus group

Setting: A bare room in an old building, with a few chairs and a table. Narrator turns up the light as he enters, arranges chairs in a semi-circle. Researcher and artist enter and the three sit down.

Researcher: At the end of my visit I organised a focus group. I was advised by ██████ who I could invite and whose presence would shut down any sharing. ████████ trickled in, I asked lots of questions.

Narrator: For an hour-and-a-half, they shared stories, then they started to share their hopes, dreams, and fears. They began tentatively, then, when one person confided something, the next person continued, until they were speaking freely.

Artist: We were just getting warmed up when the researcher thanked us for coming, and waited for people to start to leave – but no one moved.

Narrator: They sat there in silence for a moment, and then ████ started talking again, this time at even deeper levels of sharing. They kept going for another hour-and-a-half, until finally the group felt that they were truly done.

Artist: It felt so good to be able to speak from the heart. When we left this cocoon to go back into the real world, we checked to see if we were being followed. We were all nervous about what the consequences might be later, but at that moment, we didn't care.

Scene 3: Follow-up

Narrator: A second research trip made some issues even less clear.

Researcher: I came away from this follow-up visit with a different perspective on security concerns. It was obvious from both visits that being involved in the activities under investigation could put people at risk – physically, psychologically and emotionally. So I listed this as a negative effect of participation, assuming that any level of risk was unacceptable.

Artist: But, when she asked us if we would keep going even with security risks, we all said, 'Yes!'

Researcher: One community activist challenged my assumption:

Artist: 'People know their safe spaces. Don't be condescending, community is more resilient than you think.'

Narrator: Despite the insecurity, they all felt that the benefits of participation outweighed any risks.

Researcher: Questions this raises for me are to what extent I am responsible for the security of people who do not want to be protected, and to what extent I can take security advice from people who are so habituated to living in unsafe circumstances.

Scene 4: Departure

Researcher sits centre-stage facing the audience. The narrator has moved his chair slightly behind. The artist's chair is at the side.

Narrator: The risk is not limited to country nationals. She had her own security scare, and narrowly avoided being detained and deported herself.

Researcher: Even though I had the privilege of embassy protection, I was nervous right until the moment of leaving the country. Sitting in the airport departure lounge, I kept looking over my shoulder to make sure that no government security agent was approaching me in long strides. I didn't realise that I had been holding my breath until the plane started down the runway, and I finally exhaled.

Narrator: What is really amazing is that these artists keep going, despite the personal risks, despite the years of violence, they choose to keep performing. Their resilience is summed up in this defiant line: ███████████████

█████████████████████████.

[Artist plays the drum, and the readers dance out]

****

Every black mark in this script is a visual protest.

I am haunted by the faces and stories of the people I have met. Sometimes the accounts shared with me are so deeply personal and painful that I feel like a voyeur. Despite the desire of people to have their stories told, much must remain unpublished. I am humbled by the people who trusted me enough to share their stories with me, and motivated to find creative ways to honour this sharing. I am disturbed that I could not publish all my research findings, ironically, including my full contribution in this book. As well, I am left with more questions than answers: How do I unravel the complexity of findings without over-simplifying and without over-explaining? Whose voice is heard and whose voice is repressed? How do I avoid re-traumatising people when I ask them even simple questions about past events that become triggers for them? After returning from this research site, the refrain kept repeating itself in my head, 'I am not neutral; I am not neutral; I am not neutral.' How can one be neutral about human rights abuses? I am angry. And I am amazed by the courage of those I interviewed, and eventually befriended. They must stay behind while I safely leave, passport in hand, unscathed. It's not true though; I am 'scathed'.

Section II
Uncertainty

3

Ambivalent reflections on violence and peacebuilding: Activist research in Croatia and the wider post-Yugoslav space[1]

Paul Stubbs

Introduction

I came to Croatia for the first time in May 1993, to work as a volunteer with the Croatian non-governmental organisation (NGO) Suncokret (Sunflower). I spent some nine months in total in a refugee camp in Savudrija, on the Istrian coast close to Slovenia, temporary home to some 2,000 refugees, mainly from central Bosnia. I moved to the Croatian capital Zagreb in 1994 working on a UK government-funded research project 'Social Reconstruction and Social Development in Croatia and Slovenia', later extended to cover Bosnia and Herzegovina. I continued to be active in and around Suncokret and the Anti-War Campaign, Croatia, helping to form, in 1997, the Centre for Peace Studies, a Croatian NGO that continues to exist today.[2] Between 1998 and 2003 I worked intensively on designing, implementing and evaluating social welfare reform projects in Bosnia-Herzegovina, Croatia and Serbia.[3] In November 2003, I was appointed to a research position in the Institute of Economics, Zagreb,[4] a public research institute. I continue to be based there, researching, among other themes, social policy; activism and social movements; clientelism and political capture; poverty and social exclusion; and policy translation.

Rather than exploring a single, time-limited, period of fieldwork, my chapter addresses some of the deep uncertainties and heartfelt dilemmas inherent in living, acting, observing and writing in conflict and post-conflict environments over a long period of time. My combination of activist, advocacy, consultant and academic roles, the fact that however much I integrate into Croatian society I remain a foreigner fully formed as a scholar in the imperialist-colonialist West, and the ways in which I have intervened critically in a number of debates in Croatia and the wider post-Yugoslav space all serve to multiply the 'messiness' inherent in research in and on violent spaces that is a recurring theme throughout this book.

This chapter applies a post-disciplinary perspective to researching violent conflict, emphasising political and ethical dilemmas. It is organised around the concepts of 'ambivalence' and 'positionality' that have helped to frame some of my interventions in the public sphere. I refer to these in the plural form in this text as part of an ongoing commitment to pay attention to 'the multiple, the plural, the contradictory and the awkward' (Clarke et al, 2015a, p 44). I am seeking to produce a 'writerly' text (Barthes, 1990, p 5), whose function 'is less to fully explicate and more to sow seeds that might evoke new lines of thought in the reader' (Bainton, 2015, p 171). The section on 'ambivalences' explores the dilemmas of action or activist research within grass-roots initiatives and the problems of international interventions and framings in a 'crowded playground' of humanitarian and related initiatives in a 'new war' setting. This is followed by a section on 'positionalities' that is a plea for a kind of 'multi-voiced reflexivity' in researching violent conflicts. A brief, concluding section ties the threads together and re-emphasises the political and ethical choices inherent in developing a different kind of conflict and post-conflict research agenda.

In the spirit of the work of Stuart Hall, my aim here is to try to understand the social, political and cultural 'work' that goes into any hegemonic project, understanding conjunctures as spatial-temporal moments that consist of diverse, even contradictory, elements never determined by a single factor or element (Hall, 2016). The condensation of forces during conflicts matter, of course, for the new social configurations that are possible in post-conflict environments where sometimes, to reverse the old adage, politics becomes 'the waging of war by other means'. At the same time dominant forces and practices are never all-consuming, and the room for, in Williams' terms, the 'residual' and the 'emergent' is such that there are always other possibilities at stake (Williams, 1978), which it is the task of an activist researcher to articulate, and support, albeit critically.

Backstories

My chapter here shares the sensibility that the editors of the book have both for this 'messiness' and for the importance of 'reflective, emotive and critical enquiry'. While my reflections are analytical in intent, they are also based on 'aesthetic and evocative thick descriptions of personal and interpersonal experience' (Ellis et al, 2011, p 14) as equally valid. Throughout, the use of the term 'I' risks understating the importance of numerous direct research, activist and professional collaborations, many of which have been of vital importance to me. In addition, the identity term 'researcher' connotes someone with the opportunity, even privilege, to be able to author texts based on a myriad of conversations with multiple others who go unrecognised.

Of course, rendering accounts more 'personalised' does not, in and of itself, transcend the 'hierarchies and divisions' of mainstream scholarship (Bilić and Janković, 2012, p 29). For, just as nationalist politicians in Bosnia-Herzegovina or Croatia rank answers to the question 'Where were you during the height of the war?' in order to create moral hierarchies regarding the right to speak on certain issues, there is a more subtle, but no less divisive, ranking using 'time served' in war zones, and even the extent of direct exposure to violence, as 'proxy indicators' of whether one merits fully the title of 'conflict researcher'. Indeed, in preparing this chapter, I was reminded of a comment made in a text on the ZaMir computer-mediated communication network[5] discussed further below, suggesting that 'Zagreb is a uniquely nice place to fight against a war' (Gessen, 1995) and, by extension, to research it from. During my time in Zagreb, the direct impacts of war were felt for only a couple of days in May 1995, when 'rebel' Croatian Serb forces shelled parts of the city after Croatian government forces retook one of the so-called United Nations Protected Area (UNPA) zones. The war in Croatia effectively ended following military action in two more UNPA zones in August 1995, although it took until January 1998 for the Eastern Slavonia region to be 'peacefully reintegrated' under Croatian government sovereignty. I did not venture into Bosnia-Herzegovina until after the Dayton Peace Agreement signed in December 1995, and had only visited Serbia twice before the fall of the Milošević regime.

In addition, although one of my early activist research interests was on 'peacebuilding', much of my subsequent work has had little direct engagement with the field of 'peace and conflict studies'. During this period, I got used to the idea that being 'a researcher in social policy' (Large, 1997, p 14) was not held in high esteem by true 'peace and conflict researchers', one of whom seemed to hold me responsible for the fact that, in her view: 'By 1996/7 the social and public policy issues almost seemed to dominate research concerns over ex-Yugoslavia. (Whatever happened to political violence and war?)' (Large, 1997, p 14). It is important to declare, also, that I have never worked in other conflict or post-conflict arenas outside of the post-Yugoslav space, so there is little or no comparative conflict dimension to my work. At the same time, a commitment to multi-disciplinarity, if not 'post-disciplinarity', has meant that I have long held a deep distrust of the boundaries between social scientific themes and fields of interest. Sum and Jessop (2003) suggest that a 'multi-disciplinary' approach still tends to start 'from a problem located at the interface of different disciplines and typically combines it in a rather mechanical, additive fashion … to produce "the big picture" through "joined up thinking"' (Sum and Jessop, 2003, p 5). In contrast, 'post-disciplinarity' is marked by 'a principled rejection of the legitimacy of established disciplinary boundaries and (the) adoption of a more problem-oriented approach' (Sum and Jessop, 2003, p 6), creating the space for 'more open-textured, more concrete, and more complex analyses that may also be more relevant to political and ethical issues' (Sum and Jessop, 2003, p 6).

Ambivalences

Activist researchers in conflict and post-conflict environments sometimes oscillate between 'ardent supporters' and 'transgressive critics' of the social movements they are following. Embracing 'the ambivalences and ambiguities of resistance itself' emerging 'from the intricate webs of articulations and disarticulations that always exist between dominant and dominated' (Ortner, 1995, p 190) is, I would suggest, a legitimate political and ethical standpoint. Ambivalence has the potential to 'repoliticize power relations and to embed contradictions in actual contexts, where the simple choice of "either/or" is a very rare instance for people' (Jovanović, 2016). My understanding of 'ambivalence' embraces both conceptual and affective dimensions, suggesting that much greater attention should be paid to the ways in which ambivalence 'incites, shapes and is generated by practices of meaning-making' (Gould, 2009, p 13). Homi Bhabha's suggestions that 'ambivalence introduces a performative sense of "being in the midst" of things' is persuasive, suggesting that it is only through 'working through, or living through, the process of ambivalence … that we derive a more appropriate, if agonising measure of global ethical and political conflicts' (Bhabha, 2007, p 41).

Early 'appreciative' texts about Suncokret (cf Pečnik et al, 1995; Stubbs, 1996b), for example, were followed, rather rapidly, by texts that resemble 'denunciations' (cf Stubbs, 1997). In part, this was indeed a result of a denial of the ambivalence I observed and felt, but there were clearly other factors in play. Re-reading these texts now, it is apparent that what I was struggling with was the 'disconnect' between solidarity-based, 'grass-roots', volunteer work in refugee camps and the growing 'office mentality' of a nascent Croatian NGO, experiencing a rapid increase in funding and struggling for an identity in the context of 'projectisation', replacing 'social change activism' with strategic positioning, 'a strong employment focus', professionalism and hierarchy (Bagić, 2004, p 222). Staff in the computer-rich Suncokret central office, a stark contrast to the under-funded School of Social Work in the University of Zagreb, my other workplace,[6] expended much of their energy on writing 'project proposals'. As I later wrote, 'projectisation' promoted 'technical skills at the expense of broader social goals; the empowerment of a young, urban, highly educated English speaking elite'; forced activists to 'focus on project "success" in very narrow terms' and led to 'the increasing distancing of elite NGOs from grassroots activism' (Stubbs, 2007a, p 221).

The sense that the wars of the Yugoslav succession were 'new wars' (Kaldor, 1999) or 'uncivil wars' (Keane, 2003) was certainly reflected in the themes I tried to deal with. The fact that the wars coincided with the first wave of the spreading of computer-mediated communications to significant numbers of people is of pivotal importance since, rephrasing Baudrillard, it became clear that 'war is not (only) measured by being waged but by its speculative unfolding in an abstract, electronic and informational space' (Baudrillard, 1995, p 56).[7] Having a small research grant enabled me, almost as soon as I moved to Zagreb, to purchase a laptop and modem and become connected to ZaMir, which had been established in 1992 as a Bulletin Board System (BBS) facilitating exchange between peace, human rights, women's and ecological activist groups within and beyond the post-Yugoslav space.

My sociological writings on ZaMir, computer-mediated activism, diaspora and the wars (Stubbs, 1998, 2001, 2004, 2007b) do not convey the full importance of my own ZaMir identity. Long before today's social media, I was able to use ZaMir in a way to promote my work, intervene in debates and, crucially, establish a kind of academic identity, acceptance and access within interlinked activist communities. Crucially, the language of most interactions on ZaMir was English, allowing me access to contexts, content and processes that would otherwise have been beyond me. Compounding ambivalence, some of my early shorter interventions within Zamir's 'newsgroups' also served, sometimes deliberately, to ingratiate myself to sections of the domestic peace activist constituency, not least by critiquing some of the absurdities of other foreigners' behaviour, creating an identity, achieved and ascribed, as 'not like most of the other foreigners'. Although cyberspace may well be a space in which rhetorics of violence and, indeed, of peace, become embodied (see Chapter 7, this volume), it was, for me at least, both a convenient space and an ambivalent embodiment of an emerging role as an 'activist researcher' or 'public intellectual'.[8]

The wars led to a mass influx of foreign nationals, or, as the local language(s) would have it, *stranci* (foreigners), into the region. In part this was because, as Dutch peace activist Wam Kat stated, volunteers from Western Europe could 'come hitchhiking to this war' (quoted in d'Heilly, 1996). These 'European do-gooders', 'unemployed would-be hippies', 'draft dodgers' (Gessen, 1995), and 'refugees from their own cultures' (Kat, quoted in Gessen, 1995) were joined by two other groupings: seasoned European peace and human rights activists seeking to express 'solidarity', and a vast army of so-called 'humanitarian organisations'. The best, or worst, example of so-called 'activist solidarity' concerns the by now infamous 'Peace Caravan' organised in September 1991 by the Helsinki Citizens' Assembly (hCa), a network of European intellectuals and peace activists who had been active both in the Nuclear Disarmament Movement and in supporting dissident intellectuals in Eastern Europe in the 1980s. Although set to visit several urban centres in Croatia, the Peace Caravan had not consulted with Croatian peace activists in the newly formed Anti-War Campaign, Croatia (ARK, H), which labelled the initiative 'patronising' (Teršelič, 1991, p 16). The 'caravan' fiasco eventually led to a joint statement by Croatian and Slovenian peace movements warning of 'peace tourism' and 'peace safaris' (ARK, H et al, 1992, p 27). Later, ARK, H made a radical break with more fundamentalist pacifist organisations over the issue of the use of external military force in Bosnia-Herzegovina. The crucial point here is that, although working closely with some international peace groups, notably War Resisters' International and the Quakers (cf Bennett, 2016), ARK, H was determined 'that an autonomous local interpretation of local events is *a priori* valid and legitimate' (Stubbs, 2012, p 18).

The 'novelty' of the sheer number and diverse character of international actors gathered around the conflicts and immediate post-conflict development in the post-Yugoslav space is difficult to assess. It was a deeply felt experience, however, especially when visiting parts of Bosnia-Herzegovina and later, Kosovo. The major cities and symbolic locations of the post-Yugoslav space certainly became what one journalist called 'acronym cities', or 'crowded playgrounds' (Arandarenko and Golicin, 2007, p 182), consisting of all manner of actors and agencies. Crucially, work for one of these international organisations became one of the few avenues of earning income for a young, educated population able to speak English, leading to a joke that 'Bosnia-Herzegovina has the best qualified drivers and interpreters in the world.' This 'projectariat' (Baker, 2014) formed a distinct employment sector, alongside a distinctive rental sector, as some of their fellow citizens rented their large city centre apartments to international organisations. More importantly, as international organisations scaled down and pretended to have an exit strategy, many new organisations were formed by the local staff left behind. Agendas became extremely 'donor-driven' and many organisations became 'multi-mandated' (Duffield, 1994), engaging in an ever wider, and ever more rapidly changing, range of 'projects' to try to survive as donors' interests dwindled, morphed and changed.

From quite early on, my work connected with others, notably Mark Duffield (1994), who saw the international focus on 'humanitarianism' – the delivery of 'humanitarian aid' by supposedly neutral 'humanitarian organisations' – as a poor substitute for political initiatives to stop the wars. Later, of course, US-led support for military interventions combined with externally driven political engineering to create protectorates and semi-protectorates in Bosnia-Herzegovina and Kosovo. These cumbersome political arrangements served to stop the wars by rewarding (most of) the nationalist elites with the prospect of reaping the profits of peace as much as they had the profits of war. This helped to create regimes of 'liberal peace' underpinned by a new 'development-security nexus' (Duffield, 2001) in which 'the duty to protect' was never principled but always instrumentalised in the context of geo-political power relations. Richmond's plea (2010) to focus less on 'sovereign peaces organised around states and their territories' and more on 'individual and community conditions of peace' (Richmond, 2010, p 668) derived from social advocacy and concern for the marginalised echoes some of my positions from this time.

Another theme where early certainty was replaced by cautious ambivalence was my critique of the framing of interventions overwhelmingly towards 'psycho-social support' based on the identification of massive numbers suffering from 'war trauma', including 'post-traumatic stress disorder' or 'syndrome' (PTSD or PTSS). Initially, I traced this focus as a result of importing Western therapeutic models and contributing to an over-professionalisation, medicalisation and pathologisation of service delivery at the expense of more holistic community development approaches (cf Stubbs and Soroya, 1996). However, later I came to a more nuanced position, framed in terms of the paradoxical combination of progressive and reactionary elements within both the discourse and movement (cf

Stubbs, 2005). Although remaining convinced that the medicalisation of trauma should be seen as a disciplinary technology (Edkins, 2003), the close connection between a trauma focus and some feminist human rights practitioners advocating linkages between trauma therapy and social activism (Webster and Dunn, 2005) at least makes one pause to consider the contradictory forces impinging on the trauma 'field'. The ambivalence here is compounded by the fact that, as international actors moved away, both from the region and from their support for psycho-social programmes, the 'trauma' space became occupied by state bodies paying passive disability benefits to war veterans able to claim a trauma diagnosis (Stubbs and Zrinščak, 2015).

Nothing was more controversial, however, than my critique which, more than many of my interventions, has remained more or less consistent over time, of a misplaced faith in 'civil society' as a kind of panacea or 'golden key' for overcoming all the social ills of conflict and post-conflict societies. The critique focused on the essentialist and ahistorical nature of the use of the concept, never able to be more than a poor translation term, alongside other empty signifiers such as 'transition' and 'democratisation', for far more complex, context-specific, power-laden, processes. The fact that many of those enrolled in newly formed NGOs first heard of the concept of 'civil society' in USAID-organised workshops represented a kind of 'amnesia international' (Stubbs, 2003). It is a little known fact that the idea of civil society was not only 'debated in ... academic conferences organised in socialist Yugoslavia throughout the 1980s' (Bilić, 2012a, p 54), but was also an important *leitmotif* for social movements and formal Party structures in, at least, the Socialist Republic of Slovenia at the same time (Stubbs, 1996a).

In retrospect, my concern was to both map and critique the wide array of NGOs rapidly developing across the post-Yugoslav space, including those merging a kind of liberal human rights and liberal democratic tradition, conceiving of the task in hand as a long march from nationalist authoritarianism to dialogue-based democracy, in which neither the nature of the economic system, nor even a conjunctural understanding of state power, were ever addressed explicitly. Perhaps most problematic was the way in which the positions and practices of this NGO elite bordered on 'elitism', defined by Bojan Bilić and myself recently as 'an assemblage of dispositions, discourses, and performativities which serve to marginalise, undermine and sometimes silence other voices' (Bilić and Stubbs, 2016b, p 234). Of course, just as this elite tended to treat ordinary people as 'cultural dopes', the critique can serve to treat NGO activists in the same way, denying their agency in making choices in rather complex and constrained environments. There was still ambivalence here, however. On the one hand, I was extremely critical of the 'liberal' elements of ARK, H, not least in terms of their adherence to 'non-violent conflict resolution', 'mediation' and such like, focused on the interpersonal at the expense of the structural and transformative. On the other hand, I supported and worked with many of the projects associated with ARK, H, notably Volunteer Project Pakrac, a model of grass-roots peacebuilding later consolidated in Gornji Vakuf-Uskoplje and Travnik in Bosnia-Herzegovina (cf Pierce and Stubbs, 2000). These, together with the magazine *Arkzin* (Bilić, 2012b) and the early work of the Centre for Peace Studies, represented 'living experiments' (Lovink, 2002, p 268), and important lessons in courage and creativity.

Positionalities

An important linkage between the principle of 'ambivalence' and that of 'positionality' can be made through the concept of 'reflexivity'. Reflexivity both 'heightens awareness of one's own ... biases' and 'facilitates dialogue' (Rothman, 2014, p 113) in conflict environments. In many ways, a stance of 'reflexive ambivalence' may be one of the most productive positions from which to conduct social research, even if it is rather weak as a call to a political project. This goes beyond the understanding that all reflexive practices are, inevitably, ambivalent in the sense that the author's voice is always both authentic and inauthentic (Davies et al, 2004, p 384). Whether the ambivalence both of researchers and their subjects, together with the affective mobilisation of this ambiguity, is stronger or weaker in conflict settings, is less important than a recognition of 'positionality', a naming of the '"somewhere" that we write to and from' and those we do not (2004, p 384), discussed below. Davies et al's text implores us to 'occupy an ambivalent position of competent agent and transgressive critic' (2004, p 385), acknowledging our political orientation, revealing the limits of our knowledge, and opening up 'the possibilities of thinking otherwise' (2004, p 386).

Deriving from post-colonial perspectives in development studies, the idea of 'policy otherwise' was central to our 'ethico-political project' (Rojas, 2007, p 585) in writing the book *Making policy work*, offering 'a way in to the full possibility of a view of translation as a site of struggle' (Clarke et al, 2015b, p 194). A translation lens should sensitise social researchers to the 'double movement' of power and politics, 'attentive to interruptions, disjunctures and complexities' (Clarke et al, 2015b, p

195), framed by a kind of '"relational attentiveness"beyond the confines of a singular epistemological and ontological world' (Clarke et al, 2015b, p 196). Again, a translation lens directs us to the everyday, emphasising the need to dig deeply for what Freire calls 'generative themes', 'a complex of ideas, concepts, hopes, doubts, values, and challenges in dialectical interaction with their opposites, striving towards plenitude' (Freire, 1998, p 82) rather than an uncritical acceptance of dominant or grand narratives.

'Positionality' is a concern that is not limited to methodology and inexorably goes hand in hand with 'reflexivity', recognising the 'everyone is positioned', albeit in complex ways. Describing myself, since around 2000, as 'a sociologist with anthropological tendencies', a sensibility to 'ethnography' has been fundamental to my commitment to action-oriented, activist or advocacy research. In our work on policy translation, Noémi Lendvai and I referred to the importance of 'bending and blending' positions and perspectives, constantly moving between formal, institutionalised and informal practices (Lendvai and Stubbs, 2007). Jeremy Gould's play on the notion of 'hunter gathering' (Gould, 2004) also points to creative ways in which boundaries between research and other roles are broken down. I have rarely, if ever, probably through a combination of choice and circumstance, engaged in the old anthropological *rite de passage* of 'intensive fieldwork' in 'strange locations', at the same time trying to avoid writing from a position, all too common in institutionalist social and public policy texts, pretending to 'a perspective from above or from "nowhere"' (Marcus, 1995, p 112).

In conflict and post-conflict settings, an adherence to 'multi-voiced ethnography' (Jambrešić Kirin, 1999) or multiple positionalities is not easy to maintain, not least as one struggles to balance and combine 'critical abilities', 'emotional commitment', 'moral indignation' and 'political analysis' in ways that do not 'suspend the possibility of judgement' (Povrzanović and Jambrešić Kirin, 1996, p 5). Thinking through the relationship between 'the somewheres' we come from, the 'somewheres' we write from (Davies et al, 2004, p 384), and the seemingly endless 'elsewheres' of which we have no direct lived experience is particularly necessary, and astonishingly difficult, for researchers in/of violent conflicts. Stef Jansen's ethnography of anti-nationalist activism in Belgrade and Zagreb (Jansen, 2005) illustrates the importance of tracing 'everyday practices of resistance, channelling solidarity, care, outrage and indignation' (Jansen, 2008, p 76), while at the same time re-working both an idealistic 'past' in which conflicts were supposedly absent and invoking a superior urban sensibility. Linking 'anti-nationalism' and 'urbanity' in this way, insofar as both were 'anchored in a certain popular cultural "scene" and an unwritten code of local "etiquette"' is crucial for understanding the lack of a significant 'widening of the base of anti-war and anti-nationalist activism' (Bilić and Stubbs, 2016a, p 122).

There is a certain irony in referring to the geographical focus of this chapter as 'Croatia and the wider post-Yugoslav space'. The notion of the 'post-Yugoslav space' was an outcome of an early discussion on ZaMir in which many of us expressed concerns about the constant use of terms such as 'former-' or 'ex-Yugoslavia'. At the same time, a degree of Croatian centeredness is inevitable in my work simply as a result of the positionality of being based in Zagreb. I would claim, however, that this is not a full-blown 'methodological nationalism' if what is meant by the term is that which 'normalises the current post-Yugoslav situation, perceiving the newly generated and largely still incompletely consolidated nation-states as "natural" results of long-term historical processes' (Bilić, 2012a, p 44). In conceptual terms, I remain committed to the idea that 'the variable geometry and discursive claims of space, scale and reach need to be studied without imposing an *a priori* nation-state container limit' (Stubbs, 2012, p 14). Positionalities are also 'ascribed' as much as 'achieved'. Someone labelled a Croatian nationalist by some outside Croatia may be considered the ultimate 'Yugo-nostalgic' by nationalists within. Whether one calls the wars 'civil wars' or 'wars of aggression' is important not merely as a fact of international law. Even the Anti-War Campaign, Croatia, given its title, may have contributed to a state-building process, but not in the same way as the nationalist politicians they were opposing, of course.

My work has never been primarily about 'understanding the wars', at least not in any 'grand narrative' or geo-political sense. Indeed, in an early text I expressed dismay at the 'millions of words that have been written about the "destruction" (Magas, 1993), the "breakdown" (Yugofax, 1992), the "tragic death" (Denitch, 1994), the "disintegration" (Cohen, 1993), the "fall" (Glenny, 1992), the "ending" (Thompson, 1992) or the "unmaking" (Wheeler, 1993) of Yugoslavia' (Stubbs, 1996a, p 2). All accounts are, of course, partial and yet, explicitly or implicitly, one inevitably takes a position somewhere in between relativising the wars on the one hand, and suggesting that the cause of the wars was straightforward and that all blame must be attached to a single, named, 'aggressor' on the other. Alongside hitchhiking volunteers, of course, many high-profile foreign intellectuals did 'take sides', not always based on nuanced arguments or long-standing familiarity with the contexts.

A positionality as a foreign-, indeed Western-, born and educated activist researcher needs reflection, beyond crude labels of having a 'colonial mentality', having 'sold out to the devil' and/or of 'going native'. First, confronting the concept of 'global social policy' from a vantage point in Croatia may have helped me to detect and decentre the implicit colonialism of the definition of what is to constitute social policy (cf Lendvai and Stubbs, 2009). At the same time, a concern with the post-Yugoslav space even as a so-called 'semi-periphery' can reproduce an implicit 'West is best' conceptualisation that understands processes of modernisation in the region as slow, distorted or partial, and that fails to connect with dynamics in other elsewheres, including Latin America and Africa. Just as during the wars the multiplication of diverse 'political imaginaries' continue to create what Pugh has termed an 'intermestic sphere' (Pugh, 2000), not fully domestic or fully international, creating new assemblages of governance across unstable sites, in which interpreters, intermediaries and 'flex actors' (Stubbs and Wedel, 2015), blurring roles and representations, play a key role.

Conclusion

Ambivalence, reflexivity and an awareness of one's positionality are necessary, but not sufficient, principles for a 'post-colonial' perspective. The 'post-colonial turn' has become increasingly influential in the social sciences, including in international relations and peace and conflict studies, as well as in my own work on global social policy and on policy translation (Lendvai and Stubbs, 2009; Clarke et al, 2015a, b). While 'the relative neglect of local approaches to conflict resolution is bound up with the legacy of European colonialism' (Brigg and Bleiker, 2011, p 19), there is a danger of essentialism in the search for 'non-Western cultural traditions of conflict resolution' (Brigg and Bleiker, 2011, p 19). Without 'fetishising the local', then, I am arguing for a praxis of 'reflexive ambivalence', a search for new 'arenas of possibility' (Bainton, 2015, p 171) and new forms of 'collective disidentification' (Butler, 1993).

Of course, the unconscious reproduction of domination, especially by those whose first language is English, will continue to occur even among those 'well intentioned' who seek to 'do no harm' (Anderson, 1999), and not just in research in violent conflicts. There are worse starting points, or perhaps worse ending points, than with 'humility', a refusal to occupy a position that states 'you must' and that 'derives from knowing – and acknowledging – that we do not know what should be or will be' (Clarke et al, 2015b, p 207). Humble activist research works with 'glimpses' not 'engineered certainties', speaks with a 'whisper' rather than a 'scream', 'engages' rather than 'judges prematurely', and is open to 'irony', 'humour' and 'play' even in, or maybe especially in, spaces of violent conflict and cultural contexts in which such expressions in academia and activism are seen as transgressions.

Notes

[1] I am grateful to Althea-Maria Rivas, Bojan Bilić, Bob Deacon, Andrew Hodges, Azra Hromadzić, Vanja Nikolić, Jasmina Papa, Maja Povrzanović Frykman, Mike Pugh and Andreja Rafaelić for helpful comments on an earlier draft. Responsibility for what follows is, of course, mine alone.

[2] See www.cms.hr/en

[3] This work, together with work for UNICEF on childcare reform in 2007, is discussed extensively elsewhere, particularly in Stubbs (2015).

[4] See www.eizg.hr/default.aspx?lang=2

[5] ZaMir (meaning 'for peace' in Bosnian/Croatian/Serbian) was a computer network facilitating communication between peace groups across the post-Yugoslav space. See Stubbs (2004) for an historical overview.

[6] It is also important to note, of course, that a number of those working in universities also had their 'own' NGO, a phenomenon not merely a result of the impossibility of material security, at that time, from an academic post alone.

[7] I have added the word 'only' to Baudrillard's original text, albeit thereby altering its meaning appreciably.

[8] Jana Bacevic (2017) has recently written that, by engaging in critique on social media, 'intellectuals are, essentially, doing what they have always been good at – engaging with audiences and in ways they feel comfortable with.' In this context, comfort is also a source of ambivalence, of course.

References

Anderson, M. (1999) *Do no harm: How aid can support peace – or war*, Boulder, CO: Lynne Reiner.

Arandarenko, M. and Golicin, P. (2007) 'Serbia', in B. Deacon and P. Stubbs (eds) *Social policy and international interventions in South East Europe*, Cheltenham: Edward Elgar, pp 167–86.

ARK, H et al (1992) 'Pismo namjera' ['Letter of intent'], *ARKzin*, vol 4, p 26.

Bacevic, J. (2017) '@Grand Hotel Abyss: Digital university and the future of critique', *Discover Society*, Blog post, 3 January (http://discoversociety.org/2017/01/03/grand-hotel-abyss-digital-university-and-the-future-of-critique/).

Bainton, D. (2015) 'Translating education: Assembling ways of knowing otherwise', in J. Clarke, D. Bainton, N. Lendvai and P. Stubbs (eds) *Making policy move: Towards a politics of translation and assemblage*, Bristol: Policy Press, pp 157–86.

Bagić, A. (2004) 'Women's organizing in post-Yugoslav countries: Talking about "donors"', in J. Gould and H. Secher Marcussen (eds) *Ethnographies of aid: Exploring development texts and encounters*, Occasional Paper No 24, Roskilde: IDS, pp 194–226 (http://ojs. ruc.dk/index.php/ocpa/issue/view/809/showToc).

Baker, C. (2014) 'The local workforce of international intervention in the Yugoslav successor states: "Precariat" or "projectariat" towards an agenda for future research', *International Peacekeeping*, vol 21, no 4, pp 91–106.

Barthes, R. (1990) *S/Z*, Oxford: Blackwell.

Baudrillard, J. (1995) *The Gulf War did not take place*, Indiana, IN: Indiana University Press.

Bennett, A. (2016) *To trust a spark: Living links with community peacebuilders in former Yugoslavia: A Quaker initiative*, London: Post-Yugoslav Peace Link.

Bhabha, H. (2007) 'Notes on globalisation and ambivalence', in D. Held and H. Moore (eds) *Cultural politics in a global age: Uncertainty, solidarity and innovation*, Oxford: One World, pp 36–47.

Bilić, B. (2012a) *We were gasping for air: (Post-)Yugoslav anti-war activism and its legacy*, Baden-Baden: Nomos.

Bilić, B. (2012b) 'Islands of print media resistance: ARKzin and Republika', in B. Bilić and V. Janković (eds) *Resisting the evil: (Post-) Yugoslav anti-war contention*, Baden Baden: Nomos, pp 159–74.

Bilić, B. and Janković, V. (2012) 'Recovering (post-)Yugoslav anti-war activism: A Zagreb walk through stories, analyses and criticisms', in B. Bilić and V. Janković (eds) *Resisting the evil: (Post-)Yugoslav anti-war contention*, Baden Baden: Nomos, pp 25–36.

Bilić, B. and Stubbs, P. (2016a) 'Unsettling "The urban" in post-Yugoslav activisms: "Right to the City" and Pride parades in Serbia and Croatia', in K. Jacobsson (ed) *Urban grassroots movements in Central and Eastern Europe*, Abingdon: Routledge, pp 119–38.

Bilić, B. and Stubbs, P. (2016b) 'Beyond EUtopian promises and disillusions: A conclusion', in B. Bilić (ed) *LGBT activism and Europeanisation in the post-Yugoslav space: On the rainbow way to Europe*, London: Palgrave Macmillan, pp 231–48.

Brigg, M. and Bleiker, R. (2011) *Mediating across difference: Oceanic and Asian approaches to conflict resolution*, Honolulu: University of Hawaii Press.

Butler, J. (1993) *Bodies that matter: On the discursive limits of sex*, Abingdon: Routledge.

Clarke, J. et al (2015a) 'Translation, assemblage and beyond: Towards a conceptual repertoire', in J. Clarke, D. Bainton, N. Lendvai and P. Stubbs (eds) *Making policy move: Towards a politics of translation and assemblage*, Bristol: Policy Press, pp 33–64.

Clarke, J. et al (2015b) '"Policy otherwise": Towards an ethics and politics of policy translation', in J. Clarke, D. Bainton, N. Lendvai and P. Stubbs (eds) *Making policy move: Towards a politics of translation and assemblage*, Bristol: Policy Press, pp 187–228.

Cohen, L. (1993) *The disintegration of Yugoslavia*, Boulder, CO: Westview.

d'Heilly, D. (1996) Wam Kat interview (www.nettime.org/nettime/DOCS/1/wamkat.html).

Davies, B., Browne, J., Gannon, S., Honan, E., Laws, C., Mueller-Rockstroh, B. and Bendix Petersen, E. (2004) 'The ambivalent practices of reflexivity', *Qualitative Enquiry*, vol 10, no 3, pp 360–89 (http://journals.sagepub.com/doi/pdf/10.1177/1077800403257638).

Denitch, B. (1994) *Ethnic nationalism: The tragic death of Yugoslavia*, Minneapolis, MS: University of Minnesota Press.

Duffield, M. (1994) 'Complex emergencies and the crisis of developmentalism', *IDS Bulletin*, 25.4 (www.ids.ac.uk/files/dmfile/duffield254.pdf).

Duffield, M. (2001) *Global governance and the new wars: The merging of development and security*, London: Zed Books.

Edkins, J. (2003) *Trauma and the memory of politics*, Cambridge: Cambridge University Press.

Ellis, C., Adams, T. and Bochner, A. (2011) 'Autoethnography: An overview', *Forum: Qualitative Social Research*, vol 12, no 1 (www.qualitative-research.net/index.php/fqs/article/view/1589/3095).

Freire, P. (1998) *Pedagogy of the oppressed*, New York: Continuum [first published 1970].

Gessen, M. (1995) 'In the trenches with the warriors fighting one of the nastiest information wars of the late 20th century', *Wired 3.11* (www.wired.com/1995/11/zamir/).

Glenny, M. (1992) *The fall of Yugoslavia: The third Balkan war*, London: Penguin.

Gould, D. (2009) *Moving politics: Emotion and ACT UP's fight against AIDS*, Chicago, IL: University Press.

Gould, J. (2004) 'Positionality and scale: Methodological issues in the ethnography of aid', in J. Gould and H. Secher Marcussen (eds) *Ethnographies of aid: Exploring development texts and encounters*, Roskilde: Institute for Development Studies.

Hall, S. (2016) 'Lecture 7, Domination and hegemony', in J. Slack and L. Grossberg (eds) *Cultural studies 1983: A theoretical history – Stuart Hall*, Durham, NC: Duke University Press, pp 155–79.

Jambrešić Kirin, R. (1999) 'Personal narratives on war: A challenge to women's essays and ethnography in Croatia', *Estudos de Literatura Oral*, vol 5, pp 73–98.

Jansen, S. (2005) *Antinacionalizam: Etnografija otpora [Anti-nationalism: An ethnography of resistance]*, Belgrade: XX Vek.

Jansen, S. (2008) 'Cosmopolitan openings and closures in post-Yugoslav anti-nationalism', in M. Nowicka and M. Rovisco (eds) *Cosmopolitanism in practice*, Aldershot: Ashgate, pp 75–92.

Jovanović, D. (2016) 'Ambivalence and the study of contradictions', *Journal of Ethnographic Theory*, vol 6, no 3 (www.haujournal.org/index.php/hau/article/view/hau6.3.002/2589).

Kaldor, M. (1999) *New and old wars: Organized violence in a global era*, Stanford, CA: Stanford University Press.

Keane, J. (2003) *Global civil society?*, Cambridge: Cambridge University Press.

Large, J. (1997) *The war next door: A study of second-track intervention during the war in ex-Yugoslavia*, Stroud: Hawthorn Press.

Lendvai, N. and Stubbs, P. (2007) 'Policies as translation: Situating transnational social policies', in S. Hodgson and Z. Irving (eds) *Policy reconsidered: Meanings, politics and practices*, Bristol: Policy Press, pp 173–89.

Lendvai, N. and Stubbs, P. (2009) 'Globale Sozialpolitik und Governance: Standpunkte, Politik und Postkolonialismus' ['Global social policy and governance: Positionality, politics and post-colonialism'], in H.-J. Burchardt (ed) *Nord-Sud Beziehungen im Umbruch: Neu Perspektiven auf Staat und Demokratie in der Weltpolitik*, Frankfurt: Campus Verlag, pp 219–44.

Lovink, G. (2002) *Dark fiber: Tracking critical internet culture*, Cambridge, MA: MIT Press.

Magas, B. (1993) *The destruction of Yugoslavia*, London: Verso.

Marcus, G. (1995) 'Ethnography on/of the world system: The emergence of multi-sited ethnography', *Annual Review of Anthropology*, vol 24, no 1, pp 95–117.

Ortner, S. (1995) 'Resistance and the problem of ethnographic refusal', *Comparative Studies in Society and History*, vol 37, no 1, pp 173–93.

Pečnik, N., Soroya, B. and Stubbs, P. (1995) 'Sunflowers of hope: Social work with refugees and displaced persons in Croatia', *Practice*, vol 7, no 2, pp 5–12.

Pierce, P. and Stubbs, P. (2000) 'Peacebuilding, hegemony and integrated social development: The UNDP in Travnik', in M. Pugh (ed) *Regeneration of war-torn societies*, New York: St Martin's Press, pp 157–76.

Povrzanović, M. and Jambrešić Kirin, R. (1996) 'Negotiating identities? The voice of refugees between experience and representation', in R. Jambrešić Kirin and M. Povrzanović (eds) *War, exile, everyday life: Cultural perspectives*, Zagreb: Institute of Ethnology and Folklore Research, pp 3–22.

Pugh, M. (2000) *Protectorates and spoils of peace: intermestic manipulations of political economy in South-East Europe*, Copenhagen: Peace Research Institute.

Richmond, O. (2010) 'Resistance and the post-liberal peace, *Millennium: Journal of International Studies*, vol 38, no 3, pp 665–92.

Rojas, C. (2007) 'International political economy/development otherwise', *Globalizations*, vol 4, no 4, pp 573–87.

Rothman, J. (2014) 'Reflexive pedagogy: Teaching and learning in peace and conflict studies', *Conflict Resolution Quarterly*, vol 32, no 2, pp 109–28.

Stubbs, P. (1996a) 'Nationalisms, globalization and civil society in Croatia and Slovenia', *Research in Social Movements, Conflicts and Change*, vol 19, pp 1–26.

Stubbs, P. (1996b) 'Creative negotiations: Concepts and practice of integration of refugees, displaced persons and local communities in Croatia', in R. Jambrešić Kirin and M. Povrzanović (eds) *War, exile, everyday life*, Zagreb: Institute of Ethnology and Folklore Research, pp 31–40.

Stubbs, P. (1997) 'NGO work with forced migrants in Croatia: Lineages of a global middle class?', *International Peacekeeping*, vol 4, no 4, pp 50–60.

Stubbs, P. (1998) 'Conflict and co-operation in the virtual community: Email and the wars of the Yugoslav succession', *Sociological Research Online*, vol 3, no 3 (http://socresonline.org.uk/3/3/7.html).

Stubbs, P. (2001) 'Imagining Croatia? Exploring computer-mediated diasporic public spheres', in M. Povrzanović Frykman (ed) *Beyond integration: Challenges of belonging in diaspora and exile*, Lund: Nordic Academic Press, pp 195–224.

Stubbs, P. (2003) 'Towards a political economy of civil society', in M. Meštrović (ed) *Globalization and its reflections on (in) Croatia*, New York: Global Scholarly Publications, pp 149–72.

Stubbs, P. (2004) 'The *ZaMir* (for peace) network: From transnational social movement to Croatian NGO', in A. Brooksbank Jones and M. Cross (eds) *Internet identities in Europe*, Sheffield: ESCUS (http://bib.irb.hr/datoteka/233303.stubbs.pdf).

Stubbs, P. (2005) 'Transforming local and global discourses: Reassessing the PTSD movement in Bosnia and Croatia', in D. Ingleby (ed) *Forced migration and mental health: Rethinking the care of refugees and displaced persons*, New York: Springer, pp 53–66.

Stubbs, P. (2007a) 'Civil society or Ubleha?', in H. Rill et al (eds) *20 pieces of encouragement for awakening and change: Peacebuilding in the region of the former Yugoslavia*, Belgrade: Centre for Nonviolent Action, pp 215–28.

Stubbs, P. (2007b) 'Revisiting computer-mediated anti-war activism: The ZaMir network in post-Yugoslav countries', in H. Swoboda and C. Solioz (eds) *Conflict and renewal: Europe transformed – Essays in honour of Wolfgang Petritsch*, Baden-Baden: Nomos, pp 322–30.

Stubbs, P. (2012) 'Networks, organisations, movements: Narratives and shapes of three waves of activism in Croatia', *Polemos*, vol 15, no 2, pp 11–22 (http://hrcak.srce.hr/index.php?show=clanak&id_clanak_jezik=145099).

Stubbs, P. (2015) 'Performing reform in South East Europe: Consultancy, translation and flexible agency', in J. Clarke, D. Bainton, N. Lendvai and P. Stubbs (eds) *Making policy move: Towards a politics of translation and assemblage*, Bristol: Policy Press, pp 65–94.

Stubbs, P. and Soroya, B. (1996) 'War trauma, psycho-social projects and community development in Croatia', *Medicine, Conflict and Survival*, vol 12, pp 303–14.

Stubbs, P. and Wedel, J. (2015) 'Policy flexians in the global order', in A. Kaasch and K. Martens (eds) *Actors and agency in global social governance*, Oxford: University Press, pp 214–32.

Stubbs, P. and Zrinščak, S. (2015) 'Citizenship and social welfare in Croatia: Clientelism and the limits of "Europeanisation"', *European Politics and Society*, vol 16, no 3, pp 395–410.

Sum, N.-L. and Jessop, B. (2003) 'On pre- and post-disciplinarity in (cultural) political economy', Mimeo (https://core.ac.uk/download/pdf/71859.pdf).

Teršelič, V. (1991) 'O Karavani mira: neke dileme ['On peace caravans: Some dilemmas'], *ARKzin*, vol 1, no 16, 23 October.

Thompson, M. (1992) *A paper house: The ending of Yugoslavia*, London: Hutchinson.

Webster, D. and Dunn, E. (2005) 'Feminist perspectives on trauma', *Women and Therapy*, vol 28, no 3-4, pp 111–42 (www.researchgate. net/publication/254379205_Feminist_Perspectives_on_Trauma).

Wheeler, M. (1993) 'The unmaking of Yugoslavia: A comparative perspective', *Journal of Area Studies*, vol 3, pp 40–9.

Williams, R. (1978) *Marxism and literature*, Oxford: University Press.

Yugofax (1992) *Breakdown: War and reconstruction in Yugoslavia*, London: IWPR.

4

Intervention, autonomy and power in polarised societies

Corinna Jentzsch

Introduction

The secretary of a small village in Murrupula district in northern Mozambique received my research assistant and I with a concerned expression on his face when we visited the village for a second time. Following our first visit, four people from the area had been arrested and incarcerated for six days. During our first stay, we had conducted extensive interviews with former members of a community-initiated militia, the Naparama, active during the country's civil war (1976–92). We were interested in how the militia had emerged and what role it had played during the war between the party in power, Frelimo, and the rebel group, Renamo (today the main opposition party). The group was disbanded at the end of the war, but since then, some units have tried to lobby for recognition of their war effort to receive demobilisation benefits.

The village secretary linked these imprisonments to our visit since the four residents were arrested while helping with the registration of former Naparama members (and other militia men as well) in the context of their efforts to lobby the government for recognition. The registration had been organised by the Naparama leader of Nampula province from Nampula city, who had introduced us to the Naparama in Murrupula district. After the provincial Naparama leader had collected names and a fee from about 250 militiamen and left, the police charged the local Naparama leadership of the area, who had helped with the registration, with betrayal, and arrested them. According to the police, the collection of money along with the registration process was unlawful. The arrested men were released after paying a high fine to the municipality, paid by the provincial Naparama leader. Afterwards, people came to the local Naparama leaders to ask where their money was.

This story from my fieldwork in rural Mozambique in 2011–12 demonstrates the ways in which fieldwork in the aftermath of war can have unintended consequences and create ethical and methodological dilemmas for the research process. The researcher's activities may provide a backdrop for social mobilisation and opportunities for personal enrichment for interlocutors, who decide to play with people's hopes of future benefits. Nampula's Naparama leader had not visited the local Naparama community in Murrupula since the general elections in 1994. Only when I asked him to introduce me to that community and we went there together did he re-establish contact with the former militia unit. In a way, I had encouraged the re-establishment of that contact, which led to abuse by the provincial Naparama leader for his own personal benefit. That benefit had monetary and political meaning. During our conversations, he had tried to establish himself as the primary Naparama leader during the war, a fact that is contested by information from many other sources. It is likely that through this registration process, he was trying to mobilise Naparama to bolster his claim of being the one and only Naparama leader. As with other Naparama members (and also former members of the armed forces), he was disappointed about the lack of recognition as a war veteran and the lack of demobilisation payments. In fact, a considerable portion of members of the armed forces who were demobilised before the end of the war, and of Frelimo's auxiliary forces such as the Naparama and the 'popular militias', were not recognised as demobilised soldiers as part of the peace agreement signed in Rome in 1992, and thus not eligible for demobilisation benefits.

These unintended consequences are linked to how legacies of war – social, economic and political polarisation and historical marginalisation – influence how communities make sense of researchers' activities in their midst. As Sluka reminds us, research participants 'are naturally going to try to figure out what you are doing here', and previous experiences with strangers in the community provide categories such as 'spy, journalist, policeman, tax collector, and missionary' that may be mistakenly applied to the researcher (Sluka, 1995, p 283). Experiences from the war in Mozambique continue to impact daily lives, and contemporary concerns about the distribution of social, economic and political benefits all contribute to the perception of the researcher as a powerful and ambiguous figure that can influence people's lives in positive as well as negative ways. Although some community residents may feel disempowered by the researcher's presence, others may attempt to manipulate the researcher's work for the purpose of their own economic and political empowerment.

This chapter reflects on my attempt to navigate the polarised political landscape in Mozambique's postwar society. I conducted fieldwork in Zambézia and Nampula provinces in Mozambique to analyse the emergence of armed groups formed by communities to defend themselves against insurgent violence during the country's post-independence war (1976–92). The 'Naparama', as these militia groups were called, formed in central and northern Mozambique towards the end of the 1980s and, within a short time period, fought back against the rebel group Renamo. Renamo was supported by the governments of Rhodesia (today's Zimbabwe) and Apartheid South Africa that sought to destabilise the socialist government of Frelimo, the successor party of the liberation movement of Mozambique (Vines, 1991). Contrary to commonly held beliefs, the war was not just a proxy war fought in the shadow of the Cold War, but provided an opportunity to settle local conflicts and thus pitched 'brother against brother' (Geffray, 1990).

Although I encountered many challenges along the way, I succeeded in collecting more than 10,000 pages of documents in government archives and more than 250 interviews and oral histories with community members, former militia members, former rebel combatants, former soldiers, (former) government officials, politicians and academics in five districts and the capital. I worked together with a Mozambican research assistant who spoke all the necessary local languages and had experience in data collection for international projects. He helped me with arranging interviews, translating from local languages into Portuguese and explaining cultural particularities. As a Mozambican from the central province of Zambézia, but a long-term resident in the province of Nampula, my assistant was well suited to be sufficiently knowledgeable about the two provinces we worked in (and their languages), but considered enough of an outsider not to be identified with a certain political position.

Conflict researchers have recognised the ethical and practical challenges that research on violence entails (Nordstrom and Robben, 1995; Wood, 2006; Sriram et al, 2009; Fujii, 2012; Mazurana et al, 2013). However, as Malejacq and Mukhopadhyay (2016) have noted, there is still little transparency and debate on how researchers form and manage relationships in the field, and what kind of ethical compromises and methodological adaptations they have to accept in order to collect the necessary data for their projects. Researchers in political science have learned from their colleagues in anthropology (and geography) for whom the position and impact of the researcher on the local community has become a central concern for how to 'do' anthropology

(Clifford and Marcus, 1986; England, 1994; Sirnate, 2014). However, what is often obscured are the ways in which the researcher becomes a political actor capable of reinforcing existing power structures and, by disempowering or empowering local actors, influencing social realities in communities under study. This is significant, as not only the autonomy of the researched may be constrained, but also that of the researcher whose presence and work may be manipulated by local actors. This is true not only for research in today's volatile conflict zones (Malejacq and Mukhopadhyay, 2016), but also for research in (postwar) polarised societies[1] in which political conflicts linger on and reinforce economic, social and political inequalities (Gerharz, 2009, p 2).

The limited understanding of the workings of power, and by extension the limits of researcher neutrality, is often due to the fact that the usual concern in Political Science when conducting field research is not with what happens to the field site (during and after fieldwork), but surprisingly with the data that researchers extract from it and how to mitigate systematic bias. This means that challenges of access to research participants or the 'subtext' or 'meta-data' (Fujii, 2010) from conversations, such as lies, silences and evasions, are considered 'obstacles' rather than 'a source of knowledge for ethnographers' (Wedeen, 2010, p 256). In fact, researchers may alter the field site and the data in ways that are difficult to account for and 'reverse' during data analysis. As Goodhand argues, such intervention in conflict settings is not only a methodological challenge, but also an ethical issue, as it 'may affect the incentive systems and structures driving violent conflict or impact upon the coping strategies and safety of communities' (Goodhand, 2000, p 12).

In the context of Mozambique, the impact of the social, economic and political legacies of the war on my interactions with rural communities were puzzling to me, as the country is often hailed as a successful example of postwar peacebuilding and reconciliation (UN, 1995). One could expect that (unofficial) reconciliation processes, national reconstruction and the passing of time would have helped create confidence in people's futures (Honwana, 2002; Igreja et al, 2008). However, the country remains polarised even 20 years after the end of the war (Weinstein, 2002; Darch, 2015). Fear of renewed violence still influences political and social life in rural Mozambican communities – for good reason, as the current resurgence of violence in the centre of the country demonstrates (Darch, 2015). Moreover, the spoils of recent finds of natural resources have not (yet) reached the ordinary citizen, leading to increases in already high levels of inequality (IMF, 2016).

In a society seeking to overcome its violent past and advance economic development, the ways in which communities tried to make sense of my (and my research assistant's) presence had two major consequences for the (perceived) autonomy of research participants and of my own work. The first was related to a narrative of suspicion and mistrust about me and my work that stemmed from the feeling of severe disempowerment with respect to people's control over their own wellbeing. Some community residents felt threatened by my presence, as they were reminded of white foreigners mingling in their affairs over the course of the history of their community. The second narrative was related to whether and how participants could manipulate my presence and my work in a way that would benefit them economically or politically. Some research participants saw my presence as an opportunity to escape from the uncertainties of their own life regarding jobs, livelihoods and political projects. In the remainder of this chapter, I analyse these two responses and what that ambiguous response meant for the perceived autonomy of research participants in my own work. Specific examples from my fieldwork are provided to highlight the implications of residents' ambiguous response for neutrality and power during fieldwork in polarised societies.

Disempowerment and research participant autonomy

One evening in Mecubúri district in Nampula province, a local government representative, who my research assistant and I were having drinks with, told us that people had been talking and wondering what we were up to. In the days before, we had been walking through some of the neighbourhoods of the district town and conducted interviews with residents and local leaders. The government officer reported that some people were afraid we were bringing illnesses, as a number of residents had recently suffered from diarrhoea. Others thought that we might bring another war. As the officer elaborated, these fears had been triggered by several events that had occurred in the area, in the province and abroad. A few days before our arrival in Mecubúri, in October 2011, Libyan head of state Muammar Gaddafi had been killed by rebels, and the youth leader of the African National Congress in South Africa, Julius Malema, had engaged in divisive speeches (for which he was later expelled from the party) (Smith, 2011). Mozambicans follow the news of both countries closely, and in their eyes, their instability was cause for concern.

In addition, in the officer's view, some events closer to home had further made people wary of our presence. A theatre piece attempting to explain to people that 5,000 houses would be built by the Chinese and sold to the community was understood as meaning that 5,000 Chinese would come and be distributed throughout the province. Residents feared an 'invasion' of 5,000 Chinese people. People were also concerned about news that, a month before, in September 2011, one British and four Americans with heavy weapons in their luggage were held for a brief time at Nampula airport (BBC News, 2011). The men claimed that they had come to rescue a boat from Somali pirates. In the course of our conversation that evening in Mecubúri, we learned that we were not the only strangers who were treated with suspicion. Non-governmental organisation (NGO) workers of a US-funded project seeking to improve access to safe water regularly distribute 'certeza', a chlorine-based water-purifying liquid to prevent cholera outbreaks. However, whenever cholera breaks out, these workers are suspected of having brought it (Serra, 2003; AIM, 2013; Fauvet, 2013).[2]

Our presence, the presence of strangers, in the district seemed to fit into this sequence of ill-boding events whose origins and consequences remained uncertain. As Gerharz (2009) confirms, suspicion about the researcher's motives is often triggered by people's memories of past violence. In a highly polarised setting such as the civil war in Sri Lanka, residents of Colombo quickly accused Gerharz of being an LTTE (Liberation Tigers of Tamil Eelam) sympathiser when she discussed the humanitarian situation in LTTE strongholds (Gerharz, 2009, pp 5–6). Since people in the South were reminded by Gerharz' comments of their suffering from seemingly unpredictable episodes of violence, it was difficult for her to highlight the suffering of the other side and at the same time claim neutrality. Similarly, in Mozambique, people did not want a return to war, and wondered about the true meaning of my work.

Such suspicion created a situation that prevented trust and gaining access, crucial preconditions for any successful fieldwork. Drawing on research experience in Northern Ireland, Knox shows that in politically contested environments, the problem of gaining access often consists of suspicion around the real research objective, as research in such contexts is 'unlikely to be viewed by local actors as neutral or altruistic' (Knox, 2001, p 211). In the highly contested political environment of Northern Ireland, 'There was immediate suspicion about the ulterior motives of this research, which had the potential to block access at worst or severely curtail data gathering' (Knox, 2001, p 211). This is true for the context of my research. The officer we met that evening in Mecubúri was nowhere to be found when we tried to meet with him for an interview the following day.

All these concerns were troubling, as, without realising it, I had become part of a social and political context in which people feared that, as a consequence of interacting with me, they would further lose control over their health and wellbeing. The more I (or people like me) entered their lives, the less they felt in charge. At the same time, as people overestimated my power, they underestimated their own. People's responses to my presence in their communities had a similar meaning as their resistance against the distribution of chlorine, which Serra (2003) interprets as an expression of severe disempowerment. As Serra's analysis reveals, resistance against outsiders in the form of suspicion and mistrust is an expression of people's distrust in state institutions, as these have been perceived as distant and failing to deliver promised services.

The sources of such feeling of disempowerment and loss of autonomy in the central and northern provinces of Mozambique are varied. First, the history of the central and northern provinces is one of political marginalisation by the government in Maputo in the south of the country (Chichava, 2007; Do Rosário, 2009). Frelimo, the liberation movement and party in power since independence in 1975, has been perceived as a southern movement; the independence movement's penetration of both provinces during the liberation struggle was slow and ineffectual or, in the case of Nampula province, completely absent (Legrand, 1993, p 88); and the peasant population opposed Frelimo's policies after independence. In Nampula, the construction of communal villages and the abolishment of traditional authorities sparked popular discontent (Geffray, 1990). In Zambézia, it was the disrespect for traditional values more generally that had been the basis for life in the province and that, in turn, provoked opposition (Ranger, 1985, p 189; O'Laughlin, 1992, p 115). As a result, the region was and is a Renamo stronghold.

Second, the particular character of the post-independence war, a typical guerrilla war, contributed to suspicion towards strangers in rural communities. Community residents' responses to my presence during a time of uncertainty reflect Sluka's (1995, p 283) observation of the relevance of pre-existing categories misapplied to strangers who enter the community, such as being a spy, which was a common concern during the war in Mozambique, as in many other wars (Sluka, 1995; Vlassenroot, 2006). Many people referred to the war as a 'war between brothers.' In contrast to the anti-colonial struggle, members of either side could not be identified easily, as they all belonged to the same community. The enemy could always be lurking in the midst of the community. Moreover, the rebel group Renamo was actively supported by Rhodesia (today's Zimbabwe) and Apartheid South Africa. White South African advisers were regularly flown into Renamo bases. Community residents linked that experience to my presence and wondered whether I had anything to do with the war, since I was so eager to speak to them about that period of time. At the end of an interview with an older male community resident I was asked whether the war would return once I left the village. When I worked in an area in Murrupula district, Nampula, where one of the main Renamo bases was located during the war, the chief of staff of the local administration told us that there had never been a delegation with a white person staying overnight. He urged that the community police chief inform residents so that they would not think something was wrong, as this had been, 'an area of the enemy.'

Moreover, although Mozambique has received much development aid and recently also discovered more natural resources wealth, people feel they have yet to benefit from economic development. Serra's (2003) analysis points to the arrogance and distance of NGO workers that creates discontent among community residents. Examples from different regions of Mozambique, such as coal mining in Tete province or the Brazilian large-scale agribusiness project ProSAVANA, where residents are displaced to make space for the business of foreign companies, add to the impression that strangers meddle with people's affairs to the detriment of their livelihoods (Abelvik-Lawson, 2014; Zacarias, 2014; Lillywhite et al, 2015; Chichava and Durán, 2016). Finally, much of the hesitance in talking to us was connected to current party politics, and shows that the Frelimo party never lost its dominance in Mozambican politics, despite the fact that the country had introduced multiparty politics in its new constitution in 1990 (Sumich and Honwana, 2007). Some former government officials declined to be interviewed since they did not feel qualified, which suggests that they did not feel authorised and were thus afraid of violating the official party line. In other cases, these officials made sure that I had respected the administrative hierarchy and attained permission from their (former) supervisors.

This past and contemporary experience of marginalisation contributed to the perception of my research assistant and I as 'intruders'. I dealt with this situation in several ways to establish 'research legitimacy' (Knox, 2001). I always respected the social and administrative hierarchy when coming into a district I had never been to, and introduced myself and my work to local leaders to receive '"approval" from key stakeholders' (Knox, 2001, p 212). In the districts I visited after Mecubúri, I asked for an elder who was respected in the community as a guide who could introduce me to people, or asked for referrals from research participants (commonly referred to as 'snowball sampling'; Sluka, 1995, p 284; Knox, 2001, p 212; Cohen and Arieli, 2011; Romano, 2006). Mistrust between Frelimo and Renamo elites implied that I was to pursue relationships with several types of 'gatekeepers' (Campbell et al, 2006): with Frelimo party and state structures and, separately, with Renamo party structures. I also respected people's wish to not being interviewed alone; when interviewing men, their wives often sat next to them to listen in on the conversation. I tried to visit communities several times to establish a rapport (Norman, 2009; Browne and McBride, 2015).

Overall, I avoided talking about politically sensitive topics (Sluka, 1995, p 283), and avoided mentioning 'politics'. In the process of trying to make sense of my presence in their communities, residents wanted to make sure that I did not have anything to do with 'politics'. 'Politics' has negative connotations in many parts of Mozambique, as politicians are seen as people who lie and enrich themselves (as is common in many parts of Africa; see Ekeh, 1975). A businessman and veteran of the pre- and post-independence wars in Nicoadala invited me over to his house for lunch to finally "forget about politics" and "just chat". He could not understand that I was willing to "suffer" and study political history, and not do business, as Mozambique was "the place to do business." Religious community residents were concerned about my political intentions. In Murrupula, the first question of a sheikh was which party I was affiliated with.[3] In Nicoadala, a pastor only agreed to meet with me once I assured him I would not talk politics under the roof of his church.[4] I emphasised my status as a student who is independent of party politics (Knox, 2001, p 212).

But as many field researchers have recognised before me, neutrality is difficult to achieve, and sometimes not even desirable (Nash, 1976; Sluka, 1990, 1995; Gerharz, 2009; Malejacq and Mukhopadhyay, 2016). The strategies I adopted mitigated many of the concerns, but posed some new methodological and ethical dilemmas. For example, it was important to take into account the ways in which people introduced me to certain communities, and to consider whether the presence of certain people during interviews impacted and changed the conversation. As Campbell et al (2006, pp 115–16) argue, rather than trying to be 'neutral' in general, it is important to emphasise your independence from gatekeepers. It also meant that some community residents might have felt compelled to talk to me because an authority figure told them to, and not because they themselves had volunteered. Also important was the consideration of 'gatekeeper bias' (Cohen and

Arieli, 2011), and in particular, the issue of sampling bias (Groger et al, 1999). These dilemmas required much explanation on my part and transparency about my activities to make sure that people felt at ease talking to me, but also taking the emerging methodological limits into account during analysis. However, fieldwork challenges not always arose out of people's concern about their own disempowerment and the limits to their own autonomy, but also out of their hopes for political, social or economic empowerment, as the next section discusses.

Empowerment and researcher autonomy

While the reports of mistrust and suspicion in northern Mozambique were troubling, the manner in which they were communicated to my research assistant and I appeared to be for political currency. The local government representative who warned us about the concerns within the community in Mecubúri apparently used these stories to pursue his own agenda and fight a political battle against the district administrator. My research assistant found out that, for unclear reasons, the administrator was not well liked among local government employees. The officer we talked to was wary of the fact that the district administrator had given us permission to work without a guide accompanying us to interviews with community members. It seemed likely that he felt his position within the local administration was not taken seriously. As someone who was in constant contact with the local police and other local leaders, he used his monopoly on information to manipulate us for his political interests and divert attention from the fact that he himself mistrusted us. As mentioned earlier, throughout our time in that district, the officer avoided being interviewed, although he had agreed to do so earlier. This politicisation of mistrust and suspicion has a long history in Mozambique. During our conversation in Mecubúri, I learned that members of the 'opposition' sprinkle 'chlorine' (actually, they use flour), which supposedly spreads cholera, on some people's doorsteps, implying that if the residents touch it, they will be contaminated. Thus, while the initial narrative about how cholera spreads expresses disempowerment and distrust of state institutions, this counter-narrative puts blame on the 'opposition', a diffuse group of people who oppose the Frelimo government and may be sympathetic to Renamo. Overall, such suspicions feed into the reinforcement of political cleavages, which are understood in many parts of Mozambique as existential threats rather than part of democratic politics.

Politicisation can occur on several levels. Another example of the impact of current political developments was the reaction of Renamo leaders in the provincial capital of Quelimane to my request for permission to interview former Renamo combatants in the province. Since at the time of my request national Renamo leader Afonso Dhlakama had threatened to stage a (peaceful) overthrow of the government on 25 December 2011, provincial leaders of the party did not consider this a suitable time to allow such interviews.[5] When I tried again in February 2012 the provincial party leaders in coordination with Dhlakama himself granted me permission, as the political situation had since calmed. But my work was not only politicised with respect to its potential negative consequences. Others played with my work's potential positive consequences, as noted above. In a way, the Naparama leader who had organised the registration of the Naparama after our departure was manipulating people's hopes of future benefits, which I had (unwillingly) raised in the first place. Former Naparama members were surprised, but also humbled by the fact that someone wanted to talk specifically to them so long after the war had ended. This fact created the opportunity for many interviews in Mecubúri and Murrupula, since many Naparama walked many miles to meet with me. The way they made sense of this was the hope that my questions would lead to their registration as former Naparama members and eventual demobilisation benefits, or at least funds for 'projects'. In a development context, it was difficult to understand the purpose of research for the production of knowledge, and not of development outcomes.

This demand for recognition and 'projects' did not solely have meaning for the individual but for the Naparama as a whole. "You can't talk to the Naparama individually", a former commander of the government-aligned militia told my research assistant and I. We had just introduced ourselves and our project during a meeting with the group's leadership in Nicoadala in Zambézia province in Mozambique. The commander informed us that the high command of the Naparama could give us all the information we needed, and that the remaining combatants would speak to us as a group. He claimed that individual Naparama were not mentally capable of talking properly about the Naparama, which would result in contradicting stories. They sought to restrict my access and only allow me to interview former members that they could 'control', combatants of high rank, discrediting other members as not telling 'the truth'. The Naparama commander clearly sought to control what version of the history of the community-initiated militia would be told. He did not want my research project to jeopardise Naparama's ongoing struggle to receive recognition from the government and compensation for the group's wartime efforts. This concern was not completely unfounded. As the commander later explained, he had been taken to the Mozambican intelligence agency's office once, and charged for not providing a certain document that the agency had received from other sources. The commander was afraid that the intelligence agency would get access to information combatants would provide me with, and interrogate the Naparama leadership for not having disclosed this information previously.

My research assistant and I underlined that I was a student writing a thesis and that I was independent of parties or the government. However, our emphasis on my status as a student working on a degree led the leaders to conclude that the Naparama militia would not receive any benefit from the study, and thus they suddenly denied their cooperation. In a last effort to solve what at that point seemed to be an insurmountable hurdle, I explained why I found my study important: most histories of the war had focused on Frelimo and Renamo while ignoring the important contribution of the Naparama. Since the militia leaders had been in the process of demanding recognition from the government for a long time, they appreciated that I highlighted the value of their contribution, and thus agreed that all the leaders could be interviewed individually.

These examples of attempted individual and group manipulation of my research project represent another instance of the earlier-mentioned gatekeeper bias, but in a more intentional and manipulative form, which is common in fieldwork with marginalised or high-risk communities that have certain grievances that they want to see addressed. Access is traded for a certain version of representation that benefits research participants and the groups they belong to politically. Gerharz (2009), for example, mentions how the rebel group LTTE in Sri Lanka attempted to make use of the many researchers to polish its own image. In Eastern DRC (Democratic Republic of the Congo), Vlassenroot (2006, p 197), working among armed groups, experienced how his 'writings were used as proofs that [respondents'] claims or grievances were justifiable' (Vlassenroot, 2006, p 197). Researchers can thus be exploited to improve a group's or an individual's reputation. Malejacq and Mukhopadhyay report how a handshake of one of the authors with an Afghan governor was broadcast on TV to counter 'the governor's reputation as an uneducated countryman by exhibiting his connection to a foreign university professor' (Malejacq and Mukhopadhyay, 2016, p 1014).

While I was careful in all conversations to avoid the impression that talking to me would result in political or monetary benefits, this hope was difficult to dispel. Part of the problem was that local leaders who helped to connect us with former combatants were insensitive to the ways in which they might create false expectations. In a rural area in Murrupula district, the secretary of the locality had called all demobilised soldiers for a meeting. When we started our interviews with some of the demobilised soldiers, and explained what we were doing, they were disappointed since they came in the hope of finally receiving their benefits that they had waited for, for a long time. At times, it looked as if local leaders had deliberately misrepresented the purpose of such meetings, because they knew that if they had said this was for research, people would not have shown up. This created an ethical dilemma, as I was dependent on other people's help with getting introduced to community residents who had been involved in the war, but did not have complete control over how others represented the purpose of my work. Such dependence on core contacts and gatekeepers and the potential for manipulation of the researcher's presence, activities and writings inverts the power relationship between researcher and researched and constrains the autonomy of the researcher and their project (Vlassenroot, 2006). Such power asymmetries in favour of research participants are especially pronounced in dangerous settings in which researchers depend on certain elites for their personal protection (Adams, 1999; Kovats-Bernat, 2002; Malejacq and Mukhopadhyay, 2016, p 1013). But they find similar expression in polarised societies in which researchers depend on certain individuals to gain access and trust.

Conclusion

These narratives from my fieldwork demonstrate that the autonomy of the researcher and that of the researched are closely interlinked. The people I asked for an interview thought I had particular powers that could work in both directions, positive and negative. For some, my work seemed particularly threatening, as they associated my mere presence and/or the subject of my work with threats to their livelihoods and wellbeing. For others, my presence provided an opportunity to receive support for their vision of politics so that they could reach their political, social and economic goals.

In this context, the researcher becomes a political actor within the field site and fieldwork becomes 'a form of intervention' (Malejacq and Mukhopadhyay, 2016), which curtails community residents' autonomy over their lives and wellbeing. As a consequence of the researcher's presence, the field site experiences a qualitative change, which is difficult to 'factor out' of the resulting data during the process of analysis. At the same time, community residents become 'actors' in the research project, which may constrain the autonomy of the researcher (Vlassenroot, 2006) and contribute to their 'relative powerlessness', restricting their role to that of a 'mascot researcher' (Adams, 1999). The Naparama commander mentioned earlier attempted to influence the research design by limiting access to certain individuals, becoming an author of the study rather than its subject. This negotiation of the researcher's position within the field site needs to be taken into account during data analysis, beyond the considerations about potential biases due to gender and other characteristics of the researcher. Instances of empowerment and disempowerment (and their consequences) can only be recognised when discursive strategies such as rumours about the researcher, inventions, denials, evasions and silences are treated as the 'meta-data' of fieldwork (Fujii, 2010).

Rather than conceiving ourselves as external observers, analysts and critics of disempowerment, we need to take into account the ways in which we may, inadvertently, contribute to empowering some and disempowering others. Even if (or especially when) researchers try to be neutral and retain distance from community life, they unwittingly become actors in local or national conflicts (Sluka, 1990, 1995; Gerharz, 2009). Some researchers have embraced the impossibility of remaining neutral and impartial observers, in particular, in violent settings. Malejacq and Mukhopadhyay (2016), for example, discuss the ways in which they have 'intervened' in their respective field sites and engaged in 'tribal politics' during their work in Afghanistan and Somalia, creating informal networks of informants that provided access and protection. Research in violent settings is made difficult by security concerns for the researcher, but the notion that researchers intervene in local politics, even though they may 'only' intend to observe, is true for highly polarised postwar contexts as well.

Overall, the two narratives demonstrate a deeply ambiguous reaction to strangers. Community residents do not like the intrusion of strangers who bring projects, as these are contingent, conditional, subject to review, and there is no long-term investment and development of trust. Conversely, projects mean jobs and seed money, which could improve people's lives. This again confirms Serra's (2003) notion that what people ask for is not a complete absence of the state and its services, but more accountability and reliability of external interveners. By extension, what communities ask for is not that researchers stay away from them, but that they remain transparent and accountable about their activities, and aware of the political nature of their work. Researchers become part of a community and shape social realities in ways that may not be anticipated or intended, creating opportunities for both empowerment and disempowerment. Such reflection remains important, both for research transparency and research ethics.

Notes

1 By 'polarisation', I follow the definition provided by Esteban and Schneider (2008, p 133): 'the extent to which the population is clustered around a small number of distant poles. This notion of polarisation is particularly relevant to the analysis of conflict, because it stands for the idea that the tensions within a society of individuals or states result from two simultaneous decisions: identification with other subjects within the own group of reference and distancing oneself from one or several other competing groups.' In Mozambique, 16 years of war contributed to political polarisation between sympathisers of the party in power, Frelimo, and the rebel group turned opposition party, Renamo, which, during the war, was referred to as 'armed bandits' and largely seen as terrorists without a political project.

2 A related phenomenon is *chupasangue* ('drawing blood') that has recurred over decades in regions of Zambézia and Nampula province whenever government or international agencies visited rural communities during vaccination campaigns. These agencies are accused of drawing blood like vampires and thereby causing deaths in the community (Chichava, 2007, pp 392–9).

3 Interview with religious leader, Murrupula, Nampula.

4 Interview with religious leader, Nicoadala, Zambézia.

5 Renamo party leaders in Nampula province, whom I contacted a few months later, did not see the political situation at the time as a problem, and granted me permission to interview former Renamo combatants.

References

Abelvik-Lawson, H. (2014) 'Sustainable development for whose benefit? Brazil's economic power and human rights violations in the Amazon and Mozambique', *The International Journal of Human Rights*, vol 18, no 7–8, pp 795–821.

Adams, L.L. (1999) 'The mascot researcher', *Journal of Composite Materials*, vol 33, no 10, pp 928–40.

AIM (Agência de Informação de Moçambique) (2013) 'Mozambique: Cholera disinformation leads to clashes', 17 February.

BBC News (2011) 'Mozambique holds US and British "pirate hunters"', 19 September (www.bbc.com/news/world-africa-14952999).

Browne, B.C. and McBride, R. (2015) 'Politically sensitive encounters: Ethnography, access, and the benefits of "hanging out"', *Qualitative Sociology Review*, vol 11, no 1, pp 34–48.

Campbell, L.M., Gray, N.J., Meletis, Z.A. and Abbott, J.G. (2006) 'Gatekeepers and keymasters: Dynamic relationships of access in geographical fieldwork', *Geographical Review*, vol 96, no 1, pp 97–121.

Chichava, S.I. (2007) 'Le "vieux Mozambique": Étude sur l'identité politique de la Zambézie', PhD dissertation, Université Montesquieu/Bordeaux IV.

Chichava, S. and Durán, J. (2016) *Civil society organisations' political control over Brazil and Japan's development cooperation in Mozambique: More than a mere whim?*, LSE Global South Unit Working Paper Series, Working Paper no 2, London: London School of Economics and Political Science.

Clifford, J. and Marcus, G.E. (1986) *Writing culture. The poetics and politics of ethnography*, Berkeley, CA: University of California Press.

Cohen, N. and Arieli, T. (2011) 'Field research in conflict environments: Methodological challenges and snowball sampling', *Journal of Peace Research*, vol 48, no 4, pp 423–35.

Darch, C. (2015) 'Separatist tensions and violence in the "model post-conflict state": Mozambique since the 1990s', *Review of African Political Economy*, vol 43, no 148, pp 320–7.

Do Rosário, D. (2009) 'Les Mairies des "autres": Une analyse politique, socio-historique et culturelle des trajectoires locales. Le cas d'Angoche, de l'Île de Moçambique et de Nacala Porto', PhD dissertation, Université Montesquieu/Bordeaux IV.

Ekeh, P.P. (1975) 'Colonialism and the two publics In Africa: A theoretical statement', *Comparative Studies in Society and History*, vol 17, no 1, pp 91–112.

England, K.V.L. (1994) 'Getting personal: Reflexivity, positionality, and feminist research', *The Professional Geographer*, vol 46, no 1, pp 80–9.

Esteban, J. and Schneider, G. (2008) 'Polarization and conflict: Theoretical and empirical issues', *Journal of Peace Research*, vol 45, no 2, pp 131–41.

Fauvet, P. (2013) 'Mozambique: 17 People arrested for cholera riots in Nampula', Agência de Informação de Moçambique, 22 February.

Fujii, L.A. (2010) 'Shades of truth and lies. Interpreting testimonies of war and violence', *Journal of Peace Research*, vol 47, no 2, pp 231–41.

Fujii, L.A. (2012) 'Research ethics 101: Dilemmas and responsibilities', *PS: Political Science & Politics*, vol 45, no 4, pp 231–41.

Geffray, C. (1990) *La cause des armes au Mozambique. Anthropologie d'une guerre civile*, Paris: Karthala.

Gerharz, E. (2009) *Ambivalent positioning. Reflections on ethnographic research in Sri Lanka during the ceasefire of 2002*, Working Papers in Development Sociology and Social Anthropology, Working Paper no 361, Universität Bielefeld.

Goodhand, J. (2000) 'Research in conflict zones: Ethics and accountability', *Forced Migration Review*, vol 8, pp 12-15.

Groger, L., Mayberry, P.S. and Straker, J.K. (1999) 'What we didn't learn because of who would not talk to us', *Qualitative Health Research*, vol 9, no 6, pp 829–35.

Honwana, A.M. (2002) *Espíritos vivos, tradições modernas: Possessão de espíritos e reintegração social pós-guerra no sul de Moçambique*, Maputo: Promédia.

Igreja, V., Dias-Lambranca, B. and Richters, A. (2008) 'Gamba spirits, gender relations, and healing in post-civil war Gorongosa, Mozambique', *Journal of the Royal Anthropological Institute*, vol 14, no 2, pp 353–71.

IMF (International Monetary Fund) (2016) *Republic of Mozambique. Selected issues*, IMF Country Report, No 16/10, Washington, DC: IMF.

Knox, C. (2001) 'Establishing research legitimacy in the contested political ground of contemporary Northern Ireland', *Qualitative Research*, vol 1, no 2, pp 205–22.

Kovats-Bernat, J.C. (2002) 'Negotiating dangerous fields: Pragmatic strategies for fieldwork amid violence and terror', *American Anthropologist*, vol 104, no 1, pp 208–22.

Legrand, J.-C. (1993) 'Logique de guerre et dynamique de la violence en Zambézie, 1976–1991', *Politique Africaine*, June, vol 50, pp 88–104.

Lillywhite, S., Kemp, D. and Sturman, K. (2015) *Mining, resettlement and lost livelihoods: Listening to the voices of resettled communities in Mualadzi, Mozambique*, Melbourne, VIC: Oxfam.

Malejacq, R. and Mukhopadhyay, D. (2016) 'The "tribal politics" of field research: A reflection on power and partiality in 21st-century warzones', *Perspectives on Politics*, vol 14, no 4, pp 1011–28.

Mazurana, D.E., Jacobsen, K. and Gale, L.A. (eds) (2013) *Research methods in conflict settings. A view from below*, New York: Cambridge University Press.

Morier-Genoud, E., Cahen, M. and Do Rosário, D. (eds) (forthcoming) *The war within: New perspectives on the Civil War in Mozambique, 1976–1992*, Woodbridge: James Currey.

Nash, J. (1976) 'Ethnology in a revolutionary setting', in M. Rynkiewich and J. Spradley (eds) *Ethics and anthropology: Dilemmas in fieldwork*, New York: Wiley & Sons, pp 148–66.

Nordstrom, C. and Robben, A.C.G.M. (1995) *Fieldwork under fire: Contemporary studies of violence and culture*, Berkeley, CA: University of California Press.

Norman, J.M. (2009) 'Got trust? The challenge of gaining access in conflict zones', in C. Lekha Sriram, J.C. Kind, J.A. Mertus, O. Martin-Ortega and J. Herman (eds) *Surviving field research. Working in violent and difficult situations*, London: Routledge, pp 71–90.

O'Laughlin, B. (1992) 'A base social da guerra em Moçambique', *Estudos Moçambicanos*, vol 10, pp 107–42.

Ranger, T.O. (1985) *Peasant consciousness and guerrilla war in Zimbabwe: A comparative study*, London: James Currey.

Romano, D. (2006) 'Conducting research in the Middle East's conflict zones', *PS: Political Science & Politics*, vol 39, no 3, pp 439–41.

Serra, C. (2003) *Cólera e catarse*, Maputo: Imprensa Universitária.

Sirnate, V. (2014) 'Positionality, personal insecurity, and female empathy in security studies research', *PS: Political Science & Politics*, vol 47, no 2, pp 398–401.

Sluka, J.A. (1990) 'Participant observation in violent social contexts', *Human Organization*, vol 49, no 2, pp 114–26.

Sluka, J.A. (1995) 'Reflections on managing danger in fieldwork: Dangerous anthropology in Belfast', in C. Nordstrom and A.C.G.M. Robben (eds) *Fieldwork under fire: Contemporary studies of violence and culture*, Berkeley, CA: University of California Press, pp 276–94.

Smith, D. (2011) 'ANC youth leader Julius Malema thrown out of party', 10 November, *The Guardian* (www.theguardian.com/world/2011/nov/10/julius-malema-anc-expelled).

Sriram, C.L., King, J.C., Mertus, J.A., Martin-Ortega, O. and Herman, J. (2009) *Surviving field research. Working in violent and difficult situations*, London: Routledge.

Sumich, J. and Honwana, J. (2007) *Strong party, weak state? Frelimo and state survival through the Mozambican civil war: An analytical narrative on state-making*, Crisis States Working Papers Series, Working Paper No 2, London: LSE Development Studies Institute.

UN (United Nations) (1995) *The United Nations and Mozambique, 1992–1995* (United Nations Blue Books Series), New York: UN, Department of Public Information.

Vines, A. (1991) *RENAMO: Terrorism in Mozambique*, London: Centre for Southern African Studies, University of York, in association with James Currey.

Vlassenroot, K. (2006) 'War and social research. The limits of empirical methodologies in war-torn environments', *Civilisations*, vol 54, no 1-2, pp 191–8.

Wedeen, L. (2010) 'Reflections on ethnographic work in political science', *Annual Review of Political Science*, 13, pp 255–72.

Weinstein, J.M. (2002) 'Mozambique: A fading UN success story', *Journal of Democracy*, vol 13, no 1, pp 141–56.

Wood, E.J. (2006) 'The ethical challenges of field research in conflict zones', *Qualitative Sociology*, vol 29, no 3, pp 373–86.

Zacarias, A. (2014) 'Mozambique's small farmers fear Brazilian-style agriculture', 1 January, *The Guardian* (www.theguardian.com/global-development/2014/jan/01/mozambique-small-farmers-fear-brazilian-style-agriculture).

Vignette 2: Packing for Kabul

Henri Myrttinen

I was in the midst of packing my rucksack for next day's departure for Kabul when I received the email asking if I would write this short piece on emotions and fieldwork. As always before a trip to Afghanistan, I had spent the previous days and weeks emotionally charged, questioning the wisdom of my trip. My pre-trip feelings circled around, if not fear, then at least very strong apprehensions around safety and security. In my head, I played through time and again what to do in potential situations of car bombings, kidnappings and targeted attacks against guesthouses for foreigners, which had all markedly increased in Afghanistan over recent months and years. Apart from my own concerns, I was also keenly aware of the price that I was also making others close to me pay through their own apprehensions regarding my safety. Although they might not always voice it, I knew that my parents, siblings, friends and colleagues would be worried, each inevitable piece of news of yet another attack in Afghanistan putting them on edge. Agreeing to write this piece, however, also raised apprehensions of a different sort, both around opening up publicly about emotions and around the risk of navel-gazing. Nonetheless, I wanted to write this piece and own up to my own fears and weaknesses.

I chose voluntarily to go to Afghanistan and many other conflict zones over the years. Unlike most of the local Afghans, I have a European passport, a variety of credit cards, travel and health insurance, access to embassies and the ability to buy a plane ticket in minutes. I am also white and a male, both of which are identities that unfortunately still, or perhaps increasingly, give me unfair and undeserved advantages in terms of mobility and access. Therefore, I can go into, move around and also leave conflict zones when it behoves me, as soon as I start feeling too uncomfortable. Thus my apprehensions are, to a degree, of my own making and choosing, and wallowing in them at times seems like a luxury, a self-made Western problem, and a perverse self-indulgence.

At times within the non-governmental organisation (NGO) sector a working culture prevails of sucking it up, working oneself to a burnout, and having work take over one's life. Too often an 'if you can't stand the heat, get out of the kitchen' attitude still dominates in the sector and is reinforced when we tell our 'war stories' to each other at social occasions. Implicitly, we may thereby be upping the ante for others, in particular, younger colleagues, to do the same. In particular, it seems to be us middle-aged Western men who revel in the 'machismo of ... bringing back news from ... the mean streets [of the field],' to quote the sociologist David Morgan.[1] The need to question these all too common practices is becoming increasingly pressing.

Back in Kabul, as I knew they would, my apprehensions dissipated and morphed into something new as soon as I got out of the airport terminal. While the pre-trip apprehensions are more vague, 'on the ground' things become much more focused and in a sense seemingly less daunting. In what is most likely a delusional trick of the mind to conjure up a sense of control when there is none, my mind moved from vague apprehensions to focusing on practicalities. I started considering the details of what to do in case an attack happened, as if I knew what I was doing. Of course I do not, but the playing through in my mind of possible escape routes, ensuring that I had contact numbers and a grab bag ready created an illusion of control and kept the mind busy.

A car bomb on the other side of town awoke me on my second night in Kabul. Skyping with headquarters the next morning, I was given the option to cut my trip short and return to London. I knew that I would not leave. What kept me was not a sense of adventure, but rather a mixture of emotions. There was a sense of shame attached to the fact that I had the possibility of leaving at the drop of a hat, knowing that some of the Afghans I was working with were at that very moment desperately seeking a way out of the country, and that card was not one I wanted to play. There was undoubtedly also an element of pride, or perhaps cowardice – part of me was likely afraid of being seen as a coward, someone who is frightened by a minor attack on the other side of town that did not even directly endanger me. Above all, however, I felt a sense of laconic acceptance.

The following day I was in the car with one of my Afghan colleagues, sandwiched in traffic between blast walls and army vehicles pointing their heavy machine guns at us, while American Blackhawk helicopters buzzed overhead. "You know," my Afghan colleague said tiredly, summing up that laconic acceptance, mixed with a hint of exasperation that had also overtaken me, "sometimes I almost feel like I am living in a war zone."

Note

[1] See Morgan, D. (1992) *Discovering men*, London: Routledge, p 87.

Section III
Identity and power

5

Formidable fieldwork: Experiences of a lesbian researcher in post-conflict Northern Ireland

Sandra M. McEvoy

In violence, we forget who we are. (Mary McCarthy, American novelist, *On the contrary*, 1961)

Introduction

In Mary McCarthy's 1961 collection of short stories, *On the contrary*, she suggests that we can become so immersed in an activity or experience that we are transported outside of our self-awareness and lose our sense of subjectivity. McCarthy's observations, on the hypnotic nature of perception, are also illustrative of the almost transcendental capacity of wartime violence. Conflict researchers, sometimes without being aware, fail to consider how our varying identities affect our fieldwork and become secondary to project implementation. For those of us who are drawn to conducting research in communities marred by political violence, McCarthy reminds us that disassociating *from ourselves* in order to achieve our research goals creates a predicament that can be difficult to overcome. That is to say, the tension between our attempts to be present in the field and the distance we keep *from ourselves* to work efficiently in the field poses a series of personal, practical and methodological challenges to researchers.

In this chapter I draw on my 14 years of exploring gender and political violence in Northern Ireland to candidly illustrate my own predicaments, anxieties and hesitations in the field as I struggled to manage my identities as a lesbian field researcher and as a first-generation Protestant Northern Irish American with ties to Loyalism.[1] For my part, two foundational identities, 'who I am' (my sexuality) and 'where I am from' (my Northern Irish roots), were intensely difficult to manage in my first extended period of fieldwork in Northern Ireland in 2006. Despite years of research experience in Northern Ireland,

I did not really have any sense of the ways the Loyalist community conceived of the lesbian, gay, bisexual, transgender, queer, intersex, allies or asexual (LGBTQIA) population, and I worried that revealing this information might negatively affect my ability to gain access to some of the more conservative sections of the Loyalist community (McEvoy, 2015).

This chapter aims to simultaneously expose and embrace the obstacles and impediments to conducting fieldwork in a conflict-affected environment while negotiating identities that may further complicate the already difficult work of the researcher. Relying on the testimony of politically violent women and reflecting on my own field notes, this chapter explores three dominant themes that have been central in my various research journeys: my struggle to conduct fieldwork in conflict-affected environments, my process of understanding the ways that these identities have influenced my previous research, and how my own reflective process shapes my current research practice. It is important to note that this often challenging personal and professional journey could not have been possible without the continuing generosity and patience of women and men in Loyalist Belfast. In my mind, without their always honest and always patient engagement, I would be a far less effective researcher.[2]

Failures of mainstream methodologies

As the editors deftly outline in the Introduction to this volume, conducting fieldwork in conflict-affected areas is a very difficult task. It is difficult not only because of the inherent dangers present in communities without functioning (or trustworthy) security forces or judiciary systems, the presence of armed groups, or because of the fear of the re-emergence of armed violence; it is also difficult for scholars because unlike wartime correspondents, international aid workers or members of the diplomatic corps, no formal training or infrastructure is generally available to support scholars once they arrive in the field. Often work in (post)conflict zones depends on making the best decisions possible with the information at hand, and when our decision-making is insufficient, I have observed that researchers are rarely transparent enough to reflect on these processes or highlight their shortcomings. In many cases, when unexpected issues arise or when mistakes are made, consultation with a dissertation adviser or faculty colleague is a scholar's only recourse. Moreover, because context is so critical to the scholar's decision-making process, such calls, emails, exchange of voicemail or letters serve mostly as support, reassurance or reflection rather than corrections or directives on how to move forward with the research programme.

As I prepared for my field research in Northern Ireland, I felt ill equipped to access Loyalist paramilitary organisations (LPOs), and had little idea of how to 'do' fieldwork in a space where despite the signing of a peace process, intercommunal violence was still part of everyday living for many of my interviewees. It is not my intention to convey that my graduate training in feminist research methods had not been rewarding, insightful and rigorous. Instead, I suggest that at the time of my conceptualisation of the project, to my knowledge no researcher had immersed themselves in Loyalist communities in Northern Ireland, and I knew of no blueprint to guide my approach. Further complicating my preparation was an awareness that resources from traditional International Relations (IR) scholarship were largely insufficient to help me prepare for fieldwork in conflict-affected spaces. Even a cursory search of instructional materials on how to design and operate research programmes in such contexts reveals little help.[3] In most cases, students receive limited training to prepare for fieldwork, and that is particularly the case for qualitative research programmes. Sadly, even when students and scholars are encouraged to journey outside of academic halls, the focus is on what could be described as the most basic 'nuts and bolts' of field research.

Lamont (2015, p 141) outlines a simple set of instructions given to prospective researchers that includes 'practical', 'ethical' and 'security considerations'. In the category of practical considerations, field researchers are encouraged to consider, 'What questions will be asked?' 'Who do I need to talk to?' and 'How do I get access to them?' (2015, p 141). Ethical considerations include questions such as 'Will I secure informed consent of all research interviewees?' and 'What steps do I take to protect the anonymity of research interviewees?' Related to security, initial considerations for the preparation of researchers is even more sparse and lacks even the most basic concern that fieldwork can be unsafe for the researcher and dangerous to the interviewee. Here, Lamont encourages potential field researchers to assess: 'Is my field site in an insecure environment?' and 'How am I, and my research project, likely to be perceived by those on site?' and lastly, 'What does my home country's embassy advise in relation to travel to my field research site?' (2015, p 141).

While it is not my belief that researchers will descend into the field relying only on Lamont's (or similar) textbook, I do believe these texts are frequently students' first introduction to fieldwork, and the absence of a more structured, transparent and practical discussion of the difficulties and complications that can occur in violent and non-violent environments seems a rudimentary and dangerous oversight. Noticeably absent from these cursory initial questions is a curiosity about the way in which context, not to mention gender, sexuality and class, plays a role in preparing the researcher for the fieldwork. In addition, these early questions ignore the potentially negative impact on study participants beyond the basic need to maintain confidentiality. In short, this kind of preparation ignores the type of humility needed to do good research. These oversights feel especially egregious in resource-poor institutions or programmes where non-normative research projects are more likely to be conducted. The consequences of these collective oversights are grim and essentially leave academics to educate themselves on effective research practices in the field. Frequently, this self-education takes the form of an interdisciplinary review of literature in the hope of finding a scholar brave enough to document the disordered and untidy nature of fieldwork. In so doing, the pre-trip preparation for fieldwork can feel lonely and isolating to many researchers who may already feel uncertain about working in violent environments.

Depending on feminists

I recall being a young doctoral student when my dissertation adviser, Cynthia Enloe, began to pack up her university office to prepare for 'retirement'. As Cynthia sifted through materials from a lifetime of feminist research and advocacy, I was the lucky recipient of several of her 'classic' feminist texts. One of the best was *Interpreting women's lives* (1989), written by a collective of 10 feminist writers known as the 'Personal Narratives Group'. I had been thinking about Protestant women and political violence in Northern Ireland, a topic that very few scholars had taken much interest in. I thumbed through the book, feeling as excited to read about feminist narrative research as I was to try and make sense of Cynthia's famous scribbles and notes that were often written on small pieces of sticky paper, the back of envelopes and postcards and occasionally on a receipt. I came to believe that narratives could be an important part of understanding women's use of political violence. Although I had been conducting qualitative research in Northern Ireland for some time before my dissertation-related fieldwork, I realised the analytical power of women's narratives to serve as a type of antidote to normative research that was not curious about women's lives. In the first chapter, the authors sketch the 'origins' of their work:

Traditionally, knowledge, truth, and reality have been constructed as if men's experiences were normative, as if being human meant being male. *Interpreting Women's Lives* is a part of the larger effort to undermine this partial construction and to create a more inclusive, more fully human consumption of social reality. This process of reconstruction challenges what has been defined and taught as our common intellectual and cultural heritage. Throughout the world, interviewees in recent movements for social change have asserted that this heritage has excluded their experiences. They have argued, furthermore, that would have been presented as an objective view of the world with selectively a dominant white, male view. What was once accepted as normative was recognized as being the limited and limiting the perspective of a particular gender, class, and race. (Personal Narratives Group, 1989, p 3)

The text seemed to arrive at just the right time, and gave me the permission that I needed to challenge a notion that is widely accepted in Protestant Northern Ireland that only men were responsible for protecting the state, and that it was women's job to support this effort.[4] The Personal Narratives Group affirmed that interviewees from movements for change around the world themselves believed that these traditions have excluded their experiences, ignored their political agency and identities in such a systemic manner that men's experiences were understood to be their own. I wondered what I might learn by asking women themselves about their experience with political violence, what they would say and how exactly this might come about.

Fear and pressure of getting 'close' to LPO women

It was with a great deal of nervous excitement that I sought to document, explore and analyse women's experiences of their own participation in/support of LPOs in Northern Ireland in the years between 1968 and 2006. As I worked to gain the trust of this very private Loyalist community, I quickly became aware that this work would be difficult, not only in terms of the practical difficulties in conducting high-level scholarship, but much more unexpectedly, because of the cumulative personal pressure that developed over my time in the field to do the work 'right'. Over time, I found that these two dynamics were intricately intertwined in ways that were not always useful to the project.

One of the most critical components to investigating women members of LPOs was the need to gain access to and become trusted by my interviewees and the larger Loyalist community. My own direct familial ties to Loyalism were by far my greatest asset. While almost all of my paternal and maternal relatives have immigrated or have passed away, some family members and acquaintances remain in the city and were extremely helpful in making contacts. A cousin, who for a number of years worked as a computer educator with troubled Protestant youth and young adults, was very helpful in making introductions to Loyalist women. Although her help to get a local 'foot in the door' did not automatically solidify the relationship between any interviewee and me, it was a very helpful first step. Once general introductions were facilitated by my relative, further relationships and details of the interviewees were kept confidential so that security could be maintained and to reduce my relative's influence on my findings or analysis.

However, access to a larger community of LPO women remained difficult, and I quickly learned that access to these women was highly regulated by Loyalist men. Time and time again I was told by men within LPOs that "the women were never there." When I asked if I could talk to any of the women who "might have been there", the question was turned back to me and men would say, "What women are you talking about?" The first step in this process was to convince male members of LPOs and their associates that 'should' such women exist, that their experiences and contributions to 'the defence of Ulster' were important to record and to be recognised. 'Snowball' sampling was used to locate interviewees. This was considered a 'chain of referrals' whereby one person involved in the study refereed me to another person who shared 'certain attributes' (Clark, 2006). Snowball sampling was a particularly important method of locating potential study participants given the relative absence of data that affirmed the existence of women in LPOs or their approximate numbers. Equally important to research related to illegal activity of study participants was that snowballing also served as a way of building trust between me and the potential respondents. Because the women knew and trusted one another, and because there were no negative repercussions following my initial interviews, each loop in the chain of referrals made me more and more trustworthy.

Another important aspect of my fieldwork was my own familiarity with the history, streets and quirky vernacular of Belfast. My parents immigrated to Southern California in 1959 and as a child, Belfast was always referred to as 'back home' by my parents. A combination of their own homesickness, steadfast pride in their troubled homeland, and because of our own isolation as one of a few Northern Irish families in our neighbourhood, I found myself particularly interested and aware of the intricacies of Northern Irish life. By the time that I arrived in Belfast for my dissertation fieldwork in 2006, I had been to Belfast nearly a dozen times and had learned the distasteful names that one religious group had for the other, had a basic understanding of the Protestant-identified street names in Loyalist areas, knew the areas of town where Roman Catholics were the majority, and how one Belfast accent differed from another. The fact that my parents lived on specific streets and that my grandfather was both a well-respected member of several religious 'Orange' lodges and a former member of the 'B Specials'[5] made my credibility in Loyalist areas all the more reliable. During my fieldwork I carried a picture of my grandfather with his B Specials Unit as a form of 'proof' of my Northern Irish lineage. Over a period of months, I became a familiar sight in many Loyalist pubs, and as the community became more comfortable with me, interviews began.

Relying on semi-structured, open-ended research questions, women were encouraged to draw on their experiences freely.[6] The challenges of conducting research into the presence and participation of women in LPOs in Northern Ireland were considerable, especially in light of the sensitive nature of the research questions that I hoped to raise with the interviewees. For the interviewees, I realised that the project posed many challenges, including: contributing to the study would serve as a tacit acknowledgment of their participation in illegal activities or organisations; hesitancy to speak about their experiences in LPOs could be considered disloyal to their current or former group; and the potential that recalling such participation could have been emotionally or psychologically traumatic for the interviewee. Relying on a few brave women to refer other interviewees to me provided the needed momentum.

Throughout the interviewing process I encouraged my interviewees to help me appreciate *their* understanding of phenomena, events and ideas related to the study by creating a dialogical space whereby the interviewee's ideas were allowed to speak for themselves with minimal interpretation by me. I was aware of the tendency of some social science researchers to view the research as 'owned' by the researcher and, following in the footsteps of Cockburn (1998) and Kampwirth (2002), my research sought to restructure the inequality that often exists between the researcher and the participant, and to eliminate the notion of the 'ownership of knowledge' (Wolf, 1996, p 3). At the time of my field research, I was also conscious that other researchers of Northern Ireland had frequently made their own, selective meaning of the ways in which current events and general history of the province may or may not have affected their interviewees. This behaviour, combined with what locals referred to as 'parachuting in', or staying in Belfast for a few days, furiously collecting data and writing superficial accounts of their encounters, was always on my mind when I approached interviewees.

With this knowledge, I made every attempt to allow LPO women's insights and ideas to stand on their own and to allow the women to come to these understandings in the interviews in their own time. As the months passed, as trust continued to develop, and as my interviewees began to share their experiences related to their participation, I recall the moment when I allowed myself to admit that I was gradually beginning to understand LPO women. As I did so, I also began to feel a great deal of personal responsibility to convey their ideas in a way that was true to their testimonies. I grew concerned that I would not be up to the task of representing their views in ways that could preserve my academic responsibilities to critical analysis while simultaneously telling the story of LPO women in ways that would not offend or mischaracterise what I observed. No exchange of ideas is more indicative of these reservations than my July 2006 interview with 'Tracy'.

'Telling the truth'

Tracy joined a small elite unit of an LPO in her rural area of Northern Ireland when she was just 17, and by the mid-1980s had become a very active and respected member in her LPO. Two senior LPO members, 'George' and 'William', generously agreed to coordinate my visit and attended my meeting with Tracy at her rural home to the south of Belfast. At the time, four or more months into my fieldwork, I had already come to understand that Tracy was one of the organisation's most revered members. One especially memorable part of the interview came when I asked if there was a defining moment or event that had motivated her to become a member of the LPO. Her response was so impactful that I have almost memorised it. With a clear sense of purpose, she stated:

> 'Yeah, there probably was. There was a bomb in XXX and I was up! There was a wee bar at the top of the street ... and there was a bomb went off.... I put my coat on and away I went and there was a fella lying on the street and I

will never forget it till the day that God calls me. He was lying on the street and he was semi-conscious but he was gripping the pavement stones like that there [simulating the man gripping the pavement stones]. And his guts blew out.'

Tracy's comrade George queried:

'That made your mind up?'

And Tracy replied:

'That made my mind up. Then I said, "The bastards will get the same thing."'

Describing the Republican paramilitaries who planted the bomb in her small town, the anger and veracity in Tracy's voice was unmistakable, and although health issues prevented her from being more active in the LPO, Tracy appeared as committed to Loyalism as if she was still taking orders.

As I sat in her small front room, I found it difficult to be an objective observer of the exchange, and as I reflect on this pivotal interview, I now understand that there was a part of me that thought that being critical of this decisive moment in Tracy's decision to engage in political violence would somehow betray the trust she had invested in me to share her story. As I contemplated this feeling, I felt that each passing moment in the interview also complicated how I would proceed with the study once the interview ended. Hume (2007) asserts that this kind of 'epistemological negotiation' between the identity of the researcher is 'shifting and highly relational' and 'shaped by both the subject of research and its participants' (2007, p 147). I not only felt that my identity was shifting; I also felt that it was being stretched or maybe even transformed.

Throughout the remaining hour of the interview, I was cognisant of my responsibility as an academic to make distinctions between justified belief and opinion; however, I continued to feel a sense of rising expectations. This sense peaked during Tracy's detailed description of her experiences of the conflict including extended periods of interrogation at the hands of the British Army. It seemed important to Tracy to emphasise to me that despite her commitment to 'keeping Ulster British', that when in custody she was abused by the army and police as they tried to get her to confess to various paramilitary-related crimes. As the interview ended, George, William and I walked to the door to begin our journey back to Belfast. When we reached our car Tracy waved goodbye, and with a cigarette in her hand pointed to me and said, "Make sure that when you leave here that you write the truth." To me the message was clear, 'Don't waste my time or slander my service.'

I have written elsewhere (McEvoy, 2009, 2015) about the dangers of excluding politically violent women from negotiated settlements, and Tracy's many insights are pertinent in this way. However, only now have I come to recognise that in several interviews with LPO women, my Northern Irish Protestant identity, learned in childhood, unexpectedly came to the forefront, and I felt a sense of satisfaction when the women described their role in defending their communities. To me, Tracy epitomised the strong, capable, politicised, agentive and sometimes violent Northern Irish woman that I intuitively knew existed, but was not part of the comfortable Southern California lifestyle that I lived. I enjoyed seeing these women act powerfully. I realise now that my own, not unproblematic, Loyalist family history shaped the ways that I understood Republicans, including those not engaged in paramilitary violence.

At the time, this somehow meant that Republicans 'deserved' LPO violence because *their* violence was illegitimate. I was also embarrassed to admit to myself that in the moments where women described their participation in LPO activities, that it felt – good. These beliefs were so deeply embedded in what Jacoby (2006), researching her own deep family connection to the conflict in Israel and Palestine, describes as the 'centrality of my own subject position' that I used as an 'essential mythological mechanism for negotiating my relationship with those that I researched' (2006, p 157). In other words, the person I understood myself to be felt enamoured by the feeling of retribution as the women described their LPO activities. More so, their violence somehow avenged the imagined offences, insults, deprivation and victimisation that I learned from my parents recounting their lives in Belfast.

As I continue to think about my positive feelings about women and LPO violence, I am remote enough from the field to understand how undeveloped my ideas were about women's use of political violence. It seemed easy during my interviews to affirm women's choices to be violent as a way to encourage them to continue with the interview. Jacoby (2006, p 168) refers to this process as 'an extravagant form of navel-gazing', and despite my deep respect for LPO women, I was guilty of the behaviour. I am now aware of the degree to which I was entrenched in Loyalism and I was exhilarated when I began to make connections between concepts and ideas that had puzzled me in the early stages of being in the field. In these heightened periods of meaning-making it was difficult to keep track of the way that my family background was shaping my perceptions and interactions, and how important it was to me personally and professionally to validate Loyalist views. However, to whatever degree I may have understood myself to be understanding and operating within Loyalist communities, it is nearly impossible for me to understand the conditions under which these women committed acts of political violence. What LPO women were describing was not a movie or a game – the violence was real – and the truth of the matter is that had I been present for any of the activities the LPO women described, I likely would not have had the fortitude to stay present.[7]

Staying far away

Fear played a role. I have come to realise that the ways in which I actively distanced parts of myself, in particular, my lesbian identity, from these same people negatively affected my ability to solidify greater trust between myself and my interviewees. Initial impressions of doing so will seem confusing to some readers, especially given that I am not obliged to conceal my sexuality in my personal or professional life. But to others who conduct conflict fieldwork and who identify as being from the LGBTQIA community, the convoluted dance that researchers like me perform in order to mask their sexuality is a familiar one.[8] I have written previously of the risks that my identity as a lesbian posed to conducting research in post-conflict Northern Ireland (McEvoy, 2015). Drawing on Fisher's (2003) 'strategy of concealment', I contemplated the risks and benefits of outing myself to the Loyalist community, and realised that I had no idea what position, if any, the Loyalist community held on non-normative sexual or gender identities.[9]

Additional concerns for negative repercussions surrounded the worry that if potential interviewees knew that I was a lesbian, that they might question whether I could appreciate their heterosexual romantic relationships during 30-year conflict. On more than one occasion LPO women appealed to my assumed heterosexuality as they articulated how difficult it was to have their male partner and co-parent incarcerated for long periods of time. I was concerned that if the women knew that I was a lesbian, would they somehow censor their reflections about their lives during the conflict out of fear of making *me* uncomfortable? I could accept that members of the community might not want to share their experiences with me out of the concern of reliving a painful past or because I was working with the Historical Enquiries Team (HET).[10]

It was more difficult for me, however, to accept that I might miss the opportunity to talk to them because of my sexuality (McEvoy, 2015).

In an effort to try and dispel suspicions about my sexuality, I made a concerted effort to alter or change my appearance so that I could more easily blend into Loyalist working-class femininity. Over time, however, managing my appearance became laborious, and it was one of the few aspects of my fieldwork that I struggled with and that I came to resent. More than just a bothersome need to conform to meaningless gender norms, I felt resentful that these self-imposed requirements were disrupting the work that I was trying to do. As my fieldwork progressed, a feeling of cognitive dissonance formed that made it feel impossible for me to conduct fieldwork in post-conflict Northern Ireland *and* be a lesbian. I was not at all closeted in my hometown of San Diego, CA or in Massachusetts where I attended graduate school, and at the time a Google search would not have revealed my sexuality. To me this work did not seem to necessitate that I reveal this aspect of my identity. I sometimes found myself fleetingly thinking about whether today would be the day that I would come out, but the reasoning always remained the same – it was too much of a risk to my work to 'out' myself, and I was unwilling to jeopardise the relationships that I was building with the Loyalist community.[11]

Unfortunately, it simply did not occur to me at the time that allowing LPO women and men greater access to who I was beyond my Northern Irish, Loyalist-connected identity that worked most obviously to my advantage could have actually enhanced my fieldwork rather than compromised it. I wonder if perhaps the women would have considered my lack of understanding of heterosexual marriage as an opportunity to serve as 'experts' in our field relationship and equalise power relations a little more. Indeed, one of the women I sensed could be a lesbian may have found comfort in talking with me about her far less understood role in the conflict. Had I placed more emphasis on developing reflexive practice in the research process, and committed 'to being constantly aware of the ways that our own varied identities directly impact the ways we approach our investigations' (McEvoy, 2015, p 144), perhaps the issue of my sexuality would have been less fraught.

Similar to my concerns with getting too 'close' to LPO communities, I realise after all these years that many members of the LPO community were already aware that I was a lesbian and had likely known this from my earliest days in the field. As such, I was not really 'passing'. It seems naive to believe that I could do so since I had surrounded myself with people whose lives and communities depended on their careful noticing of strangers in their community. An absence of any detail related to my romantic relationships and discomfort with the topic was undoubtedly noticed by this close-knit community. For over 30 years these men and women were experts in identifying falseness, discomfort and lies. I was not fooling anyone but myself. In fact, only recent reflective practice has helped me understand that being a lesbian was not an issue for the Belfast-based conservative Northern Irish people I knew. More accurately, what appeared to really be at issue were the conservative opinions about my sexuality from the Northern Irish family members *in my hometown* of San Diego, CA.

In San Diego, there were very few people who even identified strongly as Irish American, let alone Irish immigrants. It was not until I moved to the state of Massachusetts for graduate school that I first encountered large groups of Irish people. In essence, my understanding of what it meant to be Northern Irish was filtered through a very small group composed of my family and a few of their close friends. It was based on the representations of Northern Irish men and women by this limited pool, who were also deeply uncomfortable with my sexuality, that I made assumptions about Protestant/Loyalist men and women in Belfast. I transferred this aversion onto LPO women and men, and believed that they would share the homophobia of some members of my extended family. My assumptions were especially unfair in that these men and women accepted and trusted me with exceptionally sensitive information about them, and I was not able to do this same. These kinds of insights are now only possible given that both my Mom and Dad have passed, and the recognition is bitter sweet.

These ideas were confirmed during a two-week visit to Belfast in 2014 and again in late 2016 when a trusted and well-respected member of the Loyalist community visited me in Massachusetts. The visit was the first opportunity that I have had to engage with any member of the Loyalist community on my own 'turf', and for a short time after her arrival, I had some difficulty trying to make sense of her visit. I wondered how it was possible that my two worlds, my international academic work and my domestic professional work, were colliding in such wonderful ways. As our friendship developed, I mustered my courage to ask her about what the community knew about my sexuality. She stated frankly, "Everyone knew, they know now and they do not care" and as quickly as that, in a typically quick-witted Belfast quip, I felt once again able to re-engage with Loyalism, this time on more authentic and agentive terms.

Conclusion

This chapter began by outlining some of the obstacles of conducting fieldwork in conflict-affected environments and the inadequacies of mainstream methodologies to prepare researchers for work in such spaces. I then explored the ways in which feminist research methodology offers promising tools and frameworks that can assist researchers and interviewees to act as co-creators of knowledge. Drawing on my own research in post-conflict Northern Ireland, I illustrated the ways in which my field research was difficult and often fraught with anxiety and apprehension as I struggled to candidly engage with men and women members of LPOs. In the years that have followed I continue to visit Belfast for shorter fieldwork periods that have allowed me the opportunity to come to know a few women more personally. With time and age I have become comfortable sharing my personal life with one especially important interviewee, 'Chloe'. But truthfully, I struggle to keep connections without referencing the past, and feeling embarrassed that I do not know more about their present lives. In this way, I feel like I am continuing to disproportionately benefit more from these relationships. At times, I have felt uncomfortable reconnecting when I have a burning question that I know that someone like Chloe can help me understand.

The chapter also considered the ways in which my own familial ties to Loyalism granted me unique access to the community, but also prompted a concern with my own abilities to adequately and accurately represent or 'tell the truth' about the experiences of political violence conveyed to me. Finally, the chapter outlined the ways in which my fear that the Loyalist community would learn that I was a lesbian would alienate me from those who graciously welcomed me into their homes.

As I reflect on my ongoing work in Northern Ireland, I remain motivated by Cynthia Enloe's 1989 provocation, 'Where are the women?' I know there is much more to be understood about Loyalist women's experiences of conflict and their hopes for the future. Still, I am mindful that honing my academic skills cannot alone provide the insight needed to be a successful and reflective scholar. As scholars expand their research interests to areas affected by conflict, I am persuaded more than ever of the importance of extending Enloe's curiosity to ourselves as researchers so that the question of 'Where am I?' in the research project becomes integral to our analysis.

Notes

[1]   The concept of Loyalism and those who identify as 'Loyalists' is a hotly contested term within Northern Irish Protestantism. Here the term is used to refer to those people and groups who support or are affiliated to Loyalist paramilitarism and affirm Northern Ireland's connection to the UK. For more on Loyalist identity, see Aughey (1997).

[2]   In order to maintain the confidentiality of the identities of my interviewees, I have assigned pseudonyms and removed any reference to individual organisational affiliations. Given the highly territorialised and politicised nature of Belfast, the names of meeting places have also been removed to ensure that no group or subset of the Loyalist community can be identified in this work.

[3]   An exception within traditional IR is Druckman's (2005) edited text, *Doing research: Methods of inquiry for conflict analysis*. Druckman's work is often cited as one of the earliest examples of conducting research *on* conflict. While the contribution is notable, almost none of Druckman's contributors take field research *in* conflict seriously. In fact, when searching the index of this seminal text, 'fieldwork' simply does not appear.

[4]   Feminist researchers have documented how traditional gender roles are militarised in order to both sustain wars and reify understandings of gender binaries. See Elshtain (1987), Enloe (1990, 1998, 2000), Houston (1983) and Goldstein (2001).

[5]   The controversial force, also known as the Ulster Special Constabulary, was formed by the British government in 1920 to protect Protestants from attacks from the Irish Republican Army. The force was comprised entirely of Protestant men from Northern Ireland, and although welcomed by Protestants, over time, it was frequently accused of brutal enforcement tactics (see Lundy, 2006; Lawlor, 2011).

[6]   In order to place the ideas and experiences of interviewees into an analytical context, it is important to note that these interview questions were asked of women eight years after the signing of the Good Friday Agreement in 1998 and over 30 years after the official start of 'The Troubles' in 1968. That is, interviewees were asked to reflect on their experiences of their membership in groups as many as two decades earlier and following a series of somewhat dramatic shifts in the political landscape of their country.

[7]   I am aware of studies in psychology, including Milgrim's famous prison experiment. Milgrim convincingly illustrates that individuals are likely to commit acts of violence and will justify this violence as long as this behaviour is understood as an act of obedience to a group or cause. Perhaps I would have felt a similar need to engage in violence.

[8]   Field research by members of the LGBTQIA community in conflict-affected environments is still in its infancy, and an area where there are significant gaps in our understanding of the complicated nature of negotiating sexual identity in unsafe environments by individuals who can often feel unsafe even outside of these spaces.

[9]   Importantly, in the last few years several lesbian candidates have successfully run for office in Loyalist-aligned parties in Northern Ireland. Two of the highest profile women are Julie-Anne Corr Johnston, Belfast City Councillor and Sophie Long, representative for Upper Bann, and both are from the Progressive Unionist Party.

[10] The HET is an effort by the British government to investigate unsolved high-priority crimes committed during the conflict, focusing largely on crimes

committed by paramilitary organisations. For more information on the HET team inquiries, see Lundy (2011).

[11] Historically, a small handful of researchers in the fields of Political Science and International Relations have focused on the experiences of LGBTQIA researchers in conflict-affected environments.

References

Aughey, A. (1997) 'The character of Ulster Unionism', in P. Shirlow and M. McGovern (eds) *Who are 'The people'? Protestantism, Unionism and Loyalism in Northern Ireland*, London: Pluto Press, pp 16–33.

Clark, J. (2006) 'Field research methods in the Middle East', *PS: Political Science and Politics*, vol 39, no 3, pp 417–23.

Cockburn, C. (1998) *The space between us: Negotiating gender and national identities in conflict*, London: Zed Books.

Druckman, D. (2005) *Doing research: Methods of inquiry for conflict analysis*, London and Thousand Oaks, CA: Sage Publications.

Elshtain, J. (1987) *Women and war*, Chicago, IL: University of Chicago Press.

Enloe, C. (1990) *Bananas, beaches, and bases: Making feminist sense of international politics*, Berkeley, CA: University of California Press.

Enloe, C. (1998) 'All the men are in the militias, all the women are victims: the politics of masculinity and femininity in nationalist wars', in L. Lorentzen and J. Turpin (eds) *The women and war reader*, New York: New York University Press, pp 50–62.

Enloe, C. (2000) *Maneuvers: The international politics of militarizing women's lives*, Berkeley, CA: University of California Press.

Enloe, C. (2014) *Bananas, beaches, and bases: Making feminist sense of international politics* (2nd edn), Berkeley, CA: University of California Press.

Fisher, D. (2003) 'Immigrant closets: Tactical-micro-practices-in-the-hyphen', in A. Yep (ed) *Queer theory and communication: From disciplining queers to queering the discipline(s)*, Binghamton, NY: Harrington Park Press, pp 171–92.

Goldstein, J. (2001) *War and gender: How gender shapes the war system and vice versa*, Cambridge and New York: Cambridge University Press.

Houston, N. (1983) 'Tales of war and tears of women', in J. Stiehm (ed) *Women and men's wars*, Oxford: Pergamon Press, pp 271–82.

Hume, M. (2007) 'Unpicking the threads: Emotion as central to the theory and practice of researching violence', *Women's Studies International Forum*, vol 30, pp 147–57.

Jacoby, T. (2006) 'From the trenches: Dilemmas of feminist IR fieldwork', in B. Ackerly and M. Stern (eds) *Feminist methodologies for international relations*, Cambridge and New York: Cambridge University Press, pp 153–73.

Kampwirth, K. (2002) *Women and guerrilla movements: Nicaragua, El Salvador, Chiapas, Cuba*, Pennsylvania, PA: Pennsylvania University Press.

Lamont, C. (2015) *Research methods in international relations*, Los Angeles, CA: Sage Publications.

Lawlor, P. (2011) *The outrages 1920–1922: The IRA and the Ulster Special Constabulary in the Border Campaign*, Cork: Mercier Press.

Lundy, D. (2006) *Men that God made mad: A journey through myth and terror in Northern Ireland*, London: Jonathan Cape Publishers.

Lundy P. (2009) 'Can the past be policed?: Lessons from the Historical Enquiries Team Northern Ireland.' *Journal of Law and Social Challenges* 11(2): pp. 109-156.

Lundy, P. (2011) 'Paradoxes and challenges of transitional justice at the "local" level: Historical enquiries in Northern Ireland', *Contemporary Social Science*, vol 6, no 1, pp 89–105.

McCarthy, M. (1976) *On the contrary: Articles of belief, 1946–1961*, London: Octagon Books.

McEvoy, S. (2009) 'Loyalist women paramilitaries in Northern Ireland: Beginning a feminist conversation about conflict resolution', *Security Studies*, vol 18, no 2, pp 262–86.

McEvoy, S. (2015) 'Queering security studies in Northern Ireland: Problem, practice and practitioner', in M.L. Picq and M. Thiel (2015) *Sexualities in world politics: How LGBTQ claims shape international relations*, New York: Routledge, pp 135–4.

Personal Narratives Group (eds) (1989) *Interpreting women's lives: Feminist theory and personal narratives*, Bloomington and Indianapolis, IN: Indiana University Press.

Wolf, D. (1996) 'Situating feminist dilemmas in fieldwork', in D. Wolf (ed) *Feminist dilemmas in fieldwork*, Colorado, OH: Westview Press.

6

Insider-outsider reflections on terrorism research in the coastal region of Kenya

Fathima Azmiya Badurdeen

Introduction

Navigating one's positionality while researching on terrorism can be particularly challenging when working in regions vulnerable to religiously motivated ideologies on violent extremism, where suspicion and access present barriers to engaging with the participants (Dolnik, 2013; Nielsen, 2014). Even if the researcher shares the same religion as that of the participants and is acquainted with the culture wherein relational aspects could be addressed, the religious identity within an insider-outsider perception remains a barrier, which is a precondition for exploitation in the research process (Mednicoff, 2015). This chapter examines how the researcher's religious positionality matters in studies on violent extremism or terrorism by drawing on reflections from research conducted in Kenya on the radicalisation and recruitment of youth for the al-Shabaab terrorist organisation.

Kenya has been vulnerable to the recruitment of youths by the al-Shabaab terrorist organisation due to its close proximity to Somalia and the large Muslim populations living close to its borders, such as in the country's north-eastern and coastal regions. Al-Shabaab emerged in 2006 as an offshoot of the Islamic Courts Union in Somalia, while its origins can be traced as far back as 1991 in the wake of a destabilised social structure in Somalia (Hansen, 2013). In 2012, the Muslim Youth Centre in Kenya pledged its alliance to al-Shabaab, paving the way for the radicalisation and recruitment of Swahili-speaking Africans for violent military activities in Somalia (Anzalone, 2012). The coastal region of Kenya comprises six counties, and is the hub for economic activities due to its vibrant port and tourism trade. Amidst such a development, however, the region has been marked by poverty and marginalisation due to discriminative policies by successive governments since independence. Studies reveal that the resulting socioeconomic environment that influenced religious–cultural norms inclined towards radicalisation as part of a larger response to stressful collective circumstances (Badurdeen, 2012; IRIN, 2013).

Through an exploration of the concept of positionality, this chapter probes into an array of debates centred round my religious identity and the research process. I use my own experiences of doing research on Islamic radicalisation or extremism with al-Shabaab members in the coastal region of Kenya as a case study. The basis of this chapter is an ethnographic research study that I conducted on the process of youth radicalisation and recruitment by al-Shabaab in the coastal region of Kenya (Mombasa, Lamu, Kilifi and Kwale) as part of my doctoral research. The study engaged Muslim youth and key informants such as Muslim clergies, madrasa leaders, law enforcement officials, youths labelled as radicals and parents of young people recruited by the al-Shabaab terrorist organisation from locations identified as hotspots for radicalisation. The target population was radicalised youths who ascribe to radical Islamist beliefs in line with al-Shabaab's ideology.

The chapter begins with a discussion of positionality and the debates around insider–outsider dynamics in the context of academic research. These concepts provide a lens that I use to reflect on the dilemmas and choices that I made while conducting research. The chapter then moves on to detail my experiences with the research process in Kenya and the complexity of locating one's position when doing intra-group research. In doing so, the chapter unpacks the linkage between religion, identity and postionality in research, and in particular, on terrorism research. I conclude with reflecting on my religious positionality on navigating between terminologies of radical and moderates in shaping my study.

Positionality and the research process

Positionality in qualitative research refers to a shared space between the researcher and the researched that affects the research process (Berger, 2013). As highlighted by Bourke (2014, p 1),

> Identities come into play via our perceptions, not only of others, but of the ways in which we expect others will perceive us. Our own biases shape the research process, serving as checkpoints along the way. Through recognition of our biases, we presume to gain insights into how we might approach a research setting, members of particular groups, and how we might seek to engage with participants.

These multiple locations of sameness and difference possessed by a researcher are well reiterated by Razavi (1992, p 161) who argues: 'By virtue of being a researcher, one is rarely a complete insider anywhere.' 'By moving like a pendulum along the insider-outsider continuum, a shifting interactional process in which the relationship between the researcher and the respondent is formed', there arises 'an opportunity to explore the multiple subjectivities of both researcher and respondent' (Hoel, 201, p 32). Sometimes we also become the 'stranger within' (Kristeva, 1991), when we explore unfamiliar terrain in a familiar context. Hoel (2013) also asserts that such research encounters have the potential to be co-constructions in which the insider-outsider binary can be redefined in ways that are more meaningful and inclusive than an 'either/or paradigm'.

Religious identity in shared spaces in terms of our perceptions and biases can greatly influence and shape the research process. In studies concerning religious violence or religious ideologies, the researcher's religious identity poses complex challenges (Niesen, 2014) to insightful reflections shaping the research process and its outcome. Herein, the position of 'being one of them' as an insider or 'not being one of them' as an outsider is a complicated position on studies attributed to religious violence, such as of political Islam or Islamism, which have varied dimensions. These dimensions include the religion's fundamentals, historical context and embedded politics that shape the phenomenon of Islamic radicalisation, particularly in relation to transnational, nationalist and local discourses of Islam (Chande, 2000).

In studies related to radical Islamism, the insider-outsider positioning cannot be easily defined due to its unsettled nature (Eppley, 2006). The researcher's position tends to move along a continuum rather than adopting a fixed point. The researcher may find him/herself moving between the role of a stranger and a familiar persona, a sceptic and a follower (Wiebe, 1985, p 263). The complexity and fluidity of the insider-outsider positionality is highlighted by Flood (1999, p 215) further, who cautions, however, that in contexts where violence is associated with religion or where 'religious violence disrupts dialogue or when traditions or sub-traditions seek to enforce a different ethical vision through violence…' researchers may find themselves becoming an outsider within their own religion. Therefore, the researcher, even as an insider, may resort to constructing an outsider persona for varied aspects regarding rationality and security concerns. At the same time, a researcher who has an outsider status may succumb to sympathetic concerns over the participant's views and opinions through similar shared experiences or shared subject positions, and draw him/herself into an insider perspective. I came to understand this landscape during my fieldwork.

Researching youth radicalisation in the coastal region of Kenya

Research on youth radicalisation involved interviewing participants on al-Shabaab radical ideologies, which were considered to be a sensitive issue in the coastal region due to the high rate of surveillance by the security forces. Here, the target population involved youth who ascribed to radical Islamist beliefs (al-Shabaab radicalisation). Therefore, the study described a radical in line with al-Shabaab radicalisation in the coastal region of Kenya. This labelled radicalised group only formed a minority group within a dominant cultural group of Muslims. Within the dominant group, this target group of radical Islamists is an unknown, condemned, hidden and often lived among the marginalised[1] communities. As expressed by one participant:

> 'This group of so-called radicals or extremists [al-Shabaab] live within our communities [coastal Muslim population]. We don't know who is who. It's not shown in their face, maybe sometimes their behaviour. They know how to hide from us and the police. Unfortunately they say they are Muslims. But we Muslims condemn their behaviour. They are not real Muslims. (Interview 2, 6 November 2015)

These hidden groups have learned to create a 'hidden way of life', hiding their thoughts, behaviours, attitudes and emotions, while adopting the norms and beliefs of the dominant society of the Muslim community. This hidden and inaccessible discourse creates confusion on researching the radical, as these members feel the need to protect themselves and their group members in order to defend their hidden community identity from outsiders, especially from the other 'Muslims' from the dominant cultural group (field notes, 16 January 2016). Apart from this hidden exposure, the lack of identification and definition further complicated the study of this group. For example, how do you identify or define an al-Shabaab radical or an extremist? What about sympathisers? A participant pointed out that:

> '... there are times that when a person expresses sympathy on what is going on among Muslims youth who are detained, tortured, or harassed by the police on counter

terrorism practices, the tendency is to automatically classify the person as a radical. This creates a context where people fear to express themselves in terms of rights for the fear of labelling. We have many youth labelled as radicals. Not all of them are radicals subscribing to the al-Shabaab ideology.' (Interview 6, 21 November 2015)

In an attempt to understand the radical narrative of al-Shabaab it is important to dissect the localised narratives of marginalisation and oppression in the coastal region from the al-Shabaab ideology. In my interviews, one of the ways in which this localised narrative of marginalisation and oppression was apparent was through exploring the category of al-Shabaab radical belief. Here, radical belief is meant to be 'the justification of use of violence, when their religion or the Muslim ummah [community] or their territory is at stake' (al-Shabaab magazine, *Gaidi Mtaani*). This type of radical belief seemingly became a source of strength among some of my respondents. For some, this belief of an Islamic land (Somalia) enabled them to envision a place for them 'to practice their religion fully without any impediments from non-Muslims, where external markers such as the hijab, beard and Muslim garb would not be an issue' (Interview 8, 2 December 2015). This went in harmony with the phrase echoed by Lewis (1994, p 152), in his book *Islam and the West*, describing the contemporary world as 'the prison of the believers and the paradise of the unbelievers.' For others, an Islamic state or land meant laws that were compliant with the Quran and the Sunnah of the Prophet (sal), Sharia law, which would shield them from immoral behaviours and provide a sense of security (Interview 15, 12 January 2016). Yet for others, fighting for an Islamic state meant a way to navigate through their harsh and precarious contexts,[2] or a way to liberate the entire Muslim community subjugated or oppressed by the infidels referred to as the US and the Kenyan Defence Forces (KDF) in Somalia (field notes, 16 December 2015).

Interestingly, then, by exploring the category of radical belief, different and diverse localised narratives emerged through respondents' views constituting and producing subjective, partial and situated knowledge from the community to understand the al-Shabaab radical. In the coastal region, the suffering of Muslims in terms of a deteriorating citizen-state relationship was linked to the overall narrative of Muslims being discriminated due to political, economic, cultural or social marginalisation in other parts of the world such as the hate attacks in the West (al-Shabaab magazine, *Gaidi Mtaani*). The coastal region of Kenya, with its majority Muslim population in the border regions, has remained marginalised from successive government development plans, and lags behind other regions in terms of economic development, despite its vibrant tourism and port. The resulting poverty, with a host of other issues such as ineffective development strategies on education, discriminatory employment strategies, lack of title deeds for native communities and land grabbing, has created a disgruntled youth community. A ripe context of deprivation is often exploited by al-Shabaab radical entrepreneurs to mobilise youth into their network (Badurdeen, 2012).

Within this context of radicalisation, a moderate Muslim was viewed as anyone not subscribing to the al-Shabaab ideology. In fact, communities presumed any Muslim who opposed al-Shabaab was a moderate Muslim. The term 'moderate' and 'radical' have been well articulated in the community through media and Countering Violent Extremism (CVE) projects (field notes, 6 November 2015). This affirms the identity of a good Muslim and a bad Muslim inextricably tied to terrorism (Beydoun, 2016). This can be criticised on the grounds that not all who are not al-Shabaab radicals are complete moderates. First, this continuum on moderates versus radicals has not been easy to assess as we don't know the levels of radicalisation or where we place als-Shabaab sympathisers. Second, participants subscribe to different types of reformist ideologies, not necessarily that of a particular demarcated terrorist group such as al-Shabaab (Manji and Dajani, 2015). In my fieldwork, this classification holds significant value where people place themselves at the far end of the continuum as moderates, mainly to circumvent surveillance by security personnel (field notes, 12 December 2015).

Spaces of solidarity

When I commenced fieldwork in Mombasa, I assumed that a bond would exist with the research participants based on our shared Muslim identity. Indeed, my insider status was convenient in helping me gain access to the community (Bourke, 2014). My participants and I shared a number of attributes concerning religious beliefs and practices. Raised in a traditional Muslim family, I shared commonalities with the participants in terms of practices such as Shahada (declaration of faith), daily prayers, fasting, Zakath (alms-giving) and Hajj (pilgrimage). There were also familiarities such as my name, which is a common Muslim name in the community, "Fathima … a very common name in Kenya, but we call Fatima or Fatuma … we don't have the 'h'…" (Interviewee 4, 8 November 2015). These attributes assisted in forming a connecting bond with my participants. Muslims are strongly regulated by their faith, Islam, and a common set of attributes is essential to determine the shared relationship between the researcher and the researched. Hamdan (2009) and Alzbouebi (2010) highlight the added advantage of better social interactions between a Muslim researcher and a Muslim participant in the research process, with the researcher being an insider who shares the same religion with insider knowledge and Islamic teachings.

Residing and working in a public university in the coastal region in Kenya for over four years, integrated into the Kenyan community by marriage, gave me an acceptance into the community. Another interviewee exclaimed: "… you're a Kenyan now … your husband is a Kenyan…" (Interviewee 3, 6 November 2015). As my husband is Kenyan, I was warmly accepted as Kenyan, a patriarchal statement to show that, as the wife, I belonged to the husband's land or village. Amidst such acceptance, I took my religious positionality for granted in attempting to engage Muslim youth in discussions of Islamic radicalisation in the coastal region. I acknowledge that being a Muslim woman, asking questions of a man in a patriarchal community is difficult enough, yet I believed that my sharing of the same religion would be a bridging factor. I also took my foreign identity[3] for granted, as I felt my Muslim identity would take precedence and gain acceptance for me into the community. Being an Asian resonated well among my participants who viewed me as an 'Indian' or referred to me as 'Hindi', especially in the Mombasa context, where there was a strong presence of Kenyan Indians. Within this context, sometimes their easiness was linked to the acceptance of the researcher as a member of their community. This sentiment was expressed by a Muslim youth who said: "… Your role as a Muslim [researcher] is to show these types of discrimination…" (Interviewee 4 , 8 November 2015).

This doesn't mean that the positional space that we shared was stable. On issues regarding concepts such as prayers or on how a woman should dress, I was seen as a total stranger within my own religion. Some even said explicitly to my face that: "… a Muslim women's beauty is the hijab [head cover]" (focus group discussions, women, 16 November 2015). I felt uneasy at these times as I did not wear a headscarf but had a shawl, to reveal my Asian identity. My modern[4] outlook was a matter for discussion, as one participant continued: "… you think of life as an adventure … studied in the West, learned from the West … and you call yourself modern and then start to analyse the Muslims…" (Interview 2, 12 September 2015). These were discussions that I usually tried to change midway for fear of how my religious positionality would be perceived. While these statements made me feel an outsider, the extent to which my position was perceived as an outsider is unknown. As researchers, we are frequently positioned by participants. I may wish to be perceived as an insider, but participants might, in fact, position me as an outsider amidst our shared religious positionalities.

The participants for the study were selected on the basis of their knowledge of, attitudes towards and experiences with Islamic radicalisation. Apart from building trust with the participants, my identity as a Muslim helped in approaching hard-to-reach religious leaders on understanding the radicalisation narrative in the coastal region of Kenya, and how it is pegged into the coastal grievances.[5] I was able to meet religious leaders who were labelled from either end of the moderate to radical continuum[6] as they opened up into discussions that centred on religion that better explained the origin of the radicalisation wave in East Africa and Kenya. As the researcher, I was able to hold on to conversations that centred on religion and the history of religion, constantly probing with various Ayaths (verses of the Quran) and Hadiths (collection of traditions of the Prophet Muhammad sal to understand the concept of al-Shabaab radicalisation). Hence, the assumption that I understood the various aspects of the religion was key to conducting interviews centring on religious tenets, practices and manipulative narratives. This confirms Henkel's (2011) view on the advantage of the researcher being a religious believer in order to understand the researched as well as the research context. In line with this view, Yasmeen (2008) posits that Islam inhabits the space of fundamental commitment by individuals toward their belief in certain realities, giving meaning to their identity and life experiences. This essential quality determines Muslim identity in regulating their behaviour, without which their worldview cannot be understood (Inner and Yusel, 2015). In studies on Islamic radicalisation, the knowledge of this worldview was key to understanding the radicalisation discourse as experienced by the radicals themselves.

In interviews participants were, for the most part, willing to talk to a fellow Muslim researcher on a topic that they felt affected the entire Muslim community in response to stereotypical and Islamophobic sentiments. Such an unspoken contract between the researcher and the participants implies that the research needed to address the concerns of both parties, which has eventual implications for the time and energy participants are prepared to invest in the study, so as to facilitate in-depth interviews or the data-gathering process. The participants found the study intrinsically valuable as they shared their concerns on issues such as how Muslims were portrayed globally, the difficulties that religious stereotypes posed during travel and the constant portrayal of Muslims as terror suspects. For example, during an interview, a Muslim youth expressed his concern on how the government treated him and his friends: "My friends still struggle to get their IDs [identity cards], all because we are Muslims. I fought a battle [difficulty] to get my passport … how can we think of jobs without proper documentation?... We are ill-treated by the government..." (Interviewee 2, 15 September 2015).

Being the outsider

My outsider positioning was evident and highlighted when I dealt with participants who were Muslims with a distinct culture such as that of youths labelled as 'radicals' or convicted as 'extremists'. It is vital to acknowledge this difference, because the study involves understanding the sub-group 'al-Shabaab' that remains hidden, marginalised and considered dangerous, allying to the dominant cultural group of Muslims in the coastal region of Kenya. Thus I was an outsider within this category of participants amidst my shared religious space. There was a contrast in our worldviews, attributed to the embedded historical, social, cultural and political contexts of the region as well as the politics of religion. These differences were captured through lengthy dialogues so as to learn the other and their 'symbolic worlds' (Fielding, 1993, p 157), and to understand the radicals and the radicalisation process. The outlined facts reveal how my being an outsider facilitated my knowledge and understanding of the other within the shared space of a common religion.

These regional deprivations, interpreted along the line of 'Muslims discriminated all over the world' by radical entrepreneurs, resonated easily among vulnerable youths, thus enabling their recruitment into the al-Shabaab organisation (Badurdeen, 2011). Given this backdrop, my quest to understand the radical took me to participants who gave varied community definitions. Based on my religious positionality, there were times I felt some definitions were in harmony with my views and others where I felt confused. I realised that not all Islamic radicals were al-Shabaab associates or its sympathisers despite their persistent labelling as such. The term 'radical' is a derogatory term among Muslims in Kenya, and is usually synonymous for an association with al-Shabaab. One of the participants in a focus group discussion stated, "If defending my religion makes me a radical, all of us here are radicals." Then he asked me a question: "As a Muslim, would you not do the same?" I smiled, but I did not reply, and went on to my next question. I remained cautious in dialogues in which utterances not only responded to the other speaker, but also anticipated a counter-response. According to Bakhtin (1986, p 94, as cited in Hyvarinen, 2008), an utterance is constructed in anticipation of encountering a response from the other, and in my case, a response was expected, to know whether my religious stance was that of a moderate or a radical. However, the participant's statement made me reflect on my plight as the researcher. By merely replying 'yes' or 'no' to such a question, I would have brought disastrous consequences of suspicion on myself.[7] Self-disclosure in contexts related to my religious stance was viewed with caution, and it was usually equated to my being a government informer or an al-Shabaab sympathiser (field notes, November 2015).

Next, I faced considerable challenges in classifying my participants in terms of the moderate–radical debate. The debate of Islamic moderate versus Islamic extremist is a far-reaching one (Jackson, 2007; Hopkins and Kahani-Hopkins, 2009), which is often propagated by the West and the media (Lean, 2012). I found it difficult to draw the line between the moderate, the radical and the extremist from my religious positioning of a moderate. A feeling of confusion prevailed throughout the research process regarding these definitions. This was well encapsulated by a participant's statement: "You base your opinion of me as a radical, al-Shabaab or any other name given to me [by the law enforcement, state, media] … they themselves do not know the definitions … and you [researchers] make the definitions…." In the context of Sharia law,[8] the same participant asserted:

> '… it has become a common practice to evaluate a person along their affinity towards the Sharia law. First, you should understand what this law is. It is a code of conduct for all Muslims that govern their daily life. Therefore, do you think when a person follows any part of this law; you classify him as a radical? … now violence to achieve this is wrong, but to adhere to the belief that one day Muslims will have the Sharia law to govern them is not wrong….' (Interview 7, 11 December 2015)

My position as an outsider was also highlighted as I began to probe into the core concepts related to my study. Some of the participants viewed me as questioning the core values that were unquestionable, as it was the word of God and the teachings of the Prophet. One of my key informants looked at me as if I had not understood what is in the Quran with regard to fighting the enemy, and said, "Go read the Quran and come back for the next meeting, and you will realise that it [fighting the enemies] is in the Quran" (Interviewee 3, 6 November 2015). According to al-Shabaab magazine (*Gaidi Mataani*), views to the contrary might deem one an enemy. Therefore, despite my religious identity as a Muslim, the argument that moderates were the religion's worst enemy and did nothing to protect it cautioned me to temporarily halt discussions that were sensitive to some of my participants. I stopped this particular discussion, thanked the participant for his time, and told him that I would meet him during my next visit. This resonated well with the warning given to me by one of my supervisors:

> '… ideology and religion is twisted in radical [al-Shabaab] teachings; if you hear any statement on the issue of ideology that makes you or your respondent uneasy, just divert to another topic or just stop. Never counter any statement, whether it is intentional or unintentional…. At times, it's safe not to reveal your position, as you do not know their real position….' (field notes, 12 September 2015)

Categorising and essentialing

My religious stance as being posed by my participants as a 'moderate Muslim' led to challenges in the field during the research process. Foremost, I encountered unanticipated problems wherein I was already labelled as a 'moderate' during the interview process. One participant stated, "So you are Fathima, what brings you here to work on a topic like youth radicalisation?" When I explained that it was my interest as well as my PhD research topic, the respondent did not trust (was suspicious) that my interest in the topic was only as a PhD study, and replied, "good". Then he stated, "[Me] being a moderate, just like you…. I feel that these youth who fall prey to extremist organisations [al-Shabaab] are weak in their religious faith…." While the respondent had already classified me as a moderate, I also felt that the interviewee felt safe by classifying himself as a moderate in my presence. A similar situation was evident during another interview when the respondent stated, "… as a moderate, you will never be able to talk to a radical. They are hard nuts to crack, they are crazy and confused … you will be viewed as a hypocrite according to their ideals" (Interview 13, 21 December 2015).

My selective positioning as a moderate Muslim tended to carry assumptions linked to prejudices that radicals have narrow interpretations or distorted versions of Islam. For example, I tended to assume how my participants viewed Jihad (holy war) or Hijra (the migration journey of the Prophet Muhammad sal) was an indication of their radical views. If a participant perceived Jihad in line with physical Jihad or agreed to Hijra (migration in the cause of Allah, and in this case, going to the battlefield in Somalia), the participant was viewed as an al-Shabaab radical. This was well ascertained when a participant asked me if al-Shabaab and its origins were oppressive and if the organisation's positioning of defending their 'Muslim' territory from 'invasions' from outsiders (non-Muslims) was wrong. Or, if protecting their women was wrong. The participant expressed his views on an unjust world, highlighting cases from Bosnia, Iraq, Sudan and Somalia. According to him, "… fighting against an unjust world is not wrong…. Hijra is mandatory" (Interviewee 2, 6 November 2015).

These assumptions were in themselves complex and contributed little in differentiating between moderate and radical views. The worldview of the participants was not necessarily driven by religion, but also influenced by their socioeconomic circumstances and understanding of historical and political situations. Their experiences, as are mine, were also influenced by their upbringing and opinions of friends and family. In my selective positioning, I viewed the other, 'the participant', as having a narrow perspective of the unjust situation, while the other viewed me as having a narrow interpretation due to their religious and cultural thinking. Both positions ultimately essentialised and cast suspicion on the other. I found out that during the research process it was difficult to undo bias in a study that centres on my ascribed religion. Personally, it was hard for me to tolerate how Muslims were perceived or the stigmatisation of Muslim communities promoted locally and globally. I felt the dire need myself to clear up the misconceptions and labels associated with Muslim communities. This bias made me subjective as I felt a similar resonance between the researcher and the researched, and this very act made me a total insider.

Conclusion

Conducting ethical research in volatile regions of conflict and focusing on radicalised populations requires self-reflectivity and an understanding of one's role as a researcher in this field. Such ongoing reflections bring us closer to answering the questions as to where and in which ways our actions as researchers can be useful to research on terrorism. Throughout this chapter, I have argued that the researcher's religious positionality could either facilitate or challenge the research process, which could eventually shape the research. This positioning of the researcher either as an insider or an outsider, or even being in-between, did have an impact on the researcher, the researched, the research setting and the research project. Sometimes these challenges hindered the research process, while at other times they facilitated the exploration of rich contextual knowledge that enriched the study. For example, I learned to mature emotionally in the process of hearing phrases such as 'being sympathetic', 'being radicalised in the process' and 'being biased', giving me ample opportunities to reflect on my subjectivity towards the researched. Understanding and acknowledging our subjectivities as well as the associated biases in the field can be the way forward for a meaningful research output.

During discussions and interviews, I felt myself drawn into a sympathetic complexity when I encountered discrimination or marginalisation. Being a Muslim, I felt sympathy for their marginalised contexts, whereby the participants pegged their local grievances to the international context and drew parallels on "how Muslims all over the world are suffering" (Interviewee 3, 11 November 2015). There was an internal contradiction within me of being a Muslim and labelling some of my participants as radicals. Hence, there was the possibility that I became sympathetic to the views of some participants as well, and a victim in the research process. In other instances, I could not accept certain narratives. In fact, the participants' reactions to the research were often framed on how I chose to acknowledge or address issues pertaining to my belief, identity and stance on religion (shaped by my learning on various international and local discourses on Islam).

In this case, the researcher and the participants had Islam as a common denominator; however, attributing and simplifying complex human beings and complex societies to the one single factor of politicised Islam, and determining the outcomes through this one factor, were dangerous. The diversity of views on Islamic radicalisation highlighted the futility of attempting to place the differentiation between a 'moderate' or a 'radical' in hermetically sealed boxes and is likely to affect a number of people whose identities and beliefs seem to operate across, between or simultaneously in a continuum of categories (focus discussion group, 9 February 2016). At the same time, it is not helpful to simply argue that religion or belief is complex, diverse, personal and defies categorisation altogether. Finally, the approaches to researching the 'moderate' or the 'radical' should attempt to understand the two in their own individual rights as well as in their diverse positioning. Prematurely narrowing the research approach to the 'radical' through clear and self-conscious 'moderate' perspectives on terrorism research runs the risk of missing out important research data on complex issues hinging on politicised Islam.

Notes

[1] Most of the radicals or extremists are associated with marginalised communities in the coastal region. Nevertheless, care should be taken to note that not all labelled or identified as al-Shabaab radicals come from marginalised, poverty-stricken communities (field notes, 12 December 2015).

[2] Narratives used by al-Shabaab on the harsh realities for Muslims in the coastal region and in other regions of the world (al-Shabaab magazine, *Gaidi Mataani*).

[3] I was born in Sri Lanka and have since settled in Kenya.

[4] 'Modern women' was a term used to refer to those who imitated women from the West.

[5] I refer to hard-to-reach religious leaders as the participants who feared being labelled as moderates or as sympathisers for al-Shabaab. Being labelled in either category meant surveillance on them from either the government security forces or from al-Shabaab, with a risk to their lives.

[6] Government authorities labelled some religious leaders as radical or moderate based on their views.

[7] Among my participants I did not know who was an al-Shabaab associate or a sympathiser, and my words needed to be used with the utmost care due to the prevailing security context.

[8] Sharia law is the Islamic religious law forming part of the Islamic traditions.

References

Alzbouebi, K. (2010) 'The splintering selves: A reflective journey in educational research', *International Journal of Excellence in Education*, vol 4, no 1, pp 1–9.

Anzalone, C. (2012) 'Kenya's Muslim youth centre and Al-Shabaab's East African recruitment' (www.ctc.usma.edu/posts/kenyas-muslim-youth-center-and-al-shababs-east-african-recruitment).

Badurdeen, F.A. (2012) 'Youth radicalization in the coast province of Kenya', *Africa Peace and Conflict Journal*, vol 5, no 1, pp 53–8.

Bakhtin, M.M. (1986) 'Speech genres and other late essays', in C. Emerson and M. Holquist (eds) (V. McGee, translator), Austin, TX: University of Texas Press.

Berger, R. (2013) 'Now I see it, now I don't: Researcher's position and reflexivity in qualitative research', *Qualitative Research*, vol 1, no 1, pp 1–16.

Beydoun, K.A. (2016) 'The myth of the "moderate Muslim": Deconstructing the myth "good versus bad" Muslim paradigm' (www.aljazeera.com/indepth/opinion/2016/05/myth-moderate-muslim-160511085819521.html).

Bourke, B. (2014) 'Positionality: Reflecting on the research process', *The Qualitative Report*, vol 19, no 18, pp 1–9.

Chande, A. (2000) 'Radicalism and reform in East Africa', in N. Levtzion and R.L. Pouwels (eds) *The history of Islam in Africa*, Athens, OH: Ohio University Press.

Dolnik, A. (2013) *Conducting terrorism field research: A guide*, London and New York: Routledge.

Eppley, K. (2006) 'Defying insider-outsider categorization: One researcher's fluid and complicated positioning on the insider-outsider continuum', in D. Weaver-Zercher (ed) 'Review Essay: Writing the Amish: The worlds of John A. Hostetler', *Forum Qualitative Sozialforschung / Forum: Qualitative Social Research*, vol 7, no 3 (http://nbn-resolving.de/urn:nbn:de:0114-fqs0603161).

Fielding, N. (1993) 'Ethnography', in N. Gilbert (ed) *Researching social life*, London: Sage Publications, pp 154–71.

Flood, G. (1999) *Beyond phenomenology: Rethinking the study of religion*, London: Cassell.

Hamdan, A.K. (2009) 'Reflexivity of discomfort in insider-outsider educational research', *McGill Journal of Education*, vol 44, no 3, pp 377–404.

Hansen, S.J. (2013) *Al-Shabaab in Somalia: The history and ideology of a militant Islamist group 2005-2012*, New York: Oxford University Press Inc.

Henkel, R. (2011) 'Are geographers religiously unmusical? Positionalities in geographical research on religion', *Geographical Research on Religion*, vol 65, no 4, pp 389–99.

Hoel, N. (2013) 'Embodying the field: A researcher's reflection on power dynamics, positionality and the nature of research relationships', *Fieldwork in Religion*, vol 8, no 1, pp 7–26.

Hopkins, N. and Kahani-Hopkins, V. (2009) 'Reconceptualising extremism and moderation: From categories of analysis to categories of practice in the construction of collective identities', *British Journal of Social Psychology*, vol 48, no 1, pp 99–113.

Hyvarinen, M. (2008) 'Analyzing narratives and story-telling', in P. Alasuutari, L. Bickman and J. Brannen (eds) *The Sage handbook of social research methods*, Abingdon: Sage, pp 447–60.

IRIN (2013) 'Countering the radicalization of Kenya's youth', 6 May (www.irinnews.org/report/97982/countering-radicalization-kenyas-youth).

Jackson, R. (2007) 'Constructing enemies: "Islamic terrorism" in political and academic discourse, government and opposition', *An International Journal of Comparative Politics*, vol 42, no 3, pp 394–426.

Kristeva, J. (1991) *Strangers to ourselves*, New York: Columbia University Press.

Lean, N. (2012) *The Islamophobia industry: How the right manufactures fear of Muslims*, London: Pluto Press.

Lewis, B. (1994) *Islam and the west*, New York: Oxford University Press.

Manji, I. and Dajani, M.S. (2015) 'Is there a "moderate" Islam?', *Policy Watch*, The Washington Institute for Near East Policy (www. washingtoninstitute.org/policy-analysis/view/is-there-a-moderate-islam).

Mednicoff, D. (2015) 'Religious identity and social science research in the Middle East' (http://blogs.lse.ac.uk/mec/2015/08/26/religious-identity-and-social-science-research-in-the-middle-east/).

Nielsen, R.A. (2014) *Thoughts on the ethics of interventions when studying religion and politics in the Middle East, the ethics of research in the Middle East* (http://pomeps.org/wp-content/uploads/2014/07/POMEPS_ Studies_8_Ethics.pdf).

Razavi, S. (1992) 'Agrarian change and gender power: A comparative study in South Eastern Iran', DPhil dissertation, Oxford: Oxford University.

Wiebe, D. (1985) 'Does understanding religion require religious understanding?', in T. Witold (ed) *Current progress in the methodology of the science of religion: The insider/outsider problem in the study of religion*, Warsaw: Polish Scientific Publishers, pp 260–73.

Yasmeen, S. (2008) *Understanding Muslim identities: From perceived relative exclusion to inclusion* (www.dss.gov.au/sites/default/files/files/settle/ multicultural_australia/final-muslim-identities.pdf)

Vingette 3: Thinking about race and gender in conflict research

Althea-Maria Rivas

Exploring the racialised and gendered nature of the structures of power and historical processes that have justified and facilitated intervention and produced conflict in many parts of the world are central to my research and that of many critical conflict scholars. A much less explored topic is how these racialised and gendered histories enter into sites of conflict to influence the research process, and the experience of the researcher, and the perceptions of the research participants and communities of the researcher when the researcher comes from a racialised community. This vignette provides a short reflection on the ways in which race can enter into the research process, and ends with a few thoughts on the need for more discussion within academic circles about intersectionality and research praxis.

School daze: I dreaded leaving the university in the evening. I had arranged a nightly car pool with another lecturer who would wait for me outside of the school entrance until my last class had finished. Outside of the gates there were always groups of students hanging around, getting ready to go home and arranging their own rides back to the suburbs of Kabul. I enjoyed and admired the energy of the students who were usually still hyper at the end of what was for many of them a full day of work at their professional jobs followed by several hours of study and classes at the university. There were also a number of armed guards who sat drinking tea or stood by looking for signs of trouble and ensuring no one lingered too long. The guards rarely moved, and although they were heavily armed after spending a decade in conflict zones I had learned to accept guns as part of everyday life. The students and the guards, however, were not what played on my mind as I prepared to go home.

No, what I dreaded was the group of neighborhood children who had begun congregating at the gate to watch me leave at night. For many of them I suspect it was not the first time they had seen a black person, as there were many African-American, mostly male, military personnel who patrolled the city on a regular basis, and there had been for many years. I, however, was different. I was not armed or accompanied by heavy military vehicles and I was a woman. That meant my young entourage could almost come very close to me without feeling threatened, which they often did. In fact, they regularly tried to form a large circle of sorts around me, which did not restrict any movement but made the walk to the car slightly more challenging than necessary. Had it only been this odd variation of 'ring around the rosey' that entertained them, I would not have minded.

A chorus of racial slurs, however, always accompanied the circle, many of which I had not heard in years, and had never had directed at me explicitly and repeatedly in a public space in short bursts of time. The children seemed aware they were saying something insulting, but also seemed to think it was a sort of game that for much of that first term that I taught at the university they rarely tired of. I wondered if they knew the weight of the words or if they just thought that is what I was called. I cannot say over time this nightly game ever began to bother me less.

A complicating factor was that the university students and the guards who were also often present during this performance were, of course, well aware of the weight of these words. Even the guards who did not speak English picked up on what was going on. In an effort to keep the children at bay, the students usually shooed them away. One day, when the kids were particularly robust, one of the guards decided to be a little more aggressive. I immediately intervened, which created an odd scene where I had to place myself between an armed guard and a young child who was still calling me the N-word as I tried to protect them from being beaten or thrown to the ground, while suppressing my own anger and disillusionment. The students and the guards, however, were embarrassed. On my behalf, but more so because of what the chants of these children revealed about the perceptions of their older brothers and sisters, their families and certain elements with their community.

Children often learn hate from those around them. These kids had been taught at some point that people with black skin occupied a lower place in the world than they did and could be ridiculed. When I asked my Afghan colleagues where the children would have learned those words and the ideas that underlie them, the answers were varied. Some thought it was from their older siblings or people on the street who may have used derogatory terms to refer to the black American military and as an expression of anger towards the occupation. Others thought it came from music lyrics and television. In the course of those conversations, however, they tended to all agree that many people did perceive of black people as being corrupt or inferior, not just in Afghanistan, but in a global hierarchy of people. They spoke to the gendered and racialised implications of many overlapping historical processes.

It took some time for me to reconcile these events within myself. Indeed, it would be dishonest to say I did not experience shock, anger and frustration during my fieldwork at times as a result of these occurrences. I had to acknowledge, however, that it was a conscious choice to put myself in this space. Aside from the children outside of the university, however, I had very few experiences with overt racism in Afghanistan. In fact, I can think of only a few other incidents in five years, and I was more often humbled by the hospitality of people than their racism.

But race was often there, though perhaps taking different forms. It could be a surprised look as I was not what they expected when they heard a Western researcher was coming, or uncertainty about what to make of me at various events. Over time I began to realise how these constructions influenced the many relationships and modes of communication between the multiple and diverse actors who lived and worked in Afghanistan. This is an area I began to explore in my work. Ultimately, understanding how constructions of race were given meaning in this space for those I engaged with, for me and for many others, was an important part of my research process. It was essential to gaining a deeper understanding of the subjectivities of the people around me, the dynamics of the environment I was in, and developing insights on myself as a researcher.

Road trips: It was a long day and it had been a long trip. I had crossed four countries, mainly by road, in two weeks, and the logistics of this consultancy seemed more practical on paper before I left home than it was in reality. I did like being in rural Africa, though. There was something about the scent of the land, the weight of the humidity and the vividness of colour in the countryside that reminded me of the Caribbean island where I had spent parts of my childhood. As a woman of Caribbean descent, my own heritage is complex and speaks to the interactions between Caribs, African slaves and European settlers, many of which took place through violent historical processes. I consider myself, however, part of a diverse African diaspora.

In the car during the drive to the Burundi border from Congo I had a long talk with the non-governmental organisation (NGO) staff I was with about how colonialism had affected their country and the region. They spoke of the emotional and physical destruction different colonial powers brought with them and then left behind, and the violence of ongoing conflicts that were rooted in colonial legacies. I talked about growing up on an island that had made great efforts to re-write textbooks to reflect our history as we saw it, not the one given to us by the British. At the same time whenever I visited back home we drove past a large shantytown, informally called 'the beatdown', which was mainly populated by black faces. This settlement and others like it are among the poorest areas on the island and stand in stark contrast to the gated mansions and communities where the populations were mixed but also where a majority of the white islanders lived. These latter communities were often located on land that was controlled by the British and Americans before independence and had been largely restricted to foreign employees or servicemen and their families. These were areas like Forest Reserve, Vista Bella and Point-a-Pierre, in the south of the island, where the British oil companies had operated and Chagaramus, an old American military base.

It was a long trip, but we finally made it across the border and were joined by the Burundi team. I would go ahead with them to Bujumbura and the car they had brought me in would turn back. The young man driving the car decided to teach me a few words of the local language to help me get along during the coming weeks. At least the greetings were important, he suggested, and my struggle with basic words was clearly a source of mild entertainment for the other passengers.

After a few minutes of conversation, one of the female staff commented how surprising but nice it was to have a black consultant come to the office. I smiled yes, there was always some sense of familiarity there. There was also, however, much difference. The head of the office highlighted this when he turned around and responded to her comment and said, "Ah but no, this one she's white. Can't you see that. She doesn't even speak any African language." The woman sitting beside me responded with, "What are you talking about you make no sense ... but yes, it is true, she has no African language." After a quick and somewhat rhetorical glance at myself in the rearview mirror, to confirm I still looked the same as I remembered, I just smiled and sat back. It was a conversation that I had participated in many times during the years I had done research in conflict-affected areas in Africa.

The road trip was one of many of these experiences that gave me a deeper understanding of the constructed, intersecting and shifting nature of race, ethnicity and class, within different societies and across global spaces. These interactions highlighted how slavery and colonialism influenced the environments that I was researching, and the power dynamics that played out there. More so, it shed light on the way in which I was constructed, the way I constructed others, and the ways I constructed myself.

These conversations always remind me of the complicated relationship that can exist between diaspora communities and people in areas from which they originate. While there are many shared experiences, cultures develop and change separately, and a lack of appreciation for these differences can, in itself, be a manifestation of privilege, and one that local populations will be very aware of. Spivak (1990a, b) cautions researchers from the Global South or marginalised communities based at Western institutions to reflect regularly on the ways in which they represent people in the places that they are from and/or areas of the Global South. Her insights into these dilemmas have raised important questions around representation. Researchers 'doing fieldwork' have another layer of complexity to consider. The intimate in-person exchanges that take place during fieldwork can include direct encounters with experiences of racialisation that may be unexpected, enlightening and difficult. These constructions are dynamic and can raise new questions, such as, how does language relate to race? They also, however, require constant reflexivity on the assumptions, bias and power relationships in the field.

Calling the academy to account: It would be rare for a researcher to be allowed to conduct fieldwork without first completing training in their university about methodology choices and research ethics. Undoubtedly, researchers gain much from those preparatory modules. As the numbers of researchers interested in doing conflict research rises, they will increasingly come from diverse backgrounds, whether in terms of race, gender, ability, sexuality or socioeconomic background. These diverse identities produce multiple sites of privilege and oppression and unique opportunities for solidarity in conflict fieldwork. Yet these conversations, so important to preparing the researcher for the field, are too infrequently had in Western universities.

Scholars have written about the inherent irony in that, while constructions of racial difference have been central to global politics, international relations (Bell, 2013; Henderson, 2013; Shilliam, 2013) and international development (White, 1999, 2002) and feminist gender studies (Sylvester, 1995; Mohanty, 2003), there continue to be persistent silences about the issue in certain areas of academic scholarship. These silences are not only apparent in academic theorising about how to give meaning to our world; they are also present in discussions about how to go about academic fieldwork.

The circulation of power and privilege within the academy itself can have a significant influence in shaping discussions of how structures of power and privilege circulate and influence the praxis of Western researchers. Deep assumptions about who produces knowledge and the positionality of those scholars, both historically and in contemporary times, in relation to marginalised populations and global hierarchies are implicit in the ways in which academic texts are written and courses are taught. For researchers whose identity places them on the periphery of dominant knowledge paradigms of many Western universities that are still too often embedded in patriarchy and eurocentrisim, this creates frustration and anxiety. Researchers may, for example, want to acknowledge and participate in conversations about the importance of recognising the privilege that comes from being a part of the Western world and/or Western universities when conducting fieldwork in sites of conflict in the Global South, but at the same time, find they are unable to see themselves in those conversations. Frustration arises from having to locate oneself in the experiences of others to participate in the discussion and feeling that raising issues of intersectionality beyond those discussed in traditional academic texts could be seen as unimportant to 'doing' serious conflict research.

The academy needs to re-think the boundaries of the conversations that are had about academic fieldwork to take into consideration the diverse subjectivities of scholars themselves. This is particularly, but not only, the case in conflict research where emotions figure prominently and the entanglements between researchers, research participants and community members are at times marked by intensity, violence and vulnerability. Essential to this move is dismantling the power structures and knowledge frameworks that dictate what should be discussed when we talk about doing conflict research and who does conflict research.

References

Bell, D. (2013) 'Race and international relations: Introduction', *Cambridge Review of International Affairs*, vol 26, issue 1, pp 1–4.

Henderson, E. (2013) 'Hidden in plain sight: Racism in international relations theory', *Cambridge Review of International Affairs*, vol 26, issue 1, pp 71–92.

Mohanty, C. (2003) '"Under Western eyes" revisited: Feminist solidarity through anticapitalist struggles', *Signs*, vol 28, no 2, pp 499–535.

Shilliam, R. (2013) 'Race and research agendas', *Cambridge Review of International Affairs*, vol 26, issue 1, pp 152–8.

Spivak, G. (1990a) 'Criticism, feminism and the institution (with Elizabeth Grosz)', in S. Harasym (ed) *The post-colonial critic: Interviews, strategies, dialogues*, New York: Routledge, pp 1–16.

Spivak, G. (1990b) 'Gayatri Spivak on the politics of the subaltern, interview by Howard Winant', *Socialist Review*, vol 20, no 3, pp 81–97.

Sylvester, C. (1995) 'Africa and western feminisms: World traveling and the tendencies and possibilities', *Signs*, vol 20, no 4, pp 941–97.

Sylvester, C. (1999) 'Development studies and postcolonial studies: Disparate tales of the "Third World"', *Third World Quarterly*, vol 20, no 4, pp 703–21.

White, S. (2002) 'Thinking race, thinking development', *Third World Quarterly*, vol 23, no 3, pp 407–19.

Section IV
Technology and social media

7

Bodies of cyberwar: Violence and knowledge beyond corporeality

Fabio Cristiano

Introduction

During the time I spent in Palestine, I visited the Al-Quds University campus in Abu Dis on several occasions. Detached from Jerusalem as a result of the stage-two construction process of the separation wall in 2003, campus activities are often disrupted by Israeli raids and subsequent violent confrontations with Palestinian students. In the course of my latest visit in March 2017, the campus atmosphere appeared to be one of apparent calmness in the aftermath of a recent storm. Burnt tyres, tear gas canisters and stones lay scattered on the road facing the main entrance. Israeli-armoured vehicles and soldiers oversee the campus from the top of a nearby hill. After numerous Israeli raids over the preceding weeks, the usual vibrant and noisy atmosphere of the campus seemed restored. Clumps of students crowded around the steps of the main building, some of them campaigning and putting up PFLP's (Popular Front for the Liberation of Palestine) red flags for the upcoming student elections.

Situated within the grounds of the campus is the Abu Jihad Museum for Prisoner Movement, a museum that narrates Palestinian prisoners' testimony through the exhibition of pictures, letters, poems and artworks. Within the walls of the museum are located the memories of seized and tortured bodies, experiences that often escape mainstream narratives of the conflict.[1] The museum, financed by the Arab Fund in Kuwait, has few visitors: students, in fact, seem to prefer hanging out in the sun rather than being reminded of the too-familiar violence of the Israeli occupation. This thought immediately brought me back to a past conversation with a young Palestinian hacker, conducted just a few metres away from the museum and the area of the clashes, in 2013. While narrating the successes and vicissitudes of the latest attacks on Israeli cyberspace, the conversation often deviates to make space for the recurrent argument that, after all, engaging in cyberwar concedes to be part of the struggle without being violent and allowing for the alleviation of a personal risk of physical violence.

This argument appears to be consistent with mainstream scholarship on the topic. In fact, cyberwars are generally considered not to be violent because they lack those physical and corporeal elements that define war in a traditional sense. The absence of a violence that is distinctly available to sensorial experiences would relegate cyber-like types of confrontation to something short of war. Along these lines, scholarship on cyberwarfare (as well as policy and legal frameworks) recognises corporeality as a defining element for the classification of cyberattacks as actual instances of war (NATO, 2013, 2017; Schmitt, 2014). Only in the event a cyberattack causes physical damage in the 'real' world do we eventually witness cyberwar.

At the same time, many praise cyberwar for allowing operations that, albeit non-violent, function in the prevention and deterrence of war (Lucas, 2012). In line with this argument, the launch of, for example, the malicious computer worm Stuxnet in 2010 can be considered as a non-violent alternative to a possible military intervention, and as an effective measure in undermining, or at least setting back, a perceived threat that was the Iranian nuclear programme (Lindsay, 2013). Similarly, Gaza-based hackers revealed, in online interviews conducted in 2013, their rhetorical understanding of cyberwar as the means for damaging and defeating Israel, while escaping the daily violence of the blockade and occupation. In their understanding, cyberwar enables the perpetration of a violence that supersedes and reduces the risk of retaliatory physical harm.

Albeit different, each of these perspectives on the violence of cyberwar clusters around a traditional understanding of war. In line with the classical writings of Prussian General Carl von Clausewitz (1943), these discourses primarily identify war as the violent kinetic interaction of fighting bodies (which unfolds on political and sovereignty grounds). Consequently, the absence of these corporeal and embodied elements would exclude cyberattacks from the realm of war. These bodies are thought to exist in corporeal forms and function both as the target, as well as the source, of physical violence. In furthering this argument, even if aiming at bodiless targets, hackers often attribute them corporeal characteristics. Through recurring expressions – such as 'put Israel on its knees', 'stab Zionism in the back', or 'hit Israeli cyberspace in the face' – hackers tend to depict their targets in embodied and fleshy discursive forms.

A wide array of emerging scholarship on war connects to feminist perspectives on embodiment in order to suggest ways of prioritising and problematising the role of the body in the study and the framing of wars (Butler 2004a, b, 2009; Sylvester, 2013). Recognising war as a lived and embodied experience, these scholars inspire research that moves beyond concerns regarding the (failure of) political interactions of belligerent parties (see Barkawi and Brighton, 2011). Rather, the focus relapses into reflections on the ways in which violence becomes embodied in the life experiences of those who are ultimately affected by war. In this light, bodies transcend their corporeality (see Turner, 1984) and, aside from existing as terrains where these experiences disrupt in physical forms, become theorised as the social product of different discourses and experiences of war (see Wilcox, 2015). Moreover, questions pertaining to the social construction of bodies interrogate how these are made to appear or disappear in order to justify a type of violence that, without bodies on sight, appear harmless, yet necessary and just.[2] For this reason, and in order to capture the centrality of bodies in the analysis of wars, boundaries of warscapes are extended beyond their territorial and physical dimensions and include their surrounding discourses, imagery and aesthetics (Sontag, 2003). In this sense, the violence of war entails much more than its corporeal and physical manifestations.

In line with these approaches, this chapter explores how violence unfolds in the context of cyberwar in light of views of the body that transcend its corporeality. First, the question of violence is situated within those academic debates on cyberwarfare that depart from a corporeal understanding of the body. Expanding embodied violent experiences beyond the limits of corporeality, the second section rethinks cyberwar in light of violence as an experience depending on the interplay between embodied proximity and distance rather than corporeality. In the concluding section, this broader understanding of violence is reconciled with its implications for the study of war in cyberspace, oftentimes considered as a disembodied, and thus non-violent, warscape.

Violence and cyberwar

There exists wide agreement within classical scholarship around the assumption that violence is what ultimately defines war. Von Clausewitz (1943, p 87) argues, in fact, that the essence of war consists of, 'a complete, untrammelled, absolute manifestation of violence.' At the same time, the presence of absolute violence in itself is not sufficient to indicate whether a conflictual interaction constitutes an instance of war. Most cultures attribute to war qualities that define its exceptionality vis-à-vis other forms of violent exchanges. This distinction essentially refers to those political, strategic and technological elements sustaining war's dignity and legitimacy as opposed to less noble exchanges of violence (Keegan, 1993). Moreover, the creation of ethical boundaries through codification (such as the Geneva Conventions) defines limits and extents to which violence can be justified and legitimised as the continuation of politics by other means.

In the classical study *On war*, von Clausewitz separates the *nature* of war – its immutably violent and interactive essence – from its *character*, that is, its ever-changing and contextual politics, strategies and techniques. As the 'realm of physical exertion and suffering' (1943, p 122), the character of war includes those embodied experiences of war that often escape theorising to make space for studies focusing on bodies as corporeal units of measurement. In fact, traditional studies on the political violence of war account for the body solely as the numerical unit that reveals the consequences of military interventions. At the same time, these bodies of war are usually counted through categorisations (civilian, opposed armed factions, etc) that primarily consider different social constructs over corporeal sameness.

The removal of this corporeal sameness is argued to create a social distance necessary for disconnecting war, and its inherent violence, from emotional experiences (Massumi, 2010). Once bodies disappear from experiences of war, its violence becomes un-relatable and distant – thus justifiable. Creating distance from the character of war through the removal of bodies (and the creation of otherness this removal entails) functions, in fact, in sustaining the ethical and moral validity underlying the uniqueness of the violence of war (Butler, 2009). Bodies transcend their corporeal existences and their becoming legitimate targets of violence ceases to depend on this corporeality, but rather rests articulated through those components that produce subjects of war beyond their corporeal existence, thus making them 'others' and 'targets' (enemies, terrorists, etc). Moreover, in line with classical categorisations that differentiate between public and private enemy, *polemos* against *extros* for the Greeks, *hostis* against *inimicus* for the Romans, this production often sustains the moral and legal justifications for inflicting violence on some while saving and empathising with others (as strongly argued by proponents of just war theories).[3]

The relatively recent emergence of cyberwarfare interrogates theories of war on the relationship between violence and the body. In the specific context of cyberwar, physical bodies are seldom present to one another or rarely become targeted by physical violence. Confrontation, in fact, increasingly occurs in ways that remain mostly virtualised. Most advanced cyberattacks are ignited by automatised machines, thus reducing the extent and relevance of human bodily input (Singer, 2009). Programmed machines, intrusive malwares and malicious crawlers remotely carry on wide-ranging attacks, take down or deface websites, spy, leak information and damage (national) cyber infrastructures in creative ways. Similarly, attackers' quest for anonymity indicates a need, and a desire, for hiding physical bodies as well as those elements that make up for their subjectivity beyond corporeality (such as nationality, gender, etc). In other words, whereas those political and technological elements subtending war are clearly present, fighting bodies and their inherent corporeality are somewhat missing. Despite the vanishing of physical bodies in the conduct of cyberwars, as this chapter argues, violence remains.

The absence of a distinct corporeality in cyberspace, and physicality more in general, entwines with those theoretical efforts that aim to draw and capture the ontology of cyberwar through classical categories of war (see, for example, Allhoff et al, 2016). As questions pertaining to the nature of cyberwar have emerged across different disciplines (security, military and legal studies), these share a common interest in defining under which conditions a cyberattack can be associated with an act of war (and thus determining proportional military responses and appropriated legal framings). Besides attempting to draw a correspondence between national territories and cyberspace(s), these studies recur to an understanding of violence that appears limited to its physical dimension. In this light, military studies (Libicki, 2009; Rowe, 2009; Lucas, 2012), international law (Hoisington, 2009; Schmitt, 2014) and cybersecurity (Singer and Friedman, 2014) agree on a classification of cyberwar that discriminates primarily on the basis of caused physical damage.

The reduction of the question of violence to its manifestation in corporeal and physical forms also relies on a clear-cut distinction between the virtual and actual world, as two opposed characterisations of being. In this spirit, all elements residing in cyberspace (for example, websites, databases, etc) are not considered to have a physical existence of their own. As such, attacks done on these (without repercussions on elements residing outside cyberspace) are not regarded as consistent with the understanding of violence as a physical exchange – and thus a prerequisite for war. This distinction similarly separates corporeal bodies from their virtual existences and ramifications. In line with traditional theories of war, cyberwarfare scholarship attributes to the violence of cyberwar some specific qualities that, in turn, make it different from other forms of cyberattacks such as criminal theft, vandalism, malware, sophisticated espionage or intelligence operations (Ohlin et al, 2015) – in a nutshell, a perpetrator with clear national sovereign characteristics and physical or corporeal damage in the actual world (Koh, 2012).

Framing cyberwar along the lines of traditional warfare confines this phenomenon to schemes that precede its actualisation and, in fact, returning to von Clausewitz's categories, redefine its existence only with respect to its presumed nature (rather, than with regards to those contextual elements and phenomenology making up for its character). In this light, equating the violence of cyberattacks to acts of war appears to stem from the necessity of adapting existing, conceptual, legal and policy frameworks to the new emerging threat of cyberwar. To this end, research on the topic mainly focuses on state responses, prevention and preparedness – thus reflecting on ways in which traditional defence mechanisms can be adjusted for countering and deterring potential cyberattacks. In the absence of a cyberwar-specific international treaty, substantial efforts have been made in order to incorporate a definition of the violence of cyberwar by adapting existing international treaties.[4] These prescriptive understandings of cyberwar delineate a taxonomy that, rather than engaging with the phenomenology of existing experiences of cyberwar, engages with defining its nature departing from those elements that traditionally define war. As such, the expectations of a potential cyberwar, that would simply reproduce and transpose traditional elements in cyberspace, have been unattended.

The prediction of a large-scale cyberwar fought by states has, as yet, not come to fruition (see Rid, 2013). So has been the use of those conceptual categories of analysis – and policies – that were predictively developed around this imaginary and its threats, outside a phenomenology of what existed. These categories imagined a cyberwar that would simply reproduce the nature of war in the virtual realm, somehow affirming a superiority of the immutable nature of war on its actual character. In reality, however, fighting surpasses offline formations and shapes conflict in new forms and dynamics that exceeds those of territorial boundaries (Brenner, 2009). In these terms, a prescriptive equation between cyberwarfare and conventional warfare appears unfitting.

Due to a concern in rethinking categories, such as legitimate use of force, states' attribution, proportionality, espionage law and the application of international humanitarian law, relevant treaties and mainstream scholarship equate cyberwar to war, given that cyberattacks lead to consequences in the actual world (physical damage). At the same time, much less work has been devoted to defining and situating violence that occurs outside the limits of offline physical damage.

Embodied experiences of cyberwar beyond corporeality

At first glance, the absence of bodies in the context of cyberwar seems to depend on those incorporeal characteristics delineating cyberspace as a unique warscape. Contrary to the removal of bodies from the framings of traditional war, this absence does not result from a narrational or epistemic blindness. Rather, corporeal bodies – and violence that can be done upon them – seem to vanish as a result of the encounter between human experience and virtuality. In her *Cyborg manifesto*, Donna Haraway (1991) recognised the interactive merging of bodies with machines in the fabric of human experiences. In particular, cyborg theory suggests rethinking the sensorial and physical limits of corporeal bodies by reflecting on the ways in which technology intersection of virtual and real worlds, with other elements of subjectivity, thus determining and influencing human experiences. At the same time, whereas the encounter between bodies and technology forges embodied experiences at the intersection of virtual and real worlds, the corporeality of these experiences does not dissipate outright.

Engaging with similar issues, scholarship in the cognitive sciences alleges for different degrees of integration between human body, mind and computer technology – spanning from absolute disconnection to total cybernetic integration (Clark, 2004, 2016). In other words, the physical absence of bodies to one another would not determine the impossibility of corporeal experiences. These different degrees of integration presume different modes and extents in which bodies are integrated to machines or connected to virtual items, and thus contrasting ways of thinking how experiences, such as violence, become embodied in the making of subjectivity. If physical bodies are thought to have ramifications outside the limits of corporeal existences, violence done through and on these ramifications can result in bodily harm. This becomes clear, for instance, when a violation of those virtual spaces where subjectivities expand occurs (such as e-mailboxes, blogs, social media, etc). As much as these spaces do not clearly exist in physical ways, their violation might result in a type of suffering that can be experienced in corporeal forms.[5]

Feminist approaches to embodiment in general, and cyborg theory specifically – through fostering interest for discourses, imagery and the aesthetics of war – revive an interest for the body in the study of belligerent interactions. Referring to a body existing beyond its role of a physical and measurable unit targeted by the violence of war, the epistemic focus moves away from corporeal interactions to make space for those embodied experiences of violence that transcend a material interaction of bodies. At the same time, reasserting the centrality of war experiences (von Clausewitz's character of war) does not depend on discarding bodies, but rather it 'requires that human bodies come into focus as units that have war agency and are also prime targets of war violence and war enthusiasms' (Sylvester, 2013, p 484).

Besides interrogating the relationship between war and bodies beyond their physical mechanics and interaction, the character of war also unfolds in those dynamical approaches that discursively create proximity or distance from corporeal sameness.[6] While corporeal bodies possess fundamental assimilable characteristics (determining the capacity of experiencing physical harm), their social construction beyond corporeality regulates the extent to which they can be the object of physical violence. For example, in the specific context of the Israeli occupation, the enforcement of different regimes of mobility (as well as of violent punishment) for Palestinians relies on the construction of different subjectivities through regulatory and administrative apparatuses of violence.

Turning towards an epistemic interest that prioritises embodied experiences over those broader narratives of war intuitively implies engaging closely with how violence is experienced at a close proximity to the mechanics of war. However, while traditional scholarship regards this proximity in terms of corporeal closeness[7] (and thus bodies becoming measurable units that can be securitised, injured, killed, saved or displaced), a broader understanding of the body indicates that proximity to the event of war not only depends on physical closeness, but also on the interplay between distance and proximity beyond corporeality. Regardless of physical proximity, in fact, the violence of war can be experienced through the reading of a Holocaust survivor's old diary, watching a live video about a battle in East Aleppo, playing a war game wearing a virtual reality headset, or being moved emotionally by the picture of a dead Syrian boy laying on the Turkish shore.[8]

As lacking those physical characteristics that traditionally define war as violent, a physically proximate experience of cyberwar remains seldom attainable. In fact, both the immateriality of the warscape as well as the impossibility of a real-time experience of the event create physical distance. At the same time, existing experiences of cyberwar are mediated and shaped through those elements that create proximity (or distance) beyond corporeality (see Butler, 2009). In my research, I conduct interviews with Palestinian and pro-Palestinian cyber combatants that, through various hacking techniques, target Israeli national and private cyber infrastructures. They are a diverse group that spans from state cyber armies (Palestinian, Afghani, Syrian, etc) to Islamist groups (Daesh Cyber Caliphate, Palestinian al-Aqsa brigades, Hezbollah Cyber Army etc) as well as individuals and different collectives (Anonymous, Gaza Cybergang, AnonGhost, etc). While the discourses of those who are part of a national army point to an experience of cyberwar existing mainly in relation to their military engagement, Islamic cyber combatants ascribe their attacks to the realisation of a higher moral duty. Palestine-based fighters associated with small local hacking groups, or acting individually, tend to narrate their attacks in relation to the daily atrocities and injustice that the Israeli occupation subjects them to. Those connected to bigger international hacking collectives justify their attacks in light of an act of solidarity to the Palestinian cause or, in some cases, as a way to demonstrate, above all, their hacking mastery. Others engage in such activities in the pursuit and fulfilment of anti-Semitic or anti-Judean ideologies. For their part, victims – governmental and not – usually tend to minimise the impact of these attacks unless they result in serious violations of personal data, in order not to make vulnerabilities public.

As embodied experiences are dependent on being sensed, they require a degree of proximity to an event. Beside its physical dimension, however, proximity seems also to depend on perceptions and relationalities subtending these perceptions (Butler, 2009). Specifically, elements making up for individual subjectivity can bring people close to the event of war. At the same time, with technologies allowing for increasingly immersive and visible experiences of war, its violence becomes overwhelmingly available to our senses. Affective and normative positioning towards the event of war (being a fighter, a victim or a researcher) determines proximity/distance, and thus the extent in which violence becomes an embodied experience. That is to say that, embodied experiences of the violence of cyberwar in the context of Israel-Palestine remain influenced by those subjective experiences that precede and relate subjects to the conflict beyond its cyber mechanics and physical proximity. As such, the engagement in cyber activities depends on an emotional proximity to the Palestinian cause that, while transcending its territorial dimension, is manifested in political and affective terms.

Moreover, while this non-physical proximity does not seem to require bodies for its articulation and manifestation into violent cyber practices, it can, nevertheless, lead to bodily harm despite the absence of kinetic interaction. During an interview in 2014, an American-based hacker confessed he had been diagnosed as having severe depression and was subsequently hospitalised after his offline identity was made public by pro-Israeli hackers. Or, in his own words, "after being killed as a hacker". The absence of bodies does not necessarily imply an absence of physical violence if one assumes that virtual existences are just an extension of actual ones. As the violence of cyberwar manifests in ways that are primarily not physical or observable, and since bodily harm can occur outside the kinetic interaction of fighting bodies or physical proximity, the inherent violence of cyberwar can only be sensed through narrations of these embodied experiences. It is in this way that cyberwars ultimately differ from conventional wars: they are accessible only through the discourses of those directly involved. In von Clausewitz's categorisation, it exists as a war primarily in its character, albeit with the absence of corporeal bodies.

Summing up, embodied experiences of cyberwar appear to be related to all those items that create proximity to the event of war beyond corporeality. As an event existing only in post-facto narrations (or a non-event), embodied experiences and violence transcend kinetic interactions to exist as discursive items that maintain the potential of creating (physical) harm even if remaining confined to the cyber realm. In other words, considering violence in relation to the body as something that transcends corporeality, embodied experiences of cyberwar can be regarded as potentially violent.

Embodiment and knowledge

As violent warscapes unfolding at the purlieus of physical experiences, cyberwars instigate a reflection on how knowledge about this phenomenon can be produced in a manner that accounts for the positionality of the researcher and their body. In classical epistemology, experiences are commonly opposed to rationalities. The dispute pertains the modes of knowledge production, and the extent to which rationality can precede sensed experiences in theorising about a phenomenon, such as in those accounts of cyberwar that refrain from engaging with its phenomenology. In line with studies on war focusing on embodiment, instead of corporeality, this chapter proposes prioritising experiences in order to understand the violence of war. Judith Butler (2009), similarly suggests that experience must replace essence as a way to understand the nature of social constructs: the supremacy of the political on the ontological, of becoming against being.

In order to produce objective and rigorous knowledge, researchers are often reminded to distance themselves from their object of inquiry (Garfinkel, 1984; Emerson and Pollner, 1988). Lower proximity would correspond to better research, whereas subjective experiences and spaces of reflexivity would maintain a detrimental effect on the production of knowledge. However, due to the impossibility of direct observation, in a context where bodies are not physically present to one another and events only exist in the narrations of those who experienced them, claims of objectivity fade away. Conducting research in violent contexts requires an awareness of the body not only from a positionality perspective (vis-à-vis the object of study), but also for understanding our own embodied limitations, emotions and vulnerabilities (Csordas, 2008). Different methodological and phenomenological discussions argue in favour of taking our own body into account at the different stages of the research process (Weiss, 1999; Merleau-Ponty, 2006). Beyond philosophical speculations on whether an individual can ever develop full control and awareness of their own body, embodiment research has mainly advocated for studying the body as the product of those social categories that define it beyond its physical existence. Particularly with regards to the question of violence, embodiment research has primarily taken on phenomenological and reflexive approaches to study the body as the ultimate product and the site of production of social relations (see Csordas, 1994). In this sense, as much as bodies regained attention in the study of war and international relations, they also became the object of reflexive academic inquiry.

On the one hand, cyberwar challenges the realist myth of fighting physical bodies because of the absence of a corporeality that is immediately observable. Cyberwar possesses qualities that are inherently narrational – one can only provide accounts of their own experiences but nevertheless are embodied, visceral and emotional. On the other hand, as dynamics of embodiment occur through a proximity to war that defies its physical dimension, researching cyberwars seems not to pose those ethical challenges that traditionally characterise immersive research in violent settings of war (Wood, 2006). In addition, eventual belligerent interactions as well as their targets, combatants, weapons and battlefields are not based on a traditional encounter between researcher and their object of study. In fact, this makes direct observation impossible, thus belying the production of knowledge on cyberwar (and its capacity for violent impact on the individual). In the first instance, research suffers due to a lack of real-time experiences: cyberattacks are not perceptible in the moment they occur. They come into existence only through post-facto narrations, and experiences thereof, of those launching or being targeted by an attack. However, the absence of physical contact, and its deriving distance, appears to expose researchers to a violence that, albeit not immediately corporeal, is revealed in the rhetoric of narrations of war (or when becoming targeted/threatened with cyberattacks).

While conducting interviews with pro-Palestinian hackers for the last four years, very often the content of these dialogues has been characterised by an extremely violent rhetoric. From dehumanising speeches – revealed through expressions such as those invoking a 'cyber Holocaust' and 'cyber gas chambers' – to those soliciting a violence that is coherent with the anti-colonial Palestinian national aspirations, these dialogues have been diverse and signal profound discrepancies among different ways in which the same event of cyberwar is experienced and narrated. While hateful speeches mainly targeted the State of Israel, pro-Israeli hackers or Jews in general, in a number of cases I found myself to be the target of violent rhetoric and hacking threats. Often, these violent attacks would trigger an existing long-lasting sense of grief, harm and discomfort. Through an awareness of my privileged positionality vis-à-vis the violence that sets the rhythm of daily lives for Palestinians, on the one hand, I can reflexively think of this sense of grief as the feeling of becoming distant from a cause I cherish enormously. On the other, I could attribute these emotions to my daily proximity to the physical and non-physical violence of the occupation.

In this sense, the ongoing Palestinian cyberwar should be understood as an emanation of the actual violence on the ground. In fact, as much as these instances of confrontation remain confined to the cyber realm, they usually accompany actual peaks of violence and tensions of the conflict. Most recent violent events in Palestine/Israel have been parallelled – and often preceded – by violent cyber confrontations that, to different degrees, are nevertheless always latent. At the same time, the absence of bodies and their physical interaction allows for articulating and practising a type of violence that also manifests in rhetorical forms. As argued above, violence also becomes embodied outside physical interactions, as long as there exists proximity to the event of war.

Situating violence and bodies in cyberwar, however, indicates that creating distance between bodies remains a prerequisite for creating proximity to the violent event of war. When first approaching research on hackers, my preoccupation had been to strengthen my knowledge of those technological aspects and tools that are required for understanding the mechanics of these wars. In particular, understanding these mechanics also maintains an epistemological value to the extent that they allow accessing those narrations containing and redefining the existence of cyberwar. Of course, the issue of accessibility, reaching out to potential interviewees, remains intrinsically connected to the issue of their safety. Only at some level of guaranteed security are hackers potentially willing to participate in an interview. Then, creating a distance and separating bodies became the most important task in the first phases of my research planning. However, as my understanding of the violence was framed around corporeal interactions, my research design overlooked this aspect of violence, and assumed that cyberwarscapes would carry no risks for research.

Higher degrees of separation seemed to create higher levels of trust, and became necessary in order to gain access to very skilled and successful hackers. Once again, distance between bodies appears to be a peculiarity of cyberwar. It defines both the actual conduct of belligerent interactions, as well as the interaction between researcher and interviewees. At the same time, wider degrees of separation created larger spaces for extremely violent rhetoric (and emotional disengagement). In fact, those interviews conducted in safer virtual environments have been characterised by a stronger verbal violence if compared to interviews conducted in less safe virtual environments or in the 'real' world. It is, then, because of the separation of bodies that violence could emerge and be narrated, thus necessitating a reconsideration of my own relationship to body and violence.

To conclude, existing interdisciplinary scholarship draws from classical categories of war to rethink how cyberwar would exist and could be countered. As this framing confines cyberwar within the boundaries of traditional warfare, its technical and realpolitik dimensions are central in the literature when compared to its political essence. In these terms, cyberwar has been theorised as a security issue for nation-states, their sovereignty and territorial boundaries (cf Brenner, 2009). As argued in this discussion, this understanding of cyberwar not only reproduces violence and the body according to an idea of war that pre-exists, but also hardens categories that appear in my research to exist in much more fluid ways. In this sense, experiencing war depends on proximity, but a proximity that is not necessarily observable and measurable or, in other words, physically proximate. Different social constructs, such as identity or empathy, define how close subjects are to a violent event, and the extent to which they are able to perceive it in embodied forms.

Notes

[1] One interesting section of the exhibition shows how Israeli authorities – in response to increasing international monitoring – enforce violent measures that, albeit similarly cruel, are designed in ways that do not legally contravene international law. Among these, a common practice consists of lumping detainees in a small space while forcing them to stand for hours in order to take the roll; or, in case of death, returning the body to a prisoner's family only at the end of the sentenced jail time.

[2] The ambition to make bodies disappear from the realm of war is revealed both in the production of narratives that depict war as the belligerent interaction of polities or armies (thus superseding violent embodied experiences) as well as in the increasing application of unmanned machinery in military operations.

[3] This implies a differentiation between necessary, or even heroic, acts of violence from coarse ones. In other words, as violence constitutes an unavoidable condition and tendency of human nature, it is through other elements (ethics, territory, sovereignty, strategy, etc) that war traditionally discerns from its similes. For this reason, these elements – and not violence – are the primary concern of traditional theorising about war.

[4] Among these, the UN Charter, with respect to the issue of *jus ad bellum* and the 1949/77 Geneva Protocols, offer the most accurate definition of cyberwar.

[5] For example, an intrusion or unauthorised breach into sensitive personal data can be associated with an intrusion into one of the physical spaces of our lives, and questions the limits to corporeality in the definition of the conceptual boundaries of war.

[6] Corporeal sameness and relatability are what ultimately triggers affective and empathic moves.

[7] Bodies are, in fact, commonly studied and numbered in ways that prescribe them as numeric units to be counted, maintaining varying distances and functions vis-à-vis the physical mechanics of war. Different degrees of physical separation and functions distance them from war: combatants, civilians, doctors, politicians, arms contractors, mediators, researchers and journalists all physically stand at various distances from the event of war, and retain a different relationship to its inherent violence.

[8] The case of Aylan in 2015 showed how the reappearance of bodies (and the realisation of corporeal sameness) can create proximity to the event of war despite physical distance.

References

Allhoff, F., Henschke, A. and Strawser, B. (2016) *Binary bullets*, Oxford: Oxford University Press.

Barkawi, T. and Brighton, S. (2011) 'Powers of war: fighting, knowledge, and critique', *International Political Sociology*, vol 5, no 2.

Brenner, S. (2009) *Cyber threats: The emerging fault lines of the nation state*, Oxford: Oxford University Press.

Butler, J. (2004a) *Precarious life: The powers of mourning and violence*, London: Verso.

Butler, J. (2004b) 'Bodies and power revisited', in D. Taylor and K. Vintges (eds) *Feminism and the final Foucault*, Champaign, IL: University of Illinois Press.

Butler, J. (2009) *Frames of war: When is life grievable?*, London: Verso.

Clark, A. (2004) *Natural-born cyborgs: Minds, technologies, and the future of human intelligence*, Oxford: Oxford University Press.

Clark, A. (2016) *Surfing uncertainty: Prediction, action, and the embodied mind*, Oxford: Oxford University Press.

Csordas, T.J. (1994) 'The body as representation and being-in-the-world', in T. Csordas (ed) *Embodiment and experience: The existential ground of culture and self*, Cambridge: Cambridge University Press, pp 1–24.

Csordas, T.J. (2008) 'Intersubjectivity and intercorporeality', *Subjectivity*, vol 22.

Emerson, R. and Pollner, M. (1988) 'On the uses of members "responses to researchers" accounts', *Human Organization*, vol 47, no 3.

Garfinkel, H. (1984) *Studies in ethnomethodology*, Cambridge: Polity Press.

Haraway, D. (1991) 'A cyborg manifesto: Science, technology, and socialist-feminism in the late twentieth century', in D. Haraway (ed) *Simians, cyborgs and women: The reinvention of nature*, New York: Routledge.

Hoisington, M. (2009) 'Cyberwarfare and the use of force giving rise to the right of self-defense', *International & Comparative Law Review*, vol 439, no 2.

Keegan, J. (1993) *A history of warfare*, New York: Random House.

Koh, H.H. (2012) 'International law in cyberspace', *Harvard International Law Journal*, vol 54, no 1.

Libicki, M. (2009) *Cyberdeterrence and cyberwar*, Santa Monica, CA: RAND Corporation.

Lindsay, J. (2013) 'Stuxnet and the limits of cyber warfare', *Security Studies*, vol 22, no 3.

Lucas, G. (2012) *Permissible preventive cyberwar: Restricting cyber conflict to justified military targets*, UNESCO.

Massumi, B. (2010) 'The future birth of the affective fact: The political ontology of threat', in M. Gregg and G. Seigworth (eds) *The affect theory reader*, Durham, NC: Duke University Press.

Merleau-Ponty, M. (2006) *Phenomenology of perception*, New York: Routledge.

NATO (2013) *Tallinn manual on the international law applicable to cyber warfare*, Cooperative Cyber Defence Centre of Excellence, Cambridge: Cambridge University Press.

NATO (2017) *Tallinn manual 2.0 on the international law applicable to cyber operations*, Cooperative Cyber Defence Centre of Excellence, Cambridge: Cambridge University Press.

Ohlin, J., Govern, K. and Finkelstein, C. (eds) (2015) *Cyber war: Law and ethics for virtual conflicts*, Oxford: Oxford University Press.

Rid, T. (2013) *Cyber war will not take place*, London: C. Hurst & Co Publishers Ltd.

Rowe, N. (2009) 'The ethics of cyberweapons', *International Journal of Cyberethics*, vol 1, no 1.

Schmitt, N. (2014) 'The law of cyberwarfare: Quo vadis?', *Stanford Law and Policy Review*, vol 25, no 1.

Singer, P. (2009) *Wired for war: The robotics revolution and conflict in the twenty-first century*, New York: Penguin.

Singer, P. and Friedman, A. (2014) *Cybersecurity and cyberwar*, Oxford: Oxford University Press.

Sontag, S. (2003) *Regarding the pain of others*, London: Hamish Hamilton.

Sylvester, C. (2013) *War as experience: Contributions from international relations and feminist analysis*, London: Routledge.

Turner, B. (1984) *The body and society: Exploration in social theory*, Oxford and New York: Blackwell.

von Clausewitz, C. (1943) *On war*, Chicago, IL: University of Chicago Press.

Weiss, G. (1999) *Body Images: Embodiment as Intercorporeality*, New York: Routledge.

Wilcox, L. (2015) *Bodies of violence: Theorizing embodied subjects in international relations*, Oxford: Oxford University Press.

Wood, E. (2006) 'The ethical challenges of field research in conflict zones', *Qualitative Sociology*, vol 29, no 1.

8

Fields of insecurity: Responding to flows of information

Meike de Goede and Inge Ligtvoet[1]

Introduction

Information communication technologies (hereinafter ICTs) have had a far-reaching impact on the everyday life of ordinary citizens in Africa. The impact of ICTs has been particularly profound in volatile societies, where they have been shown to be an important factor in the mobilisation of people and ideas (cf the 2011 'Arab Spring' uprisings). The mobile phone influenced social life tremendously (Dibakana, 2002; Obadare, 2006; Hahn and Kibora, 2008; de Bruijn et al, 2009; Ekine, 2010), but the mediascape has changed dramatically as a consequence of the introduction of the internet and the smartphone (Cleaver, 1998; Dahlgren, 2000; Kalathil and Boas, 2003; Burrell, 2012; Gleick, 2012). The smartphone has enabled access to the internet on a mobile device, thus making the internet more broadly accessible for more people across Africa. Indeed, over 28 per cent of people on the African continent now have access to the internet (Internetworldstats, 2016). It has become an alternative technology of information exchange in an otherwise often restricted media landscape. This has transformed our fields of research as well as the lives of our informants (cf de Bruijn, 2012).

But new ICTs and the flows of information they generate also have a profound impact on how we, as researchers, can and do conduct our research in the field, and how we relate to our field. Pelckmans (2009) has observed how the appropriation of mobile telephony by both researchers and informants in the late 1990s and early 2000s enabled new forms of interaction, relating and knowing that have a profound impact on the practice of conducting research, as well as on research ethics and epistemology. Since then, the widespread use of smartphones and the internet by both researchers and informants suggests we are never really 'out of the field' (Gupta and Ferguson, 1997) because we actually carry (part of) our field in the form of our smartphone in our pockets. This continuous access brings obvious advantages, but also requires us to work with new flows of information. Working in a particularly crisis-ridden part of Africa, we have experienced that this constant flow of information through social media has had a profound impact on our perceptions of insecurity on a personal and emotional level and on our decision-making processes.

In this chapter we focus on the impact of new flows of information on the decision-making processes for researchers working in unstable, volatile regions. We draw on our personal experiences 'doing' fieldwork in Nigeria and Congo-Brazzaville. In recent years the West central African region has been plagued by violent conflict, political uprisings and a global health crisis since the start of our research in 2012. Evidently, informants were deeply affected by these developments. As a consequence, our research projects became politically more sensitive and necessary. Neither of us abandoned our research plans in response to insecurity, but we have both been faced with having to make decisions in response to changing security dynamics. We suggest that these decision-making processes are informed by flows of information about violence and insecurity that give shape to our relations with the field and with our informants. While Katz (2006) and Pelckmans (2009) have argued that the information flows generated by mobile telephony have increased the real or perceived security risks of researchers while conducting research in the field, we suggest that the new flows of information generated by the smartphone have an impact on our emotions that may alter our ability to assess security situations, and may, as such, create new fields of insecurity. This is particularly the case when not physically present in the field, but still being in the field through social media networks.

Social media, information and insecurity: making choices in the space between

While the security of the researcher is an important consideration when preparing for fieldwork, with standard practice nowadays often requiring explicit permission to visit volatile regions, questions about security and fieldwork of a more personal level are nevertheless often put aside (Sluka, 1995; Pickering, 2001). On the one hand, such questions are formalised through risk assessment forms that invite a focus on the mitigation of risks to satisfy administrative regulations in our respective research institutes, rather than a personal reflection on how these risks make us feel about our intended field research.

Moreover, the formalisation of risk assessment through forms also invites a response to officially recognised risks (violent conflict, political unrest, police repression, terrorism, criminality), while ignoring many of the more mundane and unpredictable aspects of insecurity that are often much more a reality for researchers, as well as sentiments of uncanniness that are often difficult to pin down (Dickson-Swift et al, 2009; Browne, 2013).

These personal sentiments of insecurity are, in turn, also ignored through self-censorship: when the objective risks are mitigated, there is little room for personal anxieties and fear about fieldwork in a conflict area. Confronted with implicit peer and self-pressure, we convince ourselves that fieldwork is precisely what we enjoy most in our work, even if on occasion we do not experience it as such (Shaffir and Stebbins, 2003, p 2). What we thus experience is a situation in which we develop a rational argument that risks are mitigated, while ignoring our personal emotions about security as unproductive irrationalities. Davies draws attention to these dynamics, the researcher's 'state of being' during fieldwork, and the emotions that are generated during field research (Davies, 2010). Since the inception of the Connecting in Times of Duress (CTD) research project,[2] we have developed a deeper understanding of the research environment and our position within it. It is perhaps not surprising that when researching contexts of insecurity, violence and people living under duress, personal and emotional responses of the researchers emerge. After all, the confrontation with violence, hardship and suffering in the everyday lives of our respondents with whom we spend considerable time and build up friendships is impossible to ignore. But it is not mere empathy or sympathy that we experience; instead, it affects us on a personal level.

Davies (2010) argues that these emotions offer unique insights into the understanding of the social environments we locate ourselves in for our fieldwork, and thus of the people and their everyday lives we seek to understand as anthropologists. He thus proposes radical empiricism as a methodological position that is concerned with the *spaces between*, by which he means the researcher in relation to his or her field as an object of study (Davies, 2010, p 23). These spaces between are vital for fieldwork; they are the moments when we reflect and make our choices. Focusing on these choices made in spaces between reveal implicit conclusions, insights and assertions that are important for the process of our research, and that will inevitably inform our arguments, conclusions and methodological considerations.

We experienced that it was often not episodes of conflict, violence and insecurity that directly affected our research fields, our informants and ourselves. The accumulation of historical layers of insecurity are what truly makes our region of study a field of insecurity. In both Nigeria and Congo-Brazzaville, the prolonged everyday emotional experience of non-violent hardship and uncertainty (in many cases, this included physical violence) has meant that people in these societies are living under duress. The layers of insecurity are different for each of the individuals we studied. Their personal relation to the insecure environment does, to a great extent, determine the experience of it. Each individual, researcher or informant carries a lifetime of experiences with them. These experiences with earlier crises shape their individual, emotional response to current situations. It means that the same events will affect everybody differently. A field of insecurity is, then, not only a 'physical field', but is more accurately understood as the field in which both researcher and participants are 'feeling' insecurity. This is the space between, the inter-material relation between researcher and a field of insecurity.

In this chapter we focus on the choices made in between fieldwork periods. However, due to social media the 'in between' fieldwork period is no longer such an intermediate period, as we continue to remain in our field even when physically in a different country. The field is often just a call, a click or a notification away. While the online and offline world are multiple sites of research, they are simultaneously interrelated. As such, we have to think of these multiple sites as one community that we cannot separate, analytically or methodologically (Hannerz, 2003). Leaving the field no longer means that one has finished collecting data. Depending on the accessibility of the internet in the countries we work in, information reaches us through informants' posts and tweets, chat conversations, news feeds, groups, etc. The more a researcher has subscribed to online, the more information they will be fed. This is especially true for doing fieldwork in volatile regions, from where news, eyewitness reports and other media reach us during or shortly after particular outbreaks of violence through our Facebook or Twitter accounts. Likewise, before entering the field, researchers are nowadays exposed to context and contacts online. Massive, indefinite amounts of data will reach us every day if we do not carefully assess our use of social media. We have to make clear decisions on what we read or watch online, and what we do with that information.

Feeling insecurity in Nigeria and Congo-Brazzaville

As researchers, we often rationally dismiss information that comes to us through (social) media as over-exaggerated, politicised and out of context. Yet, we are more susceptible to flows of information that circulate through (social) media than we would like to think. This implies that these flows of information not only reach us as data, but also affect us on an emotional level. The Ebola outbreak reached Nigeria when Inge Ligtvoet was 'in between' two research visits. In Brazzaville the 2016 Presidential elections were unexpectedly brought forward and held 'in between' two of Meike de Goede's research visits. They were followed by post-electoral violence in which Meike's respondents became unexpectedly implicated. While we both have extensive experience with conducting field research in volatile parts of Africa, most notably northern and eastern DRC (Democratic Republic of the Congo) and Kinshasa (2006–13), and urban south and south-east Nigeria, Calabar and Enugu (2010–15), the way we have made decisions in preparation for field research and how research can be conducted became highly influenced by new flows of information through social media, most notably Facebook, Twitter, WhatsApp and blogs.

Ebola in Nigeria, 2014

In July 2014, at the peak of the Ebola outbreak in West Africa, the crisis reached Nigeria when a Liberian who had travelled from Liberia to Lagos to visit a conference died of Ebola in a Lagos hospital (WHO, 2014b, c). The disease was quickly contained, to the surprise of the international community. There have only been 20 declared Ebola cases in Nigeria, of which eight people died, and the country was declared Ebola-free by the World Health Organization (WHO)[3] three months after patient zero had died (WHO, 2014a). But (international) panic had spread as people realised that it could mean that the disease had reached one of Africa's megacities, and that many people must have been in contact with patient zero unaware that he was severely ill. Inge was 'in between' two research visits to Enugu when patient zero was discovered.

In the first weeks following the discovery of patient zero, most international media coverage, as well as reports from Ministries of Foreign Affairs, argued that Nigeria was in control of the situation and that the spread of the disease would be limited. It quickly became clear that the real, objective risk of containing Ebola in Enugu would be negligible. Facebook, which Inge closely followed for her research on the use of new ICTs and social media among young Nigerians, was at that time filled with mostly sensible information on the prevention of contamination and many Ebola-related jokes and memes. Ebola clearly occupied the mind of most Nigerians, and people seemed to be extremely cautious.

But although social media may have been considered crucial in the rapid elimination of the disease in Nigeria (Anyaka, 2014), platforms like Facebook, Twitter, WhatsApp and other text messaging services also turned into a panic-invoking rumour machine and a source of (medical) misinformation (Oyeyemi et al, 2014). It was not long before Inge was confronted with an ongoing flow of Facebook and text messages advising her to bath in salted water before the sun came up in order to prevent Ebola infection. It went viral overnight, as one of Inge's close informants, Azu, recalls:

> 'It was complete madness that night. My neighbour knocked on my door at 3 am in the morning to ask me if I had salt. I did not know what was happening, but I gave him and then I saw all these messages on my phone. More people came for salt. I gave them. I did not bathe myself. My mum called and she said I should take a bath with salt. She had already taken hers.' (online blog post, Ligtvoet, 2014)

Judging from the messages and status updates Inge found on her Facebook page the next morning, complete chaos seemed to have indeed erupted in Nigeria at the time. People woke up in the middle of the night to bath themselves, and the rumour even included drinking salt water in versions in some parts of the country. In Plateau State two people died and 20 people were taken to the hospital because of their intake of large amounts of salt (Anyaka, 2014). The fact that the message could go viral meant that there was an inflated fear and mistrust in society, which (social) media had so far not addressed. There was a particular rumour about the disease being spread by aeroplanes in the morning and people needing to bath themselves before a particular time to avoid getting infected. This rumour placed the fear of Ebola within the wider context of insecurity and mistrust in Nigeria (Ligtvoet, 2011). The mass acceptance of this misinformation as valid and trustworthy, embedded in the context of the insecurity already existing in the country, raised strong feelings of discomfort in Inge. It made her doubt whether she wanted to be physically present in a society that was obviously strongly affected by the fear of Ebola if she didn't really have to.

The same day, Inge received a WhatsApp message from the 12-year-old daughter of one of her friends in Ibadan that increased her feelings of discomfort, and that eventually led to the postponement of her fieldwork:

Gifty:	Where are you
Inge:	I am in Congo
Gifty:	Be careful of Ebola
Inge:	I will be careful
Inge:	Will you also be careful?
Gifty:	Yes
Gifty:	There is no way of avoiding it

While Inge knew rationally the risks of contracting Ebola in Nigeria were negligible for her, the young girl's message stirred something in her. It was a discomforting confrontation with her own emotions that she had been suppressing successfully in the weeks before. She had been rationally answering her family and friends back home whenever they asked her what she thought about the situation, and whether she was planning to travel back to the field soon. She would explain to them what she knew about the media, about the exoticisation of Africa during this epidemic, and about the sensationalist reports that were exaggerated, and that Nigeria was not Liberia. Inge was rationally mitigating recognised security threats, as if filling in a risk assessment form. She could explain the situation from an informed and academic perspective, but Gifty's words confronted her with the reality of feelings of doubt and fear she also had herself. Ebola posed yet another layer to the already lingering sense of insecurity and uncertainty in Nigeria: increased mistrust towards migrants from the north in the south-eastern town of Enugu, near-daily (graphic) reports on terrorist activities in the north-east, the news about the abduction of the Chibok girls in April 2014, stories of informants greatly affected by the instability of the state, the news of several Nigerian friends having died in car accidents due to the bad conditions of the roads, etc. Over the months, this had informed her research, but it also affected her as a researcher. With Ebola, a new field of insecurity had emerged, one that was driven by Inge's emotions, fed by social media and the new forms of proximity with the field we, as researchers, experience. Inge decided not to return to Enugu in August as was foreseen, but postponed her visit by several months.

Post-electoral violence in Congo-Brazzaville

In the aftermath of the Presidential elections in March 2016 in Congo-Brazzaville, violence erupted in Bacongo, one of Brazzaville's popular quarters. It was alleged that the Ninja rebels from the Pool district had launched an attack in response to the electoral victory of Sassou Nguesso, who is highly unpopular in the south of the country (RFI, 2016a, b). The Ninjas were a rebel movement that had fought in several insurgencies in the 1990s and 2000s, but that had been officially disbanded in 2008 (Ngodi, 2009). The alleged attack in Brazzaville was quickly neutralised by the armed forces. This military response was, in effect, the launch of a military operation in the Pool district in pursuit of Pasteur Ntumi, leader of the Ninjas (International Crisis Group, 2016). Villages were bombarded, and the heavy military presence in Bacongo gave people the impression that they were under siege. It was a painful, but no doubt deliberate, reminder of the 1998 battle fought in Bacongo, when thousands were massacred by the national army, in this heavily divided country (Bernault, 1998; Bazenguissa-Ganga, 1999).

The latent political conflict between the south and the north had resurfaced. Meike's respondents became unwillingly caught up in this because her respondents all came from Bacongo and the Pool district. Moreover, Pasteur Ntumi drew from the same messianic discourse as the Matsouanists, the historic movement she was researching. In conversation, people often established a link between the current and historic problems in Pool, both in terms of how the people from the Pool district are 'always causing trouble' and in terms of how they are 'perpetually repressed' by successive governments. As a consequence, advocates of the opposition based in the Pool district found a new voice in Meike's research, which offers historical legitimation to contemporary struggles (Mâwa-Kiese, 2016; Nata Nkutu Yo, 2017). This politicisation raised new concerns about the mere feasibility of the research due to Meike's presumed political agendas and by extension, of her informants. Thus concerns about Meike's security and that of her respondents emerged.

As opposed to the situation with the Ebola outbreak in Nigeria, international media were almost silent about the events in Brazzaville. While few people in Europe may have missed the news about the Ebola crisis, hardly anybody will have been informed about the events in Brazzaville. It proved impossible to find any reliable information about what was happening in the Pool district. Internet access is limited (6.8% of Congolese people have access to the internet; Internetworldstats, 2016), particularly in the affected rural areas, so little first-hand information was posted online. Text messages between Meike and her informants were scarce, since none of them have a smartphone, and international 'sms' messages to and from Brazzaville often never reach their destination. Journalists and representatives of foreign missions and organisations were, and continue to be, prevented from visiting the Pool district. Friends and respondents spoke under self-censorship on the telephone, knowing that lines are tapped. They insisted that the troubles were over, and that the government was taking care of the situation. This narrative was well in line with the official government position that was reported on in what is paradoxically Congo's most reliable newspaper that also supports the government. When Meike later spoke to her friends face-to-face in Brazzaville, they reminded her that she should not expect an honest answer to such questions asked in telephone conversations.

Social media (mainly Facebook) and the internet, however, gave a completely different picture – bloody images of massacred people, demolished houses and villages by the bombardments, and aggressive outcries against the regime of Sassou Nguesso made it seem as if a new civil war had broken out in Congo-Brazzaville. It proved difficult to balance the different sources of information and to consider what was true and what was exaggerated. The mere idea of a government bombarding its own population in rural areas was already quite far-fetched, thereby unsettling the parameters of predictability. But without reliable information, what was true and what was exaggerated?

While being accustomed to working in volatile contexts, being confronted with a lack of information was a novelty for Meike. In this case, Meike could not make an informed, rational decision, but had to take a decision based on a lack of information and rely on instinct. It was the silence that was most disturbing. Meike understood that her research had just been given a new political angle, but the mere fact that she could not discuss this or triangulate her hunches with other information gave her an unsettled feeling. Moreover, she felt angry about the compromises she was forced to make to her research and to her informants. She decided to go to Congo for research, but instead of conducting research in the Pool district, she attempted to conduct research in the northern part of the country, far away from the political turmoil that was troubling the population of the Pool district. However, almost immediately on arrival in the north, the authorities stopped her and sent her back to Brazzaville under police escort, with the threat of accusing her of espionage. Studying the history of the Matsouanists was evidently too politically sensitive.

The emerging crises in Nigeria and Congo-Brazzaville and the flows of information about them stand in stark contrast. While the Ebola crisis sparked an overwhelming flow of information in regular and social media, the post-electoral crisis in Congo was hardly reported on, neither in social nor regular media. Yet the effects on us, as researchers, were similar to a certain extent. Either with reliable information from other sources or without it, information that reached us via social media and that we could rationally put aside as unreliable affected us strongly in our decision-making process. It created a perceived field of insecurity. But the emotions underlying these perceptions were very different, not in the least because they built on personal experiences and the ways in which Inge and Meike have been engaged with their (very different) fields of research. While Inge's emotions were sentiments of withdrawal, Meike's emotional response was primarily one of anger and frustration.

Insecurity, engagement and decision-making: anger and withdrawal as political emotions

The information flows about the emerging crises in Nigeria and Congo-Brazzaville generated by social media triggered emotional responses. That anthropologists are deeply immersed in their fields and therefore emotionally engaged has, in recent years, been given more attention (Dickson-Swift et al, 2009). Before, the need to manage emotions was emphasised, while emotionality was discussed as separate from the research itself (Pickering, 2001, p 486). We now observe a shift towards the integration of feelings in qualitative research (Gilbert, 2000, p 4). As Dickson-Swift et al have argued, research is an embodied experience, and researchers undertake emotion work throughout their projects (2009, p 73). The lived experience of the researcher is thus of crucial importance for understanding the researchers' (field)work (Hume, 2007, p 148). This not only emphasises how the researcher is part of his/her research, but also how the field and informants influence the researcher on an emotional, personal level (Hubbard et al, 2001). They can trigger anxiety, anger, frustration, self-doubt, or what we have dubbed 'a lingering sense of *je ne sais quoi*', where something indefinable tells you that something is not right.

The emotional responses we observe, and the decisions they have informed, reveal different forms of engagement, that is, how we relate to the field and to our informants, as well as to matters of security that affect us either directly or indirectly. These forms of engagement set boundaries to the depth of immersion in the field, and the ways in which we choose to be immersed in order to feel comfortable, capable to conduct our research, as well as morally right. While the researchers in both cases discussed above decided to step back, the underlying emotions that generated these decisions were of a very different nature.

The WhatsApp conversation Inge had with Gifty triggered something deep inside her. In all the months she had been doing field research, she had never really considered how insecurity in Nigeria, experienced by Nigerians, was affecting her. Quite ironically so, considering that most of her research focused on the emic of insecurity. Whenever her family back home would address issues of security in her field, she would dismiss them as irrational and based on the stereotypical image of Nigeria(ns) in the media. But when Gifty asked her to be careful of Ebola, there was no way of dismissing the message. Gifty was living in insecurity at that moment, like she had been living with layers of insecurity ever since she was born. Even though contracting Ebola could easily be avoided, Inge could not rationalise Gifty's concern in that moment. The second her message came in, the feelings of discomfort and doubt about returning to the field that had lingered for over weeks got a face: that of Gifty.

Gifty's question had triggered intersubjective reflections for Inge, which informed her about more than just how the context of the situation in Ebola affected Nigeria. It gave her insights into the emotionality of the people and their fear of the unknown, and allowed her to acknowledge the feelings of anxiety she had herself towards an increasingly insecure field, of which Ebola was just the tip of the iceberg. This brought about a state of disorientation, in which feelings of discomfort and anxiety conflicted with rational analyses on the situation in Nigeria that no longer seemed to be convincing. Even though she still tried to rationalise the situation, this event inflicted a great sense of discomfort with returning back to the field.

In the months before, while Inge had been working in the field, the mistrust among people and a general sense of insecurity in Nigerian society had greatly affected her. It was always present in her field, not least because it was exactly this sense of insecurity that she addressed in her research. During her fieldwork, she had been observing and analysing the situation as an outsider and researcher, as any ethnographer would do. But throughout her work in the field, Inge herself was also confronted with distrustful people, and instances of sudden insecure situations, as well as with daily conversations about the experience of insecurity by her research informants. She had not allowed the internalisation of feelings of insecurity of herself. The information that reached her through social media and in particular the conversation she had with Gifty made her realise that Ebola had intensified this already existing sentiment of fear and insecurity, adding to the field of insecurity already existing in Nigeria. It dawned on her that returning to the field at that particular time would mean immersion in this new layer of insecurity in society, having to live through it as well as understand it academically. Feeling disoriented, due to incompatible emotional and rational thoughts about her field, honest reflections on her experience with insecurity in Nigeria over the period of her MA and PhD research, and a sense of self-disappointment with the 'irrational doubts' she had about returning, she decided that the only way out was to not go in. She decided to temporarily withdraw from her field.

Inge could make the decision to disengage because she was outside of the country at that particular time, and there was no specific need to be in the field at that moment. Had she been in Nigeria when Ebola was brought into the country, she might have responded very differently to the situation. It might well be that the personal reflection on insecurity, that eventually led to new insights even for the analysis of her data, would have never taken place as explicitly as it had. Withdrawal here meant that Inge could physically disengage from her field, in order to avoid the exposure to insecurity that she did not want to be immersed in. However, she did decide to follow the flows of information and the discourse of informants on Ebola from a distance, through social media. This allowed her to assess the situation in the field, as well as to gather a deeper understanding about the role of social media in times of duress. Three weeks before Nigeria was officially declared Ebola-free, she travelled back to the field, not because the declaration was imminent, but because her informants provided her with the reassurance that things were 'back to normal'.

Insecurity and anger: the precarious balance between research and activism

For Meike, social media proved to be a source of information where other sources of information, including traditional media, government, international organisations and her own informants, could not offer any. Meike decided not to go to the Pool district as intended, but not because she did not want to, or because she was concerned about her own safety. Her emotions were of a political nature. The bombardments of villages in the Pool district by the government meant that the population of the Pool district was once again singled out as political opponents. Matsoua had once again become a politically loaded name, and Meike felt her informants' security would be jeopardised if she should visit the Pool district asking questions about the political repression of people following Matsoua, even if it concerned a historic case.

The events and lack of information about them thus effectively perpetuated the silencing of the Matsouanists and their history, while an objective of Meike's research into this forgotten history of Congo-Brazzaville had been to un-silence it. Meike made a rational decision to protect herself and her informants, the community of people she had befriended and who trusted her, but it was a choice that felt morally wrong, as if she had let her informants down and betrayed the objective of her research. While nobody in Congo-Brazzaville made such accusations, or even hinted in that direction, she felt the urge to apologise to everybody. Part of her wanted to go to the Pool district, and be a more activist researcher who would not allow the Congolese government to silence her research and her informants. Eventually, near the end of her stay in Brazzaville, she made a quick visit to her main informants in the Pool district and spent the afternoon with them and their families. Together with her informants she visited the local authorities to present herself as an innocent visitor who had only come to say hello to dear friends. The visit served no purpose for the research and no data were collected. However, it mitigated her decision to step away, and the sense of betrayal it had given her.

Meike's decision not to go despite her anger about what government bombs were doing to the people she cared about, and how this impacted her academic objective of giving voice to silenced subalterns, was a decision made in the blurred boundaries between intellectual inquiry and politics (Hage, 2009). When conducting anthropological research in societies under duress, we are constantly attempting to find a balance between the two. A Congolese colleague argued that he and his colleagues avoid sensitive research topics, such as the Matsouanist movement, because it is not safe for them to research it. Such realisations played an important role when deciding whether to visit the Pool district or not. Mixing politics with research in countries such as Congo-Brazzaville is always precarious. Meike chose deliberately not to become involved in the political struggles of her informants, not only because she did not want to make her informants' struggle her own, but also because she was concerned with how her more explicit engagement could negatively impact the personal security of her informants and colleagues in Congo-Brazzaville.

Conclusion

Social media has become an essential tool for researchers working in volatile areas. But it is more than a tool that gives access to information, or a medium to maintain contact with respondents and to continue to collect data while not physically present in the field. The presence of ICTs in the environments in which we conduct our research has a profound effect on the practice of research in volatile environments because, while it creates new opportunities, it also creates new dilemmas. In this chapter we have reflected on our responses to flows of information about insecurity in our research fields, and argued that new, subjective fields of insecurity emerge in response to these flows of information. We have considered the relation between the researcher and these flows of information as a space between (Davies, 2010), a vital moment when we reflect and make choices. As an inter-material space – between person and materiality or environment – it is not merely the flows of information themselves that create perceptions of insecurity. We have argued that it is the interface between information and the individual that creates unique understandings that inform further decisions about conducting research in the field. It means that insecurity is not merely a matter of risk assessment forms, in which facts and figures determine our actions geared towards risk mitigation. Instead, we have argued that perceptions of insecurity are produced by flows of information about insecurity that resonate with previous personal life experiences and personality traits. For the members of our research team, fields of insecurity thus emerged as a state of being that was triggered by flows of information about insecurity.

Social media has altered this interface between information about insecurity and the individual researcher. The information that reaches us through online platforms forces us to rethink the rationality of risk assessment practices. Social media confronts us with the 'face' of insecurity, that is, the visual, often personal, perception of the situation on the ground that is usually very different from official analyses on volatile situations. As a consequence, we respond to it very differently than we do to official 'faceless' reports about insecurity. These new flows of information shape the relation with the field and with informants, and create a deeper, emic understanding of what insecurity means for our informants, and for ourselves. No longer can we ignore the lived reality of insecurity, its state of being, as we are immersing ourselves in it when we engage in the social media discourse of our informants and those living and working in our fieldwork regions. In the CTD project, in which understanding the emic of hardship (duress) in West and Central Africa is at the core of the research, social media provided a window of analysis. However, in this chapter we have argued that as researchers we are equally susceptible to the duress that is mediated through these online platforms. Social media can have an impact on the emotions of the researcher, altering the ability to rationally assess the field of insecurity, as we know it, arguably creating a new field of insecurity 'in between'. So while social media creates new opportunities for field research, it also creates new dilemmas.

Notes

[1] This chapter draws on research done within the project 'Connecting in Times of Duress', funded by The Netherlands Organisation for Scientific Research NWO (W 01.70.600.001); Meike de Goede's research was funded by the Gerda Henkel Foundation (grant no AZ 14/V/16).

[2] See www.connecting-in-times-of-duress.nl/

[3] To be officially declared Ebola-free, the WHO used the standard of having no new cases of Ebola in a period of twice the incubation time of the disease (21 days) after the last case that was discovered. This means that Nigerians knew they would be considered Ebola-free after 42 days of the last case of confirmed Ebola in the country.

References

Anyaka, U. (2014) 'Ebola and the media – Nigeria's good news story', 30 September (www.irinnews.org/news/2014/09/30).

Bazenguissa-Ganga, R. (1999) 'The spread of political violence in Congo-Brazzaville', *African Affairs*, vol 98, pp 37–54.

Bernault, F. (1998) 'Archaïsme colonial, modernité sorcière et territorialization du politique à Brazzaville, 1959–1995', *Politique Africaine*, vol 72, pp 34–49.

Browne, B. (2013) 'Recording the personal: the benefits in maintaining research diaries for documenting the emotional and practical challenges of fieldwork in unfamiliar settings', *International Journal of Qualitative Methods, vol* 12, pp 403–19.

Burrell, J. (2012) *Invisible users. Youth and the internet cafés of urban Ghana*, Cambridge, MA: MIT Press.

Cleaver, H. (1998) 'The Zapatista effect: The internet and the rise of an alternative political fablic', *Journal of International Affairs*, vol 51, no 2, pp 621–40.

CTD (Connecting in Times of Duress) (2012) 'About CTD' (www.connecting-in-times-of-duress.nl/ctd).

Dahlgren, P. (2000) 'The internet and the democratization of civil culture', *Political Communication*, vol 17, no 4, pp 335–40.

Davies, J. (2010) 'Introduction: Emotions in the field', in J. Davies and D. Spencer (eds) *Emotions in the field: The psychology and anthropology of fieldwork experience*, Stanford, CA: Stanford University Press, pp 1–31.

de Bruijn, M.E. (2012) *Connecting in Times of Duress: Understanding communication and conflict in Middle Africa's mobile margins*, Leiden: Leiden University.

de Bruijn, M.E., Nyamnjoh, F.B. and Brinkman, I. (eds) (2009) *Mobile phones: The new talking drums of everyday Africa*, Bamenda/ Leiden: Langaa/African Studies Centre.

Dibakana, J.-A. (2002) 'Usage sociaux du téléphone portable et nouvelles sociabilités aus Congo', *Politique Africaine*, vol 85, pp 133–48.

Dickson-Swift, V. et al (2009) 'Researching sensitive topics: Qualitative research as emotion work', *Qualitative Research*, vol 9, no 1, pp 61–79.

Ekine, S. (ed) (2010) *SMS uprising: Mobile phone activism in Africa*, Cape Town: Pambazuka Press.

Gilbert, K.R. (2000) 'Introduction: Why are we interested in emotions?', In K.R. Gilbert (ed) *The emotional nature of qualitative research*, Boca Raton, FL: CRC Press, pp 3–16.

Gleick, J. (2012) *The information: A history, a theory, a flood*, London: Vintage.

Gupta, A. and Ferguson, J. (1997) *Anthropological locations: Boundaries and grounds of a field science*, Berkeley, CA: University of California Press.

Hage, G. (2009) 'Hating Israel in the field. On ethnography and political emotions', *Anthropological Theory*, vol 9, no 1, pp 59–79.

Hahn, H.P. and Kibora, L. (2008) 'The domestication of the mobile phone: Oral society and new ICT in Burkina Faso', *Journal of Modern African Studies*, vol 46, no 1, pp 87–109.

Hannerz, U. (2003) 'Being there ... and there ... and there! Reflections on multi-site ethnography', *Ethnography*, vol 4, no 2, pp 201–16.

Hubbard, G., Backett-Milburn, K. and Kemmer, D. (2001) 'Working with emotion: Issues for the researcher in fieldwork and teamwork', *International Journal of Social Research Methodology*, vol 4, no 2, pp 119–37.

Hume, M. (2007) 'Unpicking the threads: Emotion as central to theory and practice of researching violence', *Women's Studies International Forum*, vol 30, no 2, pp 147–57.

International Crisis Group (2016) *Crisis Watch, April 2016 – Republic of Congo* (www.crisisgroup.org/crisiswatch).

Internetworldstats (2016) *Internet users in Africa* (www.internetworldstats.com/stats1.htm).

Kalathil, S. and Boas, T. (2003) *Open networks and closed regimes: The impact of the internet on authoritarian rule*, Washington, DC: Carnegie Endowment for International Peace.

Katz, J. (2006) *Magic in the air. Mobile communication and the transformation of social life*, New Brunswick, NJ: Transaction Publishers.

Ligtvoet, I. (2011) *Fear and faith. Uncertainty, misfortune and spiritual insecurity in Calabar, Nigeria*, Leiden: Leiden University.

Ligtvoet, I. (2014) 'Ebola-free', The Divine Connection (http://divineconnectivities.tumblr.com/post/100667642088/ebola-free).

Mâwa-Kiese, M. (2016) 'Politique et Prophétie: Conception du Monde en Afrique Équaroriale Française', *Lettre du Pool*, vol 2–3, p 6.

Nata Nkutu Yo (2017) 'Ou sont passés les Matsouanistes qui résidaient a Djambala? Réaction d'un fervent militant de l'opposition', *Manager Horizon*, vol 7, no 100, 10-17 January, pp 1, 9, 14.

Ngodi, E. (2009) *Mouvement Nsilulu: Rupture ou continuité historique des messianismes congolais*, ASC Working Paper, 84. Leiden: African Studies Centre.

Obadare, E. (2006) 'Playing politics with the mobile phone in Nigeria: Civil society, big business and the state', *Review of African Political Economy*, vol 33, no 107, pp 93–111.

Oyeyemi, S., Gabarron, E. and Wynn, R. (2014) 'Ebola, Twitter and misinformation: A dangerous combination', *British Medical Journal*, vol 349, g6178.

Pelckmans, L. (2009) 'Phoning anthropoligists: the mobile phone's (re-)shaping of anthropological research', in M.E. de Bruijn, F.B. Nyamnjoh and I. Brinkman (eds) *Mobile phones: The new talking drums of everyday Africa*, Bamenda/Leiden: Langaa/ASC, pp 23–49.

Pickering, S. (2001) 'Undermining the sanitized account. Violence and emotionality in the field in Northern Ireland', *British Journal of Criminology*, vol 41, pp 485–501.

RFI (2016a) 'Congo: L'Armée quadrille de la ville de Brazzaville après les violences de la veille' (www.rfi.fr/afrique/20160405-congo-armee-quadrille-ville-brazzaville-apres-violences-veille).

RFI (2016b) 'Tension Congo: le pouvour denonce les ninjas, l'opposision demande des preuves' (www.rfi.fr/afriqye/20160405-tension-congo-brazzaville-ninjas-opposion-demance-preuves-kolelas).

Shaffir, W.B. and Stebbins, R.A. (2003) 'Introduction to fieldwork', in M. Pogrebin (ed) *Qualitative approaches to criminal justice: Perspectives from the field*, Thousand Oaks, CA: Sage, pp 2–16.

Sluka, J. (1995) 'Reflections on managing danger in fieldwork: Dangerous anthropology in Belfast', in C. Nordstrom and A. Robben, *Fieldwork under fire: Contemporary studies of violence and survival*, Oakland, CA: University of California Press, pp 276–94.

WHO (World Health Organization) (2014a) 'WHO declares end of Ebola outbreak in Nigeria' (www.who.int/mediacentre/news/statements/2014/nigeria-ends-ebola/en/).

WHO (2014b) *Ebola virus disease, West Africa – Update 24 July 2014* (www.who.int/csr/don/2014_07_24_ebola/en/).

WHO (2014c) *Ebola virus disease, West Africa – Update 27 July 2014* (www.who.int/csr/don/2014_07_27_ebola/en/).

Vignette 4: Visual ethnographic encounters and silence in post-conflict Banda Aceh

Marjaana Jauhola

In my urban visual ethnographic research, *Scraps of hope: An urban ethnography of peace*,[1] I focused on the gendered lived experiences of both elites and ordinary people (*orang kecil*) affected by the urban development and governance agenda known as *Kota Madani* (civilised and Islamic city of Banda Aceh), and the slogan 'Building Aceh back better', modelled on the golden age of the Sultanate of Aceh in the 16th century. Whereas the majority of previous studies on Aceh have either focused on emerging subjectivities vis-à-vis their experiences of tsunami or conflict, when approaching the lived and experienced city I practised an openness that I call ethnography of the 'here and now' (Jauhola, 2015). This method maintains that, through ethnographic encounters, other historical and personal experiences or material and spatial references may potentially emerge as significant topics or themes of discussion. Central to my approach is the respect for silence. How do we treat and interpret post-conflict silences? As oppressive, as enabling, or as forms of resilience, resistance and survivalism? I do not push for stories of violence or hold expectations of being told of them. Rather, the starting point is the everyday of now, which always consists of layers of experience. How they unfold in a research encounter is a matter of negotiation and, at times, a practice of and respect for silence (Siapno, 2009; Butalia, 2016). Here I narrate one such encounter.

Taking refuge one day from the torrential rain, and with a desire for coffee, I entered a traditional coffee shop run in their home by a man and his wife in their sixties. This became a regular stopover on my daily walks through the city. I introduced myself as a Finnish researcher, who had an interest in discussing and understanding the peace brokered by the former Finnish president, not from the point of view of elite politics or celebratory remembrance days but rather, from the perspective of those written out of the formal narratives of peace

(Jauhola, 2016a, b). I never conducted structured interviews; I even hesitated to ask questions. Over the following four years of getting to know him and his family, primarily by playing with his grandchildren, teaching them English, and telling stories of my family and life in Finland, I was told of his family's financial hardship and how they were struggling with an instable income in a bustling and expanding business and commercial part of the city. Sometimes life experiences took material and visual forms, such as the enlarged, 30-year-old, ID card photograph on their coffee shop's wall – a non-verbal, yet affective, exhibition and remembrance of armed conflict and a marker of his identity. He had joined the military structure of GAM, the AGAM (Angkatan Gerakan Atjeh Merdeka), in 1976, as a young, newly married man.

I returned to their coffee shop in December 2015 with documentarist Seija Hirstiö to record his life history. Our aim was to focus on the journey that he had taken over the 40 years from young combatant to grandfather and Sufi healer who uses traditional herbal oils and stone massage to treat people. As I was responsible for the voice recordings, I would sit at the back of the recording set-up, control the voice levels, pay attention to the spoken language and the verbally communicated meanings, and make notes of them: the classic image of an ethnographer observing the 'exotic' or 'uncivilized other' (Uddin, 2011, p 460). Yet, given my goal of providing a critique of the big narratives of making peace, I became more interested in ethnographic practices that labour over people's own wishes about 'how they would like to be represented, and how they define their world' (Uddin, 2011, p 459), and their attempts to 'unmask how they are intentionally (re)presented by others across time and space' (Uddin, 2011, p 459). Therefore, even situated encounters such as these, arguably initiated by (my) researcher's privileged position and ability to arrive at and enter research sites, can become something else and surprise us.

This was a man presenting his motivations to join the independence struggle with its Islamic ideology of economic justice and prosperity. Maintaining these ideals was narrated as a continuous struggle in the aftermath of withdrawing from the movement, and escaping the violence to the city of Banda Aceh with his family. The struggles seemed to continue despite 10 years invested in peace, especially after his withdrawal from the gangs formed by former combatants to extract money from business owners and neighbours during the post-conflict period. In this 'shack house', as he himself called it, he received his former enemies from the Indonesian police and army as his patients, treating their aching bodies and praying for their wellbeing.

A year later, in December 2016, during the video's post-production process, I watched one of our very first recording sessions where he sits in front of a backdrop of leaves and branches; indicating the oil mixtures that he prepares for massage, he narrates how the skill was essential during the years spent in the jungle as a combatant with no access to drugs or doctors. His skills were a lifesaver back then. Seija, the documentarist, changes the focus of the camera from the bucket of oil and coffee bean bag of tree leaves to his hands and the six large stone rings he has on his fingers – a common signifier of Acehnese masculinity and economic importance. The camera composition changes to a close-up of his hands. And I see, for the first time, the stump of his amputated little finger (see the photo below).

Describing his craft as *ilmu bodoh* (foolish knowledge) could be read as the words or distorted thinking of a colonised subject voluntarily embodying the position of 'uncivilized other' (Uddin, 2011). Rather, I read his demeanour in these encounters as a strategic position taken in front of the camera as a narrator of his life on his own terms: making visible his life experiences, and Acehnese and Islamic vernacular knowledge systems that were crucially important to him both during and post-conflict, but only to the point that he feels comfortable with:

'It is Allah who cures, not me. If someone is sick, it is not me who heals. And this is not just for Muslims, but also for Christians. God's creations. Same with Hindus, all are creations of God. All that exists: trees, stones and leaves are creations of Allah.

'How can the leaf of a tree turn into oil that heals? It cannot be told. That is nature's secret. If we speak about it, it no longer can heal. It's like that, just like wisdom. If we become vain, if we go on about it, it becomes egoistic.

'Those leaves become medicine.... It has helped [us] in crisis. Almost all understood leaves, the quality of this leaf. All friends understood this, during the struggle. They understood the outcome. Many died. Now those who died are already at peace; young ones died back then. The ones who are young now, I don't know them. What was done during those years; that is what cannot be spoken of.

'And now, what is the work being done? There is still conflict, what is said about it? Aceh is crowded with orphans again, victims of violence. Why does no one care?... But now, all the talk is lost. There is no point in talking even if it is the truth ... because a lot of talk will threaten one's life.

'A lot of talk will be considered traitorous. It is better I live in garbage. In a shack ... Unlike me, the palace of the ruler is not shack of suffering. But I am still alive.'[2]

Anchoring speech in the inability to speak seems to produce decisive moments that set limits on what can become knowable and shareable, thereby making lives – primarily his own and those of his loved ones – bearable and tolerable. When the first seven minutes and twenty seconds of the three documentary videos were shown to him using his daughter's mobile phone, he asked us not to distribute the video – quite wisely in this age of fast-track spread of social media video clips and their unpredictable social impacts (Miller et al, 2016). After a dialogue, it was agreed with his daughter that the videos would be kept offline and only screened outside of Indonesia, along with strict procedures ensuring his anonymity. For these reasons, ethnographic and life historical documentary videos, such as those of the ex-combatant Sufi healer, may never become consumables in open access spaces, film festivals and other events without a certain labouring over the praxis of 'Do No Harm' – but also, only after considering the primary role of the films, and what their re-presentations are there to do.

Notes

[1] A visual and textual urban ethnography that I conducted in the administrative neighbourhoods of the post-tsunami and post-conflict city of Banda Aceh in Indonesia (2012–16) on the gendered politics of everyday lives in the aftermath of the Indian Ocean earthquake and the tsunami, and the peace settlement between the Aceh Independence Movement (Gerakan Aceh Merdeka, GAM)

and the Indonesian government. The visual portfolio of the research project is accessible at http://scrapsofhope.fi/aceh/

[2] Translation from Acehnese to Indonesian by Evi Susianti and from Indonesian to English by the author.

References

Butalia, U. (2016) 'Layers of wounds: How memories unfold', Talk at Indian Languages Festival Samanvay, 7 November.

Jauhola, M. (2015) 'On "being bored" – Street ethnography on emotions in Banda Aceh after the tsunami and conflict', in L. Åhäll and T. Gregory (ed) *Emotions, politics war*, London: Routledge, pp 86–99.

Jauhola, M. (2016a) '"Conversations in silence" – Ceramic installations shaping visual and political imagination of gendered tsunami and conflict reconstruction landscapes in Aceh', in A. Peto and A. Gül Altinay (eds) *Gendered war, gendered memories*, London: Routledge, pp 229–48.

Jauhola, M. (2016b) 'Decolonizing branded peacebuilding: Abjected women talk back to the Finnish Women, Peace and Security agenda', *International Affairs*, vol 92, no 2, pp 333–51.

Miller, D., Costa, E., Haynes, N., McDonald, T., Nicolescu, R., Sinanan, J., Spyer, J., Venkatraman, S. and Wang, X. (2016) *How the world changed social media*, London: UCL Press.

Siapno, J.A. (2009) 'Living through terror: Everyday resilience in East Timor and Aceh', *Social Identities: Journal for the Study of Race, Nation and Culture*, vol 15, no 1, pp 43–64.

Uddin, N. (2011) 'Decolonising ethnography in the field: An anthropological account', *International Journal of Social Research Methodology*, vol 14, no 6, pp 455–67.

Section V
Methods

9

Writing the wrongs: Keeping diaries and reflective practice

Brendan Ciarán Browne

Introduction

Since 2009 my academic life has been dominated by travel back and forth to Palestine, usually in three-month blocks, with prolonged periods spent living in East Jerusalem and most recently, Bethlehem. While the substance of my work has changed over time, from an ethnographic analysis of Palestinian commemoration to focused qualitative research with children and young people, I have consistently endeavoured to garner a deeper understanding on issues relating to everyday life under occupation. Working in an area embroiled in an intractable conflict is not a decision one takes lightly. The opportunity to do so is a privilege, one that carries personal responsibility and a commitment to adhere to the maxim, 'Do No Harm'. Whereas much still remains to be said about how researchers can act to mitigate the harm done to a reluctant, over-researched and in many ways, exploited population, so, too, is there a need to be cognisant of the impact of such work on your own wellbeing, both physical and for the purposes of the forthcoming analysis, emotional. This chapter champions the role of diary writing as catharsis when seeking to generate reflexivity and to recover what Frey and Castro (2016, p 143) have called, 'the black box of the "inner researcher".' Fieldwork of any type, regardless of the threat of violence, is messy, generates confusion, and can lead to uncertainty of thought and action (Burgess, 1981; Silverman, 2005). When the work is conducted against the backdrop of violent and unpredictable conflict, feelings of personal uncertainty and apprehension are exponentially increased (Sriram et al, 2009). It has been suggested that fieldwork must rank as one of the most disagreeable activities humanity has fashioned for itself (Shaffir and Stebbins, 1991, p xi). Although overzealous, Shaffir and Stebbins (1991) are right to highlight that research conducted with an omnipresent threat of violence is, at best, uncomfortable. In choosing to share first-hand diary entries from my time in Palestine, this chapter responds to Malacrida's (2007, p 1334) criticism in that, 'relatively little is said about the impact of emotional topics on researchers themselves.'

With reference to personal experience, this chapter highlights the important role that diary keeping assumed when seeking to process the impact of a particularly violent spike in the conflict across Palestine. The opening section of the chapter situates the discussion within a broader literature on the role of diary keeping when engaged in conflict fieldwork. Next, the discussion moves on to consider the importance of documenting emotion when conducting fieldwork that takes place against the backdrop of conflict-related violence before providing personal first-hand diary extracts from time spent living and working in Palestine. These diary extracts, written between October and December 2015, are shared in an effort to reveal the crucial role of the diary-writing process in managing complex emotions surrounding researcher vulnerability, uncertainty, fear and apprehension. The diary was a repository for providing the space for rationalisation, generating motivation and aiding catharsis when feeling particularly overwhelmed by what was happening in close proximity.

The arguments made throughout this chapter are situated within an expansive and interdisciplinary volume of academic literature in a conscious effort to extol the virtues of diary keeping when researching violence, regardless of research experience or disciplinary background. Thinking reflexively, it is argued (Browne, 2013), ought to be a continuous process throughout fieldwork, not an activity reserved for the journey home. As such, the benefits of maintaining diaries are to be acknowledged at every stage of the fieldwork journey, in preparation, while engaged in and when departing the field. In so doing, it is hoped that a strong message can be conveyed to those who may have been reluctant to do so in the past, to make public the challenges and difficulties they faced, particularly those they were ultimately able to rationalise and overcome. Should those engaging in such work be so inclined, it will be possible to remove the unhelpful shroud of mystery surrounding the difficulties associated with researching violence.

Research diaries

From the posthumously published pages of Malinowski's diary (1967) to Rabinow's (1977) *Reflections on fieldwork in Morocco*, the craft of documenting fieldwork experiences has been a mainstay of ethnographic fieldwork. Yet despite this, there exists a dearth of insightful, illuminating and more importantly, published accounts of traditional ethnographic fieldwork diaries that are particularly focused on the emotional impact of conducting fieldwork in conflict zones. While Brewer (2016, p 3) has quite rightly acknowledged in general the existence of a great deal of reflexivity among researchers in the field of peace and conflict studies, there is an acceptance that the manner in which it has been disseminated has been disparate. It is this reticence among researchers to consistently publish the emotional toll of researching violence on their personal wellbeing that I argue adds to the murkiness surrounding the true cost of researching violence on the individual. Historically, encounters with 'the other' have found prominence in British anthropology, with semi-autobiographical writings wrapped up in the language of empire and colonialism emerging as fieldwork diaries. According to Shore (1999, p 25), 'In American anthropology, by contrast, the "self-reflexive", autobiographical account of fieldwork experiences has emerged as a distinct ethnographic genre (Stocking 1992: 13; cf. Geertz 1973; Rabinow 1977).' Regardless of their country of origin, it is unlikely that those who are conducting conflict fieldwork choose not to document personal reflections when researching in unfamiliar spaces. Despite this, there appears to exist unwillingness to make public these personal diary accounts out of a fear of, among other things, academic reprisal (Browne, 2013; Browne and Moffett, 2014). Appreciating that few of us will ever have our fieldwork experiences published alongside the diaries of the stalwarts of our discipline, one must not accept that the insights we jot down at the end of a challenging research day are any less worthwhile.

Research diaries have found prominence across a variety of disciplines; in education, teachers are often asked to maintain classroom encounters during their training so as to reflect on perceived successes and failings (Borg, 2001). In accounting and business management, scholars have found merit in keeping diaries for the benefit of encouraging reflexivity during the research process (Nadin and Cassell, 2006). Thus, 'far from being solely a repository for thoughts and courses of action taken, the diary is an integral part of a researcher's knowledge development' (Browne, 2013, p 422; see also Engin, 2011). For those whose work involves researching violence, such as is the case throughout this collection, keeping diaries can be an act of critical importance. Diaries can act as a practical resource for the documentation of facts and figures, key dates and appointments, a 'logging device' (Burgess, 1981; Lofland and Lofland, 1995, Silverman, 2005). However, they are also a space that permits the documentation of reflections, in-depth analysis of the research process and the impact of the research process on the researcher (Newbury, 2001; Engin, 2011; Browne, 2013). The role of the diary for the purposes of this chapter's analysis is to act as an emotional counter-weight, with the belief that the benefits of maintaining a research diary include the rationalisation of fieldwork anxiety, the alleviation of research frustration, and the management of uncertainty, all prevalent during sustained periods of conflict-based fieldwork (Browne, 2013). Diary writing provides an opportunity for the informal documentation of experiences and personal reflections that are more often than not absent from formulaic, research-driven field notes (Sanjek, 1990; Heller et al, 2011).

Although an appreciation of the impact of conflict fieldwork on both the burgeoning development of the research itself and on one's own emotional wellbeing is often reserved for the hidden pages of the research diary, the secrecy of this act of emotional rationalisation is disingenuous to the critical role that emotion plays in the shaping of the fieldwork process in general. The reality is that emotion shapes every decision made in relation to conducting conflict research, not solely while engaged in researching violence as it manifests itself, but also in seeking to rationalise decisions taken in advance (Borg, 2001). Moreover, as Hubbard et al (2001, p 135) have noted, it is becoming increasingly important to highlight 'that emotions have epistemological significance.' There is thus great value in shedding light on the 'hidden struggles' one experiences when researching violence (Punch, 2012).

Recording emotion in conflict fieldwork

The dangers associated with conducting fieldwork and researching violence in some of the world's most volatile regions have been well documented in an expansive and interdisciplinary literature (Sluka, 1990; Knox, 2001; Kovats-Bernat, 2002; Sriram et al, 2009; Browne and Moffett, 2014; Browne and McBride, 2015). The primary focus of much of the work has been on the methodological challenges associated with, among other things, gaining researcher legitimacy, safeguarding access, generating rapport and managing what Browne and McBride (2015) have referred to as, 'Politically sensitive encounters'. Whereas much has been published by way of a checklist of 'do's' and 'don'ts' when conducting conflict research, there are relatively few published texts by way of comparison on the emotional impact of the research on the researcher. Sluka's (1990) insights into working in the North of Ireland during the 1980s, at a time of heightened intra-Republican tension, are a candid reflection of the risks he was exposed to and how he managed to subsequently navigate them. Similarly, Kovats-Bernat (2002), concerning his work with street children in Haiti, has made public the challenges he faced with an honesty that will resonate with anyone who has chosen to research in similarly difficult spaces. For both Sluka and Kovats-Bernat, there is an emphasis placed on the need to safeguard personal safety while maintaining their good standing within the community at large. The importance attached to the relational aspect of conducting research with identified respondents in areas blighted by state surveillance is evident throughout both seminal research texts, and was an issue I was particularly sensitive to when attempting to navigate my own position as an outsider in Palestine.

Other disciplines beyond conflict studies have placed emotionality of the research process in a prominent position in terms of research design and reflective practice. Health professionals dealing with terminally ill patients, particularly researchers from the nursing tradition, have made visible by way of publication their reflections on the need to be sensitive to emotions and the impact of research on the researcher's wellbeing (Dickson-Swift et al, 2008). Literature that has focused on issues relating to emotionality and the personal impact of conducting conflict-related fieldwork includes the seminal work of Nordstrom and Antonius (1995), and Thomson, Ansoms and Murison's (2012) edited collection, with its focus on conflict research in Africa. Conflict research in an increasingly warring and uncertain world has increased, perhaps being driven by a fetishism that is beyond the scope of the current discussion (Browne and Moffett, 2014). Despite its rising popularity, there is a relative dearth in readily available, published fieldwork accounts that take seriously the emotional toils of researching violence that can lead to the unsatisfactory conclusion that the mental resolve of conflict researchers is taken for granted (Lee-Treweek and Linkogle, 2000). In advancing this argument, Borg (2001, p 164) states, 'We rarely hear about the emotional side of doing research, and the implicit message researchers may derive from this silence is that emotions have no role to play in their work and perhaps even that these should be denied and suppressed.' Corbin and Morse (2003), Grinyer (2004) and Malacrida (2007) have each outlined that the literature that takes as its focus issues related to dealing with the emotional aspects of qualitative research focuses on the ethics and effects of such research activities on research participants. While this is of undoubted importance and ought to remain a central concern for any would-be conflict fieldworker, so, too, is there a need to appreciate the impact of traumatic and mentally exhausting fieldwork on those involved in documenting and recovering harrowing narratives, particularly as it is now well established that 'the researcher is … not immune to emotional experiences in the field' (Hubbard et al, 2001, p 120).

Reflecting on the deleterious impact that conducting research was having on my own wellbeing during doctoral fieldwork when based in Palestine (2011), I turned to diary writing as a means of documenting feelings of frustration and anger. Writing acted as a form of catharsis, which allowed for 'A way to attend to the self … a place to dump anger, guilt, or fear … to clarify what it is we feel angry or guilty about' (Cooper, 1991, p 105). The pages of the research diary, far from the prying eyes of a critical academic and wider audience, permitted the expression of what were, at times, irrational, yet no less impactful, fears and anxieties. It was increasingly clear to me that in preparing to conduct my own period of fieldwork I had failed to generate any meaningful emotional awareness as to the potentially damaging impact that the work could have on me personally. On my return to Belfast I spent time reflecting on the challenges I faced. An influential and sympathetic supervisor encouraged me to challenge the unhelpful silence within the academy with regard to the personal impact that conflict research can have on the researcher. Thus, the decision was reached that I ought to analyse in excess of 60,000 words of diary entries with a view to publishing in an academic journal.

Such a proposition, publishing my inner most fears and self-deprecating revelations, has ultimately led to a greater engagement with 'in the field'-based reflection ever since. It became clear that writing in research diaries allowed for the chance to gain clarity on 'what exactly I was scared, frustrated, or angry with. More importantly, however, it gave me the clarity of thought to … work out a means of overcoming these fears, managing my frustrations, and successfully completing the task I had set out to do' (Browne, 2013, p 423). In making public these research accounts I was seeking to shine a light on what I perceived to be a hidden aspect of researching violence, and to ultimately challenge the fact that, 'Although emotional issues are often mentioned in fieldwork accounts, the literature on research methodology aimed at sociologists and other social scientists working at the "coal face", tends not to include emotional distress among the dangers which researchers may have to face' (Hubbard et al, 2001, p 120).

Writing emotion: practical examples of reflexivity in action

In 2015, during my most recent period of time living in the West Bank, my research comprised meeting with community-based organisations, youth workers and young people themselves, who were living at the sharp edge of the conflict. The work involved running focus groups with young people living in refugee camps and holding meetings with those who were responsible for delivering frontline educational services. Simultaneously, I took up a position as Assistant Professor of Law and Human Rights at the Al-Quds (Bard) University, which, in turn, presented opportunities to learn from a diverse student body coming from across the West Bank to attend college. In a relatively short space of time I formed close relationships with staff and students, and quickly became integrated into the wider university environment. During the second semester (September–December 2015), a significant escalation in hostilities and the outbreak of violent incidents, originating in Jerusalem but subsequently spreading across the West Bank, transformed the university campus in Abu Dis into a volatile and dangerous space. The impact of the violence on the student body was particularly pronounced, with a number of students who attended the university being killed. Staff and students alike attempted to navigate the additional barriers that emerged in order to get to work, with varying degrees of success. The impact of the student murders was felt acutely by all on campus, with the university becoming the focal point of violent excursions by the Israeli army.

Unsurprisingly, the violence raised safety concerns, both for myself and for the students whom I had been working with for the best part of a year. My diary entries during this time reflected this heightened sense of threat of violence and my concerns for the students with whom I had formed a strong connection; some, I noted, were struggling to cope. A subsequent content analysis of these diary entries reveals recurrent themes in the journaling that took place at the time, including fears around personal safety, feelings of frustration, apprehension about the future and critical reflections on my own involvement in what was happening around me. As has been noted above, methodological and ethical fieldwork reflections often become sanitised as a result of having been written several months after the fieldwork has taken place (Punch, 2012). The immediacy of documenting contemporaneously the raw emotion one can feel when researching violence ensures that particularly impactful personal experiences retain a sense of urgency. Conversely, documenting reflections far from the epicentre of violence that is taking place can unhelpfully lead to the rationalisation and sanitisation of potentially impactful events, with the outcome being that a careful consideration of the emotional impact of the fieldwork can essentially dissipate. In the following diary extract, taken at a time when the university campus had been raided by the Israeli army, the volume of rhetorical questions that permeate through the discourse is indicative of the immediacy of the reflection, being conducted in real time, and captures the levels of anxiety, confusion, uncertainty and apprehension I was feeling as a result of the spike in violence.

> Today the campus was attacked; we made our way up as usual for classes, but as soon as the *service* [shared taxi] pulled up at the front gates and we jumped out into the plumes of tear gas it was clear that we would have to try and get away to safety. Why were staff informed that campus was open when this was happening? What about the students? How are they supposed to get home? Questions that I doubt I will get answers to. When it was all kicking off we were standing with this young student, 19 years of age, who was visibly shaken and anxious. He suffered the dual anxiety of worrying about missing his chemistry exam, an exam that was scheduled to start in 10 minutes time. Even this evening as I sit back in the relative calm of Bethlehem I can't help but feel challenged and emotional about XXX's situation. A young guy wanting to excel in university, nervous about an exam, chain smoking, telling two random white strangers about his desires to play his self-taught violin in a European orchestra when he gets the chance to leave. Is he ok? Will he get to take the exam later? Is his family ok? Did he know the student who was killed? It makes me gut wrenchingly sad to recall his thanks to us for staying with him and shakes me to remember very clearly, never to forget our privilege here. (Research diary, Bethlehem, 4/10/15)

In documenting immediately what had happened and in becoming reflective of my own position in the events of the day, I was able to ensure that my reaction to what had been quite a violent and traumatic incident remained fresh. The exposure to this level of violence was personally uncomfortable, but ultimately the main concern to emerge from the diary entry was for the wellbeing of the student with whom we, my wife and I, had shared the tense encounter. The act of documenting reflexivity as noted in the above extract reveals an awareness of positionality during the whole encounter, and encouraged a greater sense of empathy that is often missing in more detached and superficial accounts of conflict-related fieldwork. Throughout the extract there is a clear feeling of urgency and concern for the wellbeing of staff colleagues and students with whom I had developed strong personal connections. The diary reflection thus allowed for a sharpening of my sensitivity to my privileged position as an outsider, an issue that perhaps becomes less apparent when one comes to documenting fieldwork reports further on in the research process. Rather than address bureaucratic and institutional shortcomings in a reactionary manner that perhaps would not have been appropriate in the first instance, the diary also permitted space to document frustrations, as noted above.

As the apparent spike in violent incidents across the West Bank continued, the diaries became opportunities for thought rationalisation, spaces where decisions were reached and courses of action deliberated on. Analysis of the diary extracts maintained during this period reveals feelings of frustration at an inability to successfully engage with the work that we were in Palestine to do. Despite these feelings of frustration, the diaries allowed for careful consideration of courses of action while also providing a rationalisation space to critique my response to certain problems that had arisen. Diary writing thus aided catharsis by helping to mitigate feelings of anxiety and uncertainty in my perceived inaction or inability to continue on with the work I had set out to do. The following extract highlights my attempt to manage these feelings of uncertainty and indecision:

> We have been sitting in the house now for the past five days, shops in Bethlehem were closed and, to be honest, I haven't seen them open since. It's fair to say that we are both getting itchy feet, so to speak. There is a feeling of whether or not we should/could be doing more. Ok, so travelling to college is the least we can do, but it's weighing up whether or not the place is going to be attacked again, is the main issue. Managing the risk at this stage is the main issue. But if we don't go do we just accept that education is suspended the minute that these attacks of the campus take place? Surely that is an equally unacceptable scenario? We just ought to make the journey to campus and make decisions as the fluidity of the situation unfolds. I guess we just have to make risk assessments on our own volition. (Research diary, Bethlehem, 8/10/15)

A noticeable trend in terms of documenting emotion in the diary is the link between a spike in the violence, my proximity to those involved and the subsequent attempt to come to terms with what was happening around me. Journaling in the evenings became more than solely a means of ensuring an accurate version of events was retained; diary writing was a form of catharsis that allowed me to vent feelings of anger and despair in a way that I found appropriate. Returning to the text of the diary entries by way of more structured analysis, it is clear both through use of emotive language and broken prose the extent to which I was becoming acutely impacted by the exposure to violent acts:

> There was a feeling that something crazy was happening today, and the media reports in Jerusalem I watched later that evening confirmed it. Two really challenging videos that made me explode. I tried to hide away from it, but I couldn't not relate to the wee boy in the video, spread on the pavement, clearly terrified and confused. As it transpired, he had just been hit by a car, run over and was lying, bleeding, on the pavement. The level of vitriol being hurled at him as he was bleeding made me explode and I had to stand in the dark in the bathroom unable to actually stop crying. I think that was my breaking point – 13-year-old kid being run over by settlers and then being screamed at, "die son of a who★★". F★★★ me, this place has no hope. XXXX sends me the videos that he gets in from XXXX and I understand why he does, but they're brutal. Anyways, I managed to calm down a bit, tried to watch some inane sh★★ on YouTube, had a beer and went to bed. (Research diary, Bethlehem, 14/10/15)

Borg (2001) has noted the benefits of maintaining meticulous research diaries as being the significant psycho-emotional support they can provide when working in relative isolation. Further traumatic incidents, including the death of a young boy living in a refugee camp close by to where we were living in Bethlehem, were documented in detail. The murdered young boy had been involved with the community centre that I visited regularly. The staff and young people had played a key role in helping me understand the intricacies of everyday life growing up in Palestine, and had generously spent time with me when I came to visit. Documentation of my feelings on the situation included emails I sent home and written newspaper article submissions; however, by far the most personal account of the emotion I attached to the incident was reserved for the research diary. In the extract shared below, it is clear that I am struggling to comprehend and ultimately process what was happening. My attempt at trying to rationalise and understand the nature of the arbitrary violence was proving fruitless. Interspersed within the reflections on the violent incident is an attempt to evaluate one's own position as an outsider in the region, and an effort to consider to what extent the presence of outsiders is actually doing more harm than good:

> Two children have been shot in XXXX camp. One has died as a result. The kid was 12 years of age and making his way back from school. Shot in the chest in his school uniform with a backpack on. It's hard to even begin to f***ing comprehend. I've been visiting the centre in XXXX for the last few months, holding meetings with staff and getting to know some of the young people there. Listening to their stories and seeing what life was like growing up in XXXX was a very humbling experience and to see the news today makes me sick to my stomach. Was he one of the young people who was supposed to come along to a focus group in the centre? How often did he attend the centre? What were his dreams and hopes for the future? Was he one of the kids who was unable to attend that day? The scenes on the news networks and all over Facebook are gut wrenching and I'm really struggling to find the focus to finish any meaningful work. There's a real anger swelling at the moment.... We are going to have to sit down and figure out at what stage we consider ourselves to be doing more harm than good, and also, at what stage do we think that the situation could potentially mean going home. Is it appropriate to be asking such bland and seemingly mundane questions at a time like this? (Research diary, Bethlehem, 5/10/15)

Whereas the entry above is clearly an outpouring of frustration, what is also apparent is the attempted reflexivity demonstrated throughout. In challenging my rationale for working in the area, not out of a fear for personal safety but rather being increasingly sensitive to the issue of doing more harm than good, I was reacting to events as they were unfolding, and attending to the emotional needs of the self throughout the process. The need to be continuously reflective of our engagement in the work and how it, in turn, was impacting on our emotional wellbeing is further evidenced in the following extract:

> Been thinking a lot about the fact that I had that full-on outburst yesterday after seeing the video of the kid. I

> wonder if it's not beyond the realms of possibility to think
> that maybe you can have some long-term effects of being
> involved in this and baring witness, even if you are pretty
> powerless to do anything? I'm not suggesting any form of
> PTSD or anything, but I have a deeper appreciation of the
> reasons why UN staff members get R&R every few weeks.
> It is mentally exhausting, and there's only so much you can
> do being stuck in Bethlehem. That feeling of not being able
> to do what you're here for and ultimately do more becomes
> a bit overwhelming, so I've taken to documenting things
> in as much detail as possible to try and rationalise and gain
> a sense of what is happening to me as this is all going on.
> (Research diary, Bethlehem, 15/10/15)

The feelings of guilt and frustration at my decision to take up an
academic position at home dominated the pages of the journal in
the few weeks leading up to departure. In one of my final diary
entries before leaving Palestine in December I noted my personal
anger at leaving the space that, despite being personally challenging,
had become highly important and formative over time. Those with
experience of fieldwork in conflict zones often speak of feelings of
remorse when choosing to leave, reflecting on issues such as researcher
privilege (Nilan, 2002), the subsequent impact on personal friendships
and on occasion guilt at allowing the challenging nature of the work
to result in early departure (Browne and Moffett, 2014; Sriram et
al, 2009). Whereas, I, too, had similar feelings of sadness at leaving,
my frustrations, as documented below, focus more on my fear that I
will have consigned to history this formative time living in Palestine.
Throughout the passage, feelings of guilt and frustration are coupled
with a determination to ensure that the time spent away is short-lived:

> I know that it's coming soon, we are back home on Tuesday
> and beginning to feel a lot of guilt in leaving – I wonder
> if this will all dissipate when we get the space away from
> here? I'm not so sure, and in fact I'm not so sure I want it
> to. I am trying now to put in place ways of getting back
> again as soon as we can – it's gone from being a place where
> we live to a place where we visit and that all seems a little
> surreal. How can it just become another place to visit in
> the future? No way. We need to get back and get involved
> again. I know I have to start in to work at home, but I
> need to know that the option to come back again and live

is on the table. This place is like that – it gets under the skin, and for both me and XXXX, we need to constantly be reminded of feeling a sense of connectivity to the place. (Research diary, Bethlehem, 15/12/15)

Conclusion

My goal throughout the chapter has not been to engage in what McBride (2017, p 86) has referred to as 'intellectual masturbation that decries the social and political abuses of researchers and their research.' Instead, I have sought to extol the virtues of continuous reflexive practice as a way of attending to the self and to place a greater emphasis on the crucial role that constant journal writing can play when researching violence. Journaling, I argue, can aid catharsis and help to rationalise and overcome the emotional uncertainties that permeate conflict research. The diary entries shared reveal the extent to which researching violence can be uncomfortable, potentially dangerous and ultimately challenging. Reflections on personal safety are situated alongside empathetic responses to arbitrary violence, concern over friends and colleagues, and uncertainties surrounding positionality and researcher privilege. I argue that the role assumed by research diaries in providing the space for processing raw emotion and the enhancement of critical researcher reflexivity requires greater consideration among those researching violence. Hubbard et al (2001, p 135) have further noted that,

> The more that the emotional impacts of doing research are seen as valid by the wider research community, the greater is the likelihood that research teams will take the issue seriously. Formal support may involve more literature being published about the subject of emotion, and the production of ethical guidelines to support researchers as well as respondents in these respects.

Thinking reflexively 'involves taking the unprocessed, raw material of experience and engaging with it as a way to make sense of what has occurred. It involves exploring often messy and confused events and focusing on the thoughts and emotions that accompany them' (Boud, 2001, p 10). The fieldwork diaries I maintained during my most recent period of time spent working in Palestine helped in the processing of raw first-hand experiences without the unhelpful issue of sanitisation over time. As has been noted before, 'the witnessing of violence/terror is emotionally demanding, often bequeathing the researcher with fully embodied experiences of the "real" situation on the ground' (Woon, 2013, p 31). Maintaining diaries at a time of perceived heightened violence allowed me to reflect in 'real time' in a way that allowed for the safeguarding of a feeling of exigency, and to combat amnesiac processes that would have diluted this urgency over time.

Despite being an inherently personal and at times self-deprecating exercise, I have chosen to make public the private accounts of my feelings and frustrations in an effort to provide greater transparency and to make 'visible the invisible processes of fieldwork' (Browne, 2013, p 424). The value in doing so, I argue, is that it can shine a light on the importance of processing raw emotion through the craft of journaling when involved in the researching of violence.

References

Borg, S. (2001) 'The research journal: a tool for promoting and understanding researcher development', *Language Teaching Research*, vol 5, no 2, pp 156–77.

Boud, D. (2001) 'Using journal writing to enhance reflective practice', in L.M. English and M.A. Gillen (eds) *Promoting journal writing in adult education*, San Francisco, CA: Jossey-Bass, pp 9–17.

Brewer, J.D. (2016) 'The ethics of ethical debates in peace and conflict research: Notes towards the development of a research covenant', *Methodological Innovations*, vol 9, pp 1– 11.

Browne, B. (2013) 'Recording the personal: The benefits in maintaining research diaries for documenting the emotional and practical challenges of fieldwork in unfamiliar settings', *International Journal of Qualitative Methods*, vol 12, pp 403–19.

Browne, B. and McBride, R. (2015) 'Politically sensitive encounters: Ethnography, access and the benefits of "hanging out"', *Qualitative Sociology Review*, vol 11, no 1, pp 34–48.

Browne, B. and Moffett, L. (2014) 'Finding your feet in the field: Critical reflections of early career researchers on field research in transitional societies', *Journal of Human Rights Practice*, vol 6, no 2, pp 223–37.

Burgess, R.G. (1981) 'Keeping a research diary', *Cambridge Journal of Education*, vol 11, no 1, pp 75–83.

Cooper, J.E. (1991) 'Telling our own stories: The reading and writing of journals and diaries', in C. Witherell and N. Noddings, *Stories lives tell: Narrative and dialogue in education*, New York: Teachers College Press, pp 96–112.

Corbin, J. and Morse, J.M. (2003) 'The unstructured interactive interview: Issues of reciprocity and risks when dealing with sensitive topics', *Qualitative Inquiry*, vol 9, no 3, pp 335–54.

Dickson-Swift, V., Lyn James, E. and Liamputtong, P. (2008) 'What is sensitive research?', in V. Dickson-Swift, E.L. James and P. Liamputtong (eds) *Undertaking sensitive research in the health and social sciences: Managing boundaries, emotions and risks*, Cambridge: Cambridge University Press, pp 1–10.

Engin, M. (2011) 'Research diary: A tool for scaffolding', *International Journal of Qualitative Methods*, vol 10, no 3, pp 296–306.

Frey, L.R. and Castro, N.T. (2016) 'Researchers' emotions and identities', in A. Kurylo, *Negotiating group identity in the research process: Are you in or are you out?*, London: Lexington Books, pp 143–69.

Geertz, C. (1973) *The interpretation of cultures: Selected essays*, New York: Basic Books.

Grinyer, A. (2004) 'The narrative correspondence method: What a follow-up study can tell us about the longer term effect on participants in emotionally demanding research', *Qualitative Health Research*, vol 14, no 10, pp 1326–41.

Heller, E., Christensen, J., Long, L., Mackenzie, C.A., Osano, P.M., Ricker, B. and Turner, S. (2011) 'Dear diary: Early career geographers collectively reflect on their qualitative field research experiences', *Journal of Geography in Higher Education*, vol 35, no 1, pp 67–83.

Hubbard, G., Backett-Milburn, K. and Kemmer, D. (2001) 'Working with emotion: Issues for the researcher in fieldwork and teamwork', *International Journal of Social Research Methodology*, vol 4, no 2, pp 119–37.

Knox, C. (2001) 'Establishing research legitimacy in the contested political ground of contemporary Northern Ireland', *Qualitative Research*, vol 1, no 2, pp 205–22.

Kovats-Bernat, C. (2002) 'Negotiating dangerous fields: Pragmatic strategies for fieldwork amid violence and terror', *American Anthropologist*, vol 104, no 1, pp 208–22.

Lee-Treweek, G. and Linkogle, S. (2000) *Danger in the field*, Abingdon: Routledge.

Lofland, J. and Lofland, L. (1995) *Analyzing social settings: A guide to qualitative observation and analysis* (3rd edn), London: Wandsworth Publishing Company.

Malacrida, C. (2007) 'Reflexive journaling on emotional research topics: Ethical issues for team researchers', *Qualitative Health Research*, vol 17, no 10, pp 1329–39.

Malinowski, B. (1967) *A diary in the strict sense of the word*, London: Routledge.

McBride, R.S. (2017) 'Towards hope, solidarity and re-humanisation', in S. Armstrong, J. Blaustein and A. Henry (eds) *Reflexivity and criminal justice*, London: Palgrave Macmillan.

Nadin, S. and Cassell, C. (2006) 'The use of a research diary as a tool for reflexive practice: Some reflections from management research', *Qualitative Research in Accounting & Management*, vol 3, no 3, pp 208–17.

Newbury, D. (2001) 'Diaries and fieldnotes in the research process', *Research Issues in Art, Design, and Media*, The Research Training Initiative.

Nilan, P. (2002) 'Dangerous fieldwork re-examined: The question of researcher subject position', *Qualitative Research*, vol 2, no 3, pp 363–86.

Nordstrom, C. and Robben, A. (1995) *Fieldwork under fire: Contemporary studies of violence and survival*, Oakland, CA: University of California Press.

Punch, S. (2012) 'Hidden struggles of fieldwork: Exploring the role and use of field diaries', *Emotion, Space and Society*, vol 5, no 2, pp 86–93.

Rabinow, P. (1977) *Reflections on fieldwork in Morocco*, Berkeley, CA: University of California Press.

Sanjek, R. (1990) *Fieldnotes: The making of anthropology*, Ithaca, NY: Cornell University Press.

Shaffir, W.B. and Stebbins, R.A. (eds) (1991) *Experiencing fieldwork: An inside view of qualitative research*, London: Sage Publications.

Shore, C. (1999) 'Fictions of fieldwork: Depicting the "self" in ethnographic writing (Italy)', in C.W. Watson (ed) *Being there: Fieldwork in anthropology*, London: Pluto Press, pp 25–48.

Silverman, D. (2005) *Doing qualitative research: A practical handbook*, London: Sage Publications.

Sluka, J.A. (1990) 'Participant observation in violent social contexts', *Human Organisation*, vol 49, no 20, pp 114–26.

Sriram, C.L., King, J.C., Mertus, J.A., Martin-Ortega, O. and Herman, J. (eds) (2009) *Surviving field research: Working in violent and difficult situations*, Abingdon: Routledge.

Stocking, G.W. (1992) *The ethnographer's magic and other essays in the history of anthropology*, Madison, WI: University of Wisconsin Press.

Thomson, S., Ansoms, A. and Murison, J. (eds) (2012). *Emotional and ethical challenges for field research in Africa: The story behind the findings*, New York: Springer.

Woon, C.Y. (2013) 'For "emotional fieldwork" in critical geopolitical research on violence and terrorism', *Political Geography*, vol 33, pp 31–41.

10

Abetting atrocities? Reporting the perspectives of perpetrators in research on violence

Michael Broache

Introduction

"We are happy you came to meet us. The world calls us devils, but we are only refugees who want to return to our homes. You must tell the world the truth that we are not devils." So ended my interview with a commander in the Forces démocratiques du libération du Rwanda (hereinafter FDLR), an armed group active under various guises in the conflict in the eastern Democratic Republic of the Congo (DRC) since the mid-1990s. I had interviewed this commander and other members of the FDLR for a research project examining the impact of International Criminal Court (hereinafter ICC) prosecutions on atrocities in the DRC. The ICC opened an investigation in the DRC in 2004, and the FDLR presented a useful case study for this project because the Court later issued arrest warrants for two senior FDLR leaders. Callixte Mbarushimana, a high-ranking political cadre, was apprehended in Paris in 2010, but later released after the case against him was dismissed, and Sylvestre Mudacumura, the FDLR's supreme military leader, remains at large at the time of writing. The warrants against these leaders pertained to war crimes and crimes against humanity, including attacks against civilian populations, murder, mutilation, rape, torture, inhuman treatment and pillaging, inter alia, allegedly perpetrated by the FDLR from 2009–10 in North and South Kivu provinces of the DRC (ICC, 2010, 2012). The FDLR, however, was implicated in systematic, widespread atrocities in the DRC both before and after the period covered by the ICC arrest warrants (Human Rights Watch, 2009), and the organisation originated from the Hutu extremist groups that perpetrated the 1994 Rwandan genocide (International Crisis Group, 2005).

My interviews with FDLR members were organised around a series of questions concerning their knowledge and perceptions of the ICC, and I customarily concluded interviews by asking participants if there was anything they wished to add that was relevant to the ICC. It was in response to this question that the aforementioned commander asked me to tell the FDLR's story to the world. I did not respond directly to the commander's request, not thinking much of it at the time; in the course of the 150 interviews I conducted for my research on the ICC in the DRC, many subjects – which included current and former members of various armed groups in addition to the FDLR, Congolese government officials, media and civil society activists – requested that I tell their story in some way. I simply shook the commander's hand, expressed my thanks for the interview, and proceeded on my way.

However, as I reviewed my research notes and wrote up my findings, the commander's request unsettled me. The FDLR's 'story' included what some have referred to as an extremist, ethnocentric view, and an undeniable history of atrocities in both Rwanda and the DRC based on ideology (Human Rights Watch, 2009, p 29; UN, 2010a). I had not promised anything to the FDLR commander or other interviewees in response to their request, and I intended to remain as objective as possible in reporting and analysing my interview data, focusing on any implications for my research question concerning the impact of the ICC. Even so, elements of the FDLR's 'story' were directly relevant to my research. Perceptions that the ICC (and other instruments of international justice) are part of a broader campaign of persecution against Hutus seemed to undermine the Court's legitimacy and impact vis-à-vis the FDLR. At the same time, the organisation's continuing propagation of the 'Hutu Power' ideology that motivated the Rwandan genocide suggested that international legal action had failed to alter understandings of the appropriateness of violence, as posited by some proponents of prosecutions (Sikkink, 2011). In reporting these and other elements of the FDLR's 'story' in my research, I wondered if I would be unintentionally serving as the FDLR's mouthpiece or somehow legitimising its extremist claims. In doing so, I queried whether or not I would be aiding the FDLR and serving as an unwitting accomplice in any future atrocities.

This chapter reflects on these moral conundrums in light of personal experience interviewing members of the FDLR and other armed groups implicated in atrocities in the DRC, including the national armed forces, the Forces armées de la République démocratique du Congo (hereinafter FARDC), and the rebel group Mouvement du 23-mars (hereinafter M23). I begin by describing my research in the

DRC in greater detail, reflecting on the evolution of my concerns about potentially aiding perpetrators and abetting atrocities. Then, drawing from my research and critical reflections on the use of interviews with perpetrators of various forms of illegal or illicit behaviour in criminology, history and sociology, I describe two mechanisms by which research involving perpetrators may abet atrocities. The first mechanism, which I term 'direct assistance', involves the provision of monetary compensation, material benefits or information to perpetrators. The second mechanism, 'dissemination', involves intentionally or unintentionally providing a platform for an individual or organisation's ideology or broader 'story'. I then conclude by discussing approaches for managing the concerns raised by my research, which focus principally on recognising the potential motives of perpetrators for participating and the possibilities for abetting atrocities.

Interacting with perpetrators

My motivation to pursue analysis on the effects of ICC prosecutions on atrocities was driven by the normative goal of providing insights that would help to prevent future atrocities occurring. The ICC was established in the expectation, as articulated by human rights activists, legal practitioners and scholars from the 'liberal peacebuilding' tradition, that it would contribute to the prevention of the grave crimes that fall under its jurisdiction: genocide, war crimes and crimes against humanity (Akhavan, 2001, 2009; Gilligan, 2006; Sikkink, 2011). However, sceptics (often self-proclaimed political 'realists') have questioned this claim, arguing that ICC intervention is, at best, unlikely to have any independent effect (Goldsmith and Krasner, 2003), and at worst, might exacerbate atrocities by prolonging conflicts or generating perverse incentives for belligerents to escalate violence (Snyder and Vinjamuri, 2003). At the time I began my project, there had been little research on the effects of the ICC, or transitional justice mechanisms more generally (Thoms et al, 2010), and it was my intention to generate knowledge relevant to the ongoing debate about the impact of prosecutions on atrocities.

The various mechanisms by which the ICC is posited to prevent or exacerbate atrocities depend, to a large extent, on the perceptions of the potential or actual targets of prosecutions, that is, perpetrators of atrocities. For example, the mechanism of deterrence operates by increasing the expected costs of atrocity crimes to perpetrators, and is therefore critically dependent on their knowledge of the ICC and beliefs concerning the probability and severity of legal sanctions (Kim and Sikkink, 2010). It thus became clear that it would be valuable, if not essential, to integrate the perspectives of perpetrators in my research. Initially I considered consulting publicly available court records and other secondary sources, but it quickly became clear that these sources provided only limited insight into perpetrator perspectives, and that it would be necessary to locate and interview alleged perpetrators to gather data for my project.

In planning for my interactions with perpetrators, I followed an explicitly rationalist logic, focused primarily on minimising what I perceived to be the possible risks of my research (in the unquestioned expectation, noted above, that my project would generate policy-relevant knowledge that could help prevent future atrocities). In doing so, I followed the guidance of my university's Institutional Review Board (IRB), which strongly emphasised the potential risks to interviewees arising from what would be considered the sensitivity of the topic of international criminal justice, and the possibility that interview subjects might implicate themselves in atrocity crimes (although I did not directly ask subjects about their involvement in crimes). I modelled my research on other recent studies on violence in the field of political science that use interviews with combatants (including those whose organisations were involved in atrocities), including Cohen's (2013) analysis of wartime rape incorporating interviews with ex-combatants in Sierra Leone, Weinstein's (2007) study of the organisational determinants of violence against civilians by insurgent groups in Mozambique, Peru and Uganda, and Autesserre's (2010) analysis of the failures of international peacebuilding in the DRC based on interviews with over 330 sources (including, significantly, members of the FDLR). Following the advice of my IRB and the practices employed in these studies, I took various measures to minimise risks to interviewees, including maintaining confidentiality of all sources and taking only written notes rather than recordings that could be used to identify subjects by voice.

While I focused principally on what I perceived to be the possible risks to interview subjects, I also considered whether my planned interactions might aid perpetrators, and potentially abet future atrocities. At the time, these considerations were mostly confined to legal concerns relating to the provision of material aid to individuals or groups under sanctions. The increasing use of sanctions, particularly in the context of the so-called 'War on Terror' (Drezner, 2011), has prompted concerns about their applicability to academic research and the possibility that researchers who interview sanctioned people could face legal penalties (Reno, 2013). These concerns were directly relevant to me as a US national because the US government imposed sanctions on both the FDLR and M23 shortly before I began my field research in the DRC. The US sanctions regime for the DRC prohibits 'transactions by US persons' that 'involve transferring, paying, exporting, withdrawing, or otherwise dealing in the interests or property of' identified entities. I thus designed my research to comply with this requirement (US Department of the Treasury, 2013, p 3). However, with the definition of 'transactions' not fully clear in either the relevant statute or case law, my university's research compliance office expressed concerns that interviews with active members of the FDLR or M23 might constitute prohibited transactions. I therefore applied for and obtained a licence from the US Treasury Department's Office of Foreign Assets Control (OFAC No DRC-2013-304304-1) that authorised interviews with members of these groups, conditional on not providing compensation to participants. Relieved at having obtained this licence after a long, uncertain application process, I then turned my attention to the practicalities of my research, confident that my ethical and legal obligations would be fulfilled, and that I would be doing good in some sense so long as I abided by the terms of my OFAC license and my IRB protocol.

It was only after I started conducting interviews and writing up my findings that I began to seriously consider the possibility that my research might unintentionally aid perpetrators and abet future atrocities. To the extent that my experience is reflective of the experiences of other academics who interview perpetrators and report their perspectives on violence, it would seem that ethical evaluations of such research are omitting a potentially important factor, namely, the possible mechanisms by which academic research involving interviews with perpetrators may aid perpetrators and abet future atrocities, intentionally or inadvertently.

Aiding perpetrators and abetting atrocities

A key concern that thus requires greater attention is the extent to which research incorporating interviews with perpetrators can abet future atrocities. The published versions of recent academic studies on violence have generally not addressed this question, and there has been little discussion of this question in the broader literature on the ethics and practice of researching violence and atrocities. To the extent that the authors of studies on which I modelled my research did openly discuss the potential effects of reporting perpetrators' perspectives, it was generally to express hope that their findings would yield positive benefits, similar in many ways to my expectation mentioned above. For instance, in the preface to *Inside rebellion*, Weinstein (2007, pp xvi–xvii) writes:

> I am indebted to the individuals who patiently told me their stories and answered my questions.... Although this book cannot possibly give voice to each of their individual experiences, I hope that it does make a contribution to the historical record and provide part of an explanation for the violence experienced in Uganda, Mozambique, and Peru.

However, researchers in other fields who have interviewed perpetrators of criminal or otherwise 'atrocious' behaviour, including criminologists, historians and sociologists, have considered the possibility that research may abet such behaviour more extensively. In a critical reflection on the ethics of an ethnographic study involving interactions with teenage drug dealers, Vanderstay (2005, p 372) explained how, in the course of his research he had 'inadvertently provided the funds a teenage cocaine dealer used to buy crack from his supplier', and thereby contributed to a catastrophic chain of events, including 'several drug deals, a murder, the arrest and imprisonment of my subject, and the ruin of his mother.' Drawing from this and other reflections on the ethics of interviewing perpetrators, as well as my own experiences in the DRC, the following suggests two specific mechanisms by which academic research involving interactions with perpetrators may abet atrocities: direct assistance and dissemination.

Direct assistance

The mechanism here referred to as direct assistance involves the provision of monetary compensation, other forms of material assistance or benefits and/or information to research participants, either as a condition for participation in the study, an element of the study itself or indirectly. Compensating participants is common practice in criminology, to the point that the 'ability to provide remuneration' has been characterised as a 'taken-for granted aspect of convincing active criminals to take part in social science research' (Jacques and Wright, 2008, p 30). This practice appears to be somewhat less common (or at least not widely reported) in observational research on violence and atrocities employing surveys or interviews with former or current combatants. There is no mention of participant compensation in publicly available protocols or reports of various prominent ex-combatant surveys, such as the Post-Conflict Reintegration Initiative for Development and Empowerment (PRIDE) survey in Sierra Leone (Humphreys and Weinstein, 2006) or the Aceh Reintegration and Livelihood Survey Survey (ARLS; see Barron et al, 2005). The ARLS protocol, for instance, cites the possibilities for respondents to 'help contribute to a broad understanding of the needs in your village' and 'voice their opinions about matters that are important' (Barron et al, 2005, p 19) as the sole potential benefits to participants. While seemingly less common in observational studies, the provision of money or other benefits to subjects is a central element in the burgeoning field of experimental research on political violence; indeed, such research is typically designed to evaluate the impact of an intervention involving the provision of various goods, services or information to subjects (Blattman and Annan, 2015).

As either a core element of experimental research or in observational studies employing surveys or interviews with combatants, the provision of monetary compensation or other material benefits has several important advantages for researchers. Most importantly, perhaps, is facilitating access. Like active criminals recruited for criminological studies, former (and particularly) current combatants are members of 'hidden populations' that may be otherwise difficult to locate and access (Dunlap and Johnson, 1999, p 127). The promise of compensation or other benefits can provide a useful entry point for researchers. Furthermore, prospective interviewees may expect or demand compensation for participation, resulting in foregone opportunities for researchers unwilling or unable to pay, or awkward (and potentially dangerous) encounters where targeted respondents demand compensation before or after interviews. In the course of my research several participants explicitly refused to engage without compensation, and I was accordingly forced to cancel these interviews. Beyond facilitating access, researchers who spend considerable time interacting with perpetrators may, as noted by Vanderstay (2005), develop empathy for participants and their families, and thereby feel obliged to provide some form of material assistance. While there may be legal obstacles to providing compensation or other material benefits to interview participants under sanctions (depending on the researcher's nationality and affiliation), these concerns are only applicable to a small sub-set of possible interviewees. Despite the Congolese national army's well-documented history of atrocities, I was able to interview members of this organisation without a US government licence because the army had not been formally sanctioned.

Finally, even where research protocols do not include provision of compensation or other benefits, researchers may inadvertently provide valuable information to subjects in the course of interviews or polite pleasantries. Answering seemingly innocuous questions about travel and/or conditions in other areas may provide militarily useful information to combatants involved in atrocities. I became aware of this possibility first hand during my interviews with FDLR members in North Kivu, when a commander repeatedly asked me about my travel plans and road conditions at the end of the interview. There are consequently strong incentives, only weak obstacles (at least in the case of non-sanctioned subjects), and many unintentional opportunities for researchers to provide direct assistance to perpetrators.

The provision of monetary or other forms of compensation may abet future atrocities by materially strengthening perpetrators and their organisations. The possibility has been particularly noted in reflections on the ethics of compensating drug users in criminology, specifically the potential that subjects might use payments to fund further drug purchases (Ritter et al, 2003, p 2). Applying this logic to interviews with perpetrators of atrocities, monetary or material compensation provided to research subjects could potentially be used (or converted) for a wide range of purposes that may enhance organisational capacity to commit future atrocities, including the procurement of weapons and other military supplies, paying personnel or incentivising new recruits to join. Moreover, information gleaned through conversations with researchers could be used to plan military operations that entail atrocities. In any case, researchers generally have no way of monitoring or ensuring that funds, benefits or information provided to subjects are not used for military operations involving atrocities, particularly after departing the field.

Dissemination

The dissemination of an individual or organisation's ideology or broader 'story' can be a further possible means by which research with perpetrators leads to future atrocities. Research findings that reveal aspects of the individual or group's history, current conditions and political justifications for violence can become powerful narratives if heard by sympathetic ears. This may abet atrocities by garnering support from third-party actors, thereby enhancing the individual or organisation's legitimacy, material capacity or recruitment.

Intentional dissemination may occur when researchers build rapport and begin to empathise with participants in the course of research.

This is possible even for scholars motivated by the normative goal of preventing future violence or who begin research, 'prepared to hate and fear [their] informants, to find them repellent', and accordingly expect 'no rapport, no shared assumptions, no commonality or thought or experience' (Blee, 1993, p 604). Even in such cases, interactions with perpetrators may reveal unexpected sources of shared experience that confound the researcher's expectations and provoke empathy for the individual subject or group, if not their ideology.

My experiences interviewing members of the FDLR in the DRC similarly confounded my expectations. Based on the organisation's history of atrocities, I assumed that interviewees would be hostile, overtly manipulative and evasive at best, and openly threatening or violent at worst. Although several participants did fit this bill, most interviewees were relatively polite, pleasant and seemingly forthcoming in their responses to my questions. The material conditions in which I met interviewees often provoked empathy, as in the case of FDLR members whom I met in a dilapidated, dark hut in a remote, impoverished village in the Kivus. Empathy was further provoked during this encounter through the presence of crowds of civilians whom an interviewee claimed to be Rwandan Hutu refugees under the FDLR's protection. At the same time, I was constantly reminded of the FDLR's genocidal ideology and history of atrocities as group members implicitly referenced the themes of 'Hutu Power' while discussing their perceptions of the ICC and other international courts. This tension was uncomfortable for me, as I found myself empathising on a personal level with interview subjects, but being constantly reminded of their involvement in mass violence.

Despite some empathy for the perpetrators I interviewed, I was not consciously motivated to disseminate their ideology or 'story', at least beyond the elements relevant to my research on their involvement. Even so, there remains the possibility of unintentionally disseminating an individual or organisation's ideology or story, and thereby attracting broader sympathy or support for their cause. Indeed, disseminating some aspect of the subject's story is unavoidable when researchers employ interviews, and the only sure way to avoid dissemination is to refrain from using or reporting interview data. However, this strategy raises its own ethical dilemmas, as it conflicts with a researcher's duty to report their findings and the broader research goal of furthering understandings of violence. Furthermore, the opportunity for subjects to 'tell their stories' is often presented as a possible, and sometimes the only, benefit of participation in research. Interviewing perpetrators and then refraining from using data from these interviews to avoid disseminating the subject's ideology or story may therefore conflict with promises made to interviewees and broader ethical principles relating to informed consent and the recruitment of research subjects.

Notwithstanding these potential conflicts of ethical principles, there remains the possibility that academic research will provide a forum for the dissemination of ideologies or stories that advance the interests of perpetrators and, in doing so, abet future atrocities. Beyond simply telling their stories, research participants or their organisations may perceive engagement in academic research as an opportunity to garner broader empathy and support for their causes. In reflecting on an oral history interview with a former Nazi leader in the US, Koonz (1987, p xvii, cited in Blee, 1993, p 605) noted:

> I realized that I had come to get information and she intended to give me a sanitized version of Nazism that would normalize the Hitler state in the minds of contemporaries. She saw the chance to share her views with an American as a way of taking her message to not only a younger generation, but a new audience.

Perhaps less insidiously, but no less problematic, individual participants may also present narratives reflecting deeply held, or indoctrinated, beliefs justifying participation in violence that may advance the interests of perpetrators when publicised in academic research. Ezekiel (1995) noted that neo-Nazis and KKK (Ku Klux Klan) members interviewed for a study on racism in the US typically cited experiences or perceptions of victimhood to justify participation in violence; similarly, the FDLR members I interviewed universally presented themselves as victims of oppression by the current Rwandan government or the international community. Beyond reporting the deeply held beliefs of perpetrators, and thereby advancing their justifications for violence, research that relies on interviews with perpetrators may also underestimate or under-report the severity of atrocities. Those taking part in the research may present an excessively 'cozy view of the past' that minimalises violence, either in order to impress the researcher or advance a particular version of the individual or organisation's story, or due to the psychological neutralisation of past involvement in violence (Hay, 1981, p 41). Despite evidence to the contrary, several members of the FDLR I interviewed argued that reports of their organisation's involvement in atrocities had been greatly exaggerated. In reporting such perspectives without qualification, context or verification, researchers risk indirectly advancing the narratives of perpetrators by effectively 'muting' past violence (Blee, 1993, p 601).

Minimising risk: understanding FDLR motivation for participation in my fieldwork

I began to recognise the dangers of supporting the FDLR after returning from the DRC as I wrote up my findings and reflected on the potential motives for FDLR members to participate in my research. I started by considering the objective circumstances facing the FDLR when I conducted my interviews in summer 2014. At this time, the FDLR faced increasingly dire military and political prospects. It remained a formidable force, one of 'the most significant and abusive armed groups' in the DRC, according to a non-governmental organisation (NGO) report issued in November 2014 (Enough Team, 2014, p 1). Nonetheless, the FDLR's military strength had declined from a strength of between 15,000 to 20,000 fighters in 2003 (International Crisis Group, 2003, p 5) to approximately 15,00 by the summer of 2014 (UN, 2014, para 42). This decline resulted principally from battlefield losses and attrition in the course of a series of offensives by Congolese and Rwandan government forces and the UN peacekeeping operation in the DRC from 2009 through to 2012, and as a result of fighting with various local self-defence militias (Stearns et al, 2013; DRC Affinity Group 2014). The FDLR had also lost control over major swaths of territory, and although it retained control of lucrative mining operations in eastern DRC, it had been deprived of an important source of financing from the Rwandan Hutu diaspora community – as well as important public platforms for disseminating its ideology – with the imposition of international sanctions and a crackdown against the FDLR's political leadership in Europe (UN, 2010b, 2011). Finally, shortly before I started my interviews with FDLR members in the summer of 2014, the International Conference of the Great Lakes Region (ICGLR) and the Southern African Development Community (SADC) issued a joint ultimatum for the FDLR to voluntarily surrender by January 2015 or face military action (ICGLR-SADC, 2014).

These objective circumstances suggested that FDLR members might have been motivated to participate in my research study by the prospect of material benefits to alleviate the organisation's increasingly dire circumstances and/or the opportunity to disseminate its ideology, either in order to garner third-party support or influence debates about international military action. Consistent with these inferences, multiple interviewees asked for assistance in providing material assistance or telling the FDLR's 'story' to the world. First, several FDLR members directly requested some form of monetary or material benefits (which I declined to provide, in accordance with my OFAC licence), either in exchange for their participation, as a donation to the Rwandan Hutu refugees they claimed to represent, or as a personal favour. While several subjects asked for money, others asked for basic food or medical supplies (salt was a particularly popular request). Combined with the dire circumstances confronting the FDLR and the deprivation I observed in the villages where I conducted interviews, these requests suggested individuals who perceived participation in research as an opportunity to obtain much-needed material assistance. Beyond requests for monetary and material assistance, some FDLR members, including the commander referenced at the beginning of this chapter, implored me to tell the 'truth' about their organisation to the world. In this widely discredited version of the 'truth', the FDLR is an organisation of refugees and 'freedom fighters' who seek only to return to Rwanda and establish democracy, but who have been demonised and wrongly accused of atrocities by the oppressive Rwandan government and its international supporters (FDLR, 2013).

Conclusion

This chapter has examined the ethical implications of interacting with perpetrators in the course of academic research on political violence, focusing on the possibility that such research may aid perpetrators and abet future atrocities. Based on first-hand experiences interviewing alleged perpetrators of atrocities in the DRC and studies in other fields involving interactions with perpetrators of violence or other illicit behaviour, I have identified two mechanisms by which researchers might abet atrocities: direct assistance, whereby researchers provide monetary compensation, material benefits or information that enhances an individual or organisation's capacity to perpetrate atrocities, and dissemination, whereby research provides a platform for the spread of an individual or organisation's ideology or 'story'. Given the potential for abetting atrocities, how do researchers interested in understanding violence manage these ethical sensitivities? At one extreme, researchers could forego all interactions with perpetrators of atrocities. However, even research that does not involve direct interactions with perpetrators may plausibly abet atrocities, so this 'solution' might require refraining from all research on atrocities. Furthermore, refraining from interacting with perpetrators would also forego the substantial benefits of such research for furthering understanding atrocities. At another extreme, researchers might disavow responsibility for any perverse effects of their research, particularly insofar as these effects are unintended or beyond the researcher's control. However, this approach is both normatively unsatisfying, at least for researchers motivated by the goal of preventing future atrocities, and arguably inconsistent with broader ethical principles of beneficence in research.

To manage this dilemma, it is necessary for researchers of violence to more systematically account for the possibility that their research might aid perpetrators and abet atrocities in their assessments of the ethical implications of their research. Operationally, this would involve bearing in mind the potential risks of abetting atrocities at all stages of the research process, from design to publication, and taking steps to minimise these risks. As a first, but necessarily incomplete, step toward identifying these factors, I specifically propose that researchers should be more attentive to the possible motives for perpetrators to participate in such research. Perpetrators of atrocities may have various motives for participating in academic research, and it is often difficult to discern any individual subject's precise motives, particularly insofar as subjects may conceal or misrepresent these motives. Furthermore, it is arguably impossible for an outside researcher to fully understand the motives of an individual participant. Nonetheless, knowledge about the participant's organisation and individual background, and their questions, responses and behaviour while interacting with the researcher, can suggest possible motives for participation. In turn, understanding these motives can offer insights into the benefits research participants may derive from involvement, and the possibility that research may aid perpetrators and abet atrocities.

References

Akhavan, P. (2001) 'Beyond impunity: Can international criminal justice prevent future atrocities?', *American Journal of International Law*, vol 95, no 1, pp 7–31.

Akhavan, P. (2009) 'Are international criminal tribunals a disincentive to peace? Reconciling judicial romanticism with political realism', *Human Rights Quarterly*, vol 31, no 3, pp 624–54.

Autesserre, S. (2010) *The trouble with the Congo: Local violence and the failure of international peacebuilding*, Cambridge: Cambridge University Press.

Barron, P., Humphreys, M., Paler, L., Tajima, Y. and Weinstein, J. (2005) *BRA-KDP main household and Ex-GAM survey*, Aceh Reintegration and Livelihoods Survey.

Blattman, C. and Annan, J. (2015) *Can employment reduce lawlessness and rebellion? A field experiment with high-risk men in a fragile state*, Social Science Research Network Working Paper.

Blee, K.M. (1993) 'Evidence, empathy, and ethics: Lessons from oral histories of the Klan', *The Journal of American History*, vol 80, no 2, pp 596–606.

Cohen, D.K. (2013) 'Explaining rape during civil war: Cross-national evidence (1989–2009)', *American Political Science Review*, vol 107, no 3, pp 461–77.

DRC Affinity Group (2014) *FDLR: Past, present, and policies*, SSRC: Conflict Resolution and Peace Forum.

Drezner, D.W. (2011) 'Sanctions sometimes smart: Targeted sanctions in theory and practice', *International Studies Review*, vol 13, no 1, pp 96–108.

Dunlap, E. and Johnson, B.D. (1999) 'Gaining access to hidden populations: Strategies for gaining cooperation of drug sellers/dealers and their families in ethnographic research', *Drugs and Society*, vol 14, pp 127–49.

Enough Team (2014) *How to dismantle a deadly militia*, Enough Project.

Ezekiel, R.S. (1995) *The racist mind: Portraits of Neo-Nazis and Klansmen*, New York: Penguin.

FDLR (Forces démocratiques de libération du Rwanda) (2013) *Response to the Statement of the UN Security Council President*, 30 November.

Gilligan, M. (2006) 'Is enforcement necessary for effectiveness? A model of the international criminal regime', *International Organization*, vol 60, no 4, pp 935–67.

Goldsmith, J. and Krasner, S. (2003) 'The limits of idealism', *Daedalus*, vol 132, no 1, pp 47–63.

Hay, C. (1981) 'The pangs of the past', *Oral History*, vol 9, no 1, pp 41–6.

Human Rights Watch (2009) *'You will be punished': Attacks on civilians in Eastern Congo*, HRW Document 1-56543-582-2.

Humphreys, M. and Weinstein, J. (2006) 'Handling and manhandling civilians in civil war', *American Political Science Review*, vol 100, no 3, pp 429–47.

ICC (International Criminal Court) (2010) *Decision on the Prosecutor's application for a warrant of arrest against Callixte Mbarushimana*, ICC Document No ICC-01/04-01/10-1-US.

ICC (2012) *Decision on the Prosecutor's application under Article 58* [public redacted version], ICC Document No ICC-01/04-01/12-1-Red.

ICGLR (International Conference for the Great Lakes Region)–SADC (South African Development Community) (2014) *Third Joint ICGRL-SADC meeting: Joint Communique*, Luanda.

International Crisis Group (2003) 'Rwandan Hutu rebels in the Congo: A new approach to disarmament and reintegration', Africa Briefing No 63.

International Crisis Group (2005) 'The Congo: Solving the FDLR problem once and for all', Africa Briefing No 25.

Jacques, S. and Wright, R. (2008) 'Intimacy with outlaws: The role of relational distance in recruiting, paying, and interviewing underworld research participants', *Journal of Research in Crime and Delinquency*, vol 45, no 1, pp 22–38.

Koonz, C. (1987) *Mothers in the fatherland: Women, the family, and Nazi politics*, New York: Routledge.

Reno, W. (2013) 'The problem of extraterritorial legality', in L. Mosley (ed) *Interview research in political science*, Ithaca, NY: Cornell University Press, pp 159–79.

Ritter, A., Fry, C. and Swan, A. (2003) 'The ethics of reimbursing injecting drug users for public health research interviews: What price are we prepared to pay?' *International Journal of Drug Policy*, vol 14, no 1, pp 1–3.

Sikkink, K. (2011) *The justice cascade: How human rights prosecutions are changing world politics*, New York: W.W. Norton.

Snyder, J. and Vinjamuri, L. (2003) 'Trials and errors: Principle and pragmatism in strategies of international justice,' *International Security*, vol 28, no 3, pp 5–44.

Stearns, J.K. et al (2013) *Raia Mutomboki: The flawed peace process in the DRC and the birth of an armed franchise*, Nairobi: Rift Valley Institute – Usalama Project.

Thoms, O., Ron, J. and Paris, R. (2010) 'State-level effects of transitional justice: What do we know?,' *International Journal of Transitional Justice*, vol 4, no 3, pp 329–54.

UN (United Nations) (2010a) *Report of the mapping exercise documenting the most serious violations of human rights and international humanitarian law committed within the territory of the Democratic Republic of the Congo between March 1993 and June 2003*, June.

UN (2010b) *Final report of the Group of Experts on the DRC submitted in accordance with paragraph 6 of Security Council resolution 1896 (2009)*, UN Document S/2010/596, 29 November.

UN (2011) *Final report of the Group of Experts on the Democratic Republic of the Congo submitted in accordance with paragraph 5 of Security Council resolution 1956 (2010)*, UN Document S/2011/738, 2 December.

US (United States) Department of the Treasury (2013) *Democratic Republic of the Congo sanctions program*, Washington, DC.

Vanderstay, S.L. (2005) 'One hundred dollars and a dead man: Ethical decision making in an ethnographic framework', *Journal of Contemporary Ethnography*, vol 34, no 4, pp 371–409.

Weinstein, J.M. (2007) *Inside rebellion: The politics of insurgent violence*, Cambridge: Cambridge University Press.

11

Empathy as a critical methodological tool in peace research

Sinéad Walsh

Introduction

Peace research aims to reduce violence by understanding its root causes and developing strategies for local and global justice (Galtung, 1969; Wallensteen, 2001). In practice, this normative agenda is connected to an affective economy where empathy, loosely understood as fellow feeling, is an important element (Pedwell, 2012a; see also Ahmed, 2004). Drawing on my PhD research with women's non-governmental organisations (NGOs) in Armenia and Azerbaijan, this chapter argues that critical attention to the ambiguities of empathy in and beyond the fieldwork context can yield important insights into positionality, power relations and knowledge production. This can potentially foster affective self-transformation (Bartky, 1996, cited in Pedwell, 2012b, p 164), and prompt us to think more deeply about transnational feminist solidarity (Hemmings, 2012).

Empathy is understood here as 'an active process of emotion and imagination that can play a role in catalysing thought and action' (Gray, 2011, p 226). As such, it refers to both an automatic, embodied perception of what another person is feeling, and a distinct cognitive effort to see a particular event or set of circumstances from the other's perspective. Although empathy can be a valuable research tool, it carries ethical and emotional risks that are of particular concern in peace and conflict settings. The relational nature of empathy necessitates critical reflection on the positions and politics of the researcher. To illustrate this, I focus predominantly on 12 months of fieldwork that I conducted in Azerbaijan and Armenia between September 2012 and October 2014. A reflexive narrative on this experience discusses the dangers of appropriation, exploitation and exclusion of others' experiences (Spelman, 1997; Ackerly and True, 2008), as well as the impact of role confusion and burnout (Bloor et al, 2007).

The chapter begins with an overview of the research project, emphasising the unpredictable influence that empathetic relationships had on the research process. I argue that friendships formed in the field can help to expand methodological boundaries while bringing questions about researcher privilege and positionality to the fore. This is followed by a discussion of the different ways that empathy can be invoked during ethnographic fieldwork. It highlights the impact of emotional identification and perspective-taking on peace research when violence and insecurity are woven into the fabric of everyday life. Finally, I discuss how the emotional and ethical challenges of fieldwork spill over into the process of analysis and representation. This shows how the politics of location, power and agency cut across transnational research agendas, complicating the efforts of feminists and peace researchers to bring about social change.

Contextualising research relations

The focus of my PhD was women's activism and peacebuilding in Armenia and Azerbaijan. It sought to understand how women's NGOs and civil society networks navigated the tensions between gender politics and national identity (Yuval-Davis, 1997), and what role(s) they aspired to play in the peace process. At the core of the research was the war over Nagorno-Karabakh (1988–94), which occurred when Armenians, in what was then an autonomous region of Azerbaijan, first sought unification with the republic of Armenia and later aspired to full independence. Some 30,000 people were killed, and up to a million displaced by the violence, leading to a ceasefire that has facilitated the emergence of a de facto state in Nagorno-Karabakh, while depriving hundreds of thousands of people of the right to return to their homes (de Waal, 2003). Previous research on women's activism discussed patriotic and civic initiatives, but made little or no mention of women's involvement in peacemaking (see, for example, Ishkanian, 2004; Tohidi, 2004). My research aimed to address this gap, while at the same time adopting a critical perspective on the relationship between international feminist discourse and local women's activism. A central objective was to contrast the place of home, community and nation in women's lives (Grewal and Kaplan, 1994; Mohanty, 2003) with the discursive norms of the international agenda on Women, Peace and Security (Cohn, 2008; Gibbings, 2011).

The choice of Armenia and Azerbaijan followed from five years studying the culture and politics of the former Soviet Union. Two of those years were spent living in Russia, where I was involved in intercultural dialogue and civic activism. Researching the South Caucasus would build on my attachment to Russia and at the same time complicate it by introducing the perspective of citizens in the newly independent states. While I expected my linguistic and sociocultural competences would help provide access to the urban, Russian-speaking population in Baku and Yerevan, it was unclear how my relationships with and beyond women's organisations would progress. Preliminary emails sent to women's NGOs returned some interest in the project, but respondents were reluctant to discuss the details of their peacebuilding activities before my arrival in the field. While this highlights the connections between trust, familiarity and access, it could also be considered symptomatic of a fluid environment in which the best laid plans can be derailed by political circumstances.

The research design proposed that semi-structured interviews would be carried out with a wide sample of women who were actively involved with women's NGOs, and preferably engaged in peacebuilding. This meant that the focus was drawn to relatively privileged urban elites, who were poised at the intersection of local and global civil society. Even so, I was conscious of the risks of re-traumatisation (Bell, 2001), and planned to avoid asking women direct questions about their experiences of violence and war. Instead, I hoped to build up a gradual insight into sensitive topics and to gain the trust of women who became involved in the research by spending an extended period in both field sites (Browne and McBride, 2015). This would offer opportunities for observation and participation in informal research spaces, echoing the idea of feminist researchers as supplicants, 'seeking reciprocal relationships based on empathy and mutual respect, and often sharing their knowledge with those they research' (England, 1994, p 82).

While this suggests that the research design incorporated a relational view of fieldwork, the nature and extent of those relationships was impossible to predict. Having arrived in the field with nothing more than a few phone numbers, I soon developed a warm relationship with some women who first invited me to volunteer with their NGO, and later arranged for my participation in a peacebuilding seminar for young women from Armenia and Azerbaijan. This was the first of several intensive, three- to four-day seminars that I attended over a two- year period, all the time developing my friendship with the core participants. On our return to Baku or Yerevan, I found that several of these women were increasingly open to talking about emotionally and politically sensitive topics. They also spoke about the challenges of growing up in a patriarchal and corrupt society, and asked about my personal and political experiences as young woman from an Irish background. Some of them introduced me to their friends and families, and encouraged me to travel and speak with people in rural and conflict-affected areas, including those who were opposed to peacebuilding.

As these relationships grew stronger, the scope of the research grew wider and deeper, drawing on personal resources of empathy and openness. Although this can be seen as an instinctive or personality-led approach (Moser, 2008), the risks of exploitative research relationships still demand close attention to how we negotiate our positions in the field (Browne, 2003). This methodological issue can be mapped on to political tensions found in transnational research and activism. Feminist critiques of empathy emphasise that it is often a marker of privilege, producing a liberal discourse that works to reinforce hierarchical boundaries and obscure structural injustices (Pedwell, 2012b). Clare Hemmings articulates the problem thus: on the one hand, 'empathy prioritises embodied knowledge, affective connection and a desire to transform the social terrain', but on the other, 'presumptions of empathy underplay the profound classed and raced differences within feminism that cannot simply be transcended by a feminist will to connection' (2012, pp 151–2).

While an understanding of positionality is essential to transnational feminist research, it is important to point out that identity politics are not always straightforward. As former Soviet republics, Armenia and Azerbaijan relate primarily to Russia as a (former) imperial power, and have an ambiguous relationship with Western institutions. Many of my research participants identified as culturally and politically European, and several had studied or worked for a period in Western countries. At the same time, many were disillusioned by the failure of the post-Soviet liberal transitions and critical of European policies towards regional conflicts and authoritarianism. The tensions between post-socialism and transnational feminism (Suchland, 2011), together with escalating political tensions in 2013 and 2014, led to a heightened awareness of my privileged citizenship. This, in turn, made me more conscious of risks relating to both the physical safety of participants and their emotional security in the context of unfolding research relationships.

These themes of ethical and emotional risks recur throughout the remainder of this chapter in a way that mirrors the non-linear nature of the research process itself. Ackerly and True (2008, p 694) argue that a feminist research ethic is critically aware of 'the power of epistemology, boundaries, relationships and the situatedness of the researcher', and claim that this 'requires the researcher to note points of decision, often to return to them for further reflection' (Ackerly and True, 2008, p

700). The act of returning to the site of the research, both figuratively and literally, denoted for me the over-arching function of care in feminist methodology (Robinson, 2006). This is not intended to reify gendered essentialisms, but to make a broader claim about the role of respect, empathy and trust in research relationships, and the possibility of 'empathetic cooperation' as 'a navigational method for politics at borderlands' (Sylvester, 1994, p 326).

Encountering violence in fieldwork

Despite its focus on positive social transformation, peace research operates in sites where the legacies of violence are ever present. This is true even when war and mass killing have diminished to low-intensity conflict and political stalemate, as in the case of Armenia and Azerbaijan. My interviews in Armenia and Azerbaijan provided a deeper insight into this process. One of my initial questions was concerned with establishing women's motivation for engaging in peacebuilding. This question was originally intended to help establish a positive tone for the conversation and elicit some general, shared principles before moving on to more sensitive subjects. However, it often led directly to women recounting their personal experience of conflict, and/or the continued suffering of families and villages caught in the crossfire. Many women related their participation in cross-border dialogue to a framework of community, territory and national identity rather than expressing a strong orientation towards future reconciliation (Walsh, 2015).

The stories some women told during interviews were mirrored in informal conversations that took place against the backdrop of everyday life. Although I explained that my research was about peacebuilding, and avoided asking leading questions about the war itself, it was impossible to overlook the extent to which people embraced the opportunity to share their war stories with an outsider (Wood, 2006, p 378). Their unprompted eye-witness recollections told of burning villages, bombed-out schools, civilians coming under fire, casualties of landmine explosions and families fleeing their homes and becoming destitute. Both female and male acquaintances of various ages and social backgrounds spoke to me about their family members or neighbours who were killed or had disappeared. Sometimes the same events were recounted from the perspective of two or three generations in the same family. Friends and strangers described the pain of having lost part of their childhood, their fear of forgetting what 'home' was like, and the obligations they felt towards their families and all those who struggled as a result of the conflict.

My research plan had not accounted for such vivid – and frequently harrowing – personal recollections becoming part of the data. Nevertheless, they became indicative of the context in which peacebuilding initiatives attempted to function. They illuminated the broader social discourse on violence, which included commemoration of national tragedies in prominent urban spaces (such as Martyrs' Alley in Baku and the genocide memorial complex in Yerevan) and prolific media campaigns that circulated online around the anniversaries of significant losses and victories.[1] They drew attention to ongoing structural violence endured by refugees, internally displaced people and communities living in or near the conflict zone, as well as to routine ceasefire violations, frontline casualties and the risks inherent in military conscription, which is compulsory for men in both countries. When discussing these topics, peacebuilders were often moved to express anger and despair, or to use black humour as a way of navigating difficult motions.

Christine Sylvester has used the term 'empathetic cooperation' to describe 'a process of positional slippage that occurs when one listens seriously to the concerns, fears and agendas of those one is unaccustomed to heeding when building social theory' (1994, p 317). To ignore the extent of the violence and insecurity I encountered would have been to perpetuate the silences and exclusions that have characterised international engagement with the Nagorno-Karabakh conflict for two decades. It would also have gone against a central aim of the research, which was to contextualise women's peacebuilding initiatives and account for doubt and ambivalence. Indeed, friends within this closed network frequently encouraged me to look beyond their narrow community and record the perspectives that existed both in the mainstream and on the margins of society. They saw the potential results of the research as not only speaking to international policy-makers and analysts, but as helping to advance the dialogue between women in Armenian and Azerbaijani society.

Understood in terms of relationality and reciprocity, empathy can broaden the scope of fieldwork and even realign the research aims. However, empathy can also be understood differentially in terms of various kinds of encounters. In qualitative research, empathy has been identified as a means of establishing rapport in interviews, sometimes leading to 'therapeutic opportunities', in which people reveal intimate details about their lives, including personal traumas and secrets (Dickson-Swift et al, 2007; see Chapter 1, this volume). Given the emotional risks this poses to both interviewees and researchers, Brounéus argues that empathetic listening must be accompanied by 'an ethical judgment of when it is time to stop' (2011, p 137). This 'research-therapy gap' can become even more complicated when the researcher becomes friends with participants. Over time, some people disclosed large amounts of sensitive information to me, often during informal conversations. The cumulative effect of these confidences was over-whelming, and I felt torn between the empathetic response that came to me as a friend, and the desire to record and analyse the 'data' being provided. The emotional impact their disclosures had on me was compounded by my fear that they would begin to view our relationship as an exploitative one.

While friendships work to create emotional affinity, empathy serves a wider purpose by helping us to understand the perspectives of those with whom we have less in common, or with whom we disagree on fundamental issues. In conflict settings, this can mean stepping into the shoes of someone who is an advocate of war, or who promotes an ideology of ethno-nationalism (Jacoby, 2006; Parashar, 2011). Not all violent stories are told in order to achieve emotional catharsis; some may seek to shock, enrage or shame the listener into changing their position or taking further action (Clark, 2012; see also Pedwell, 2013). On some occasions, I struggled to differentiate between a partial but honest account of conflict, and a narrative that was designed to sway my (perceived) neutrality by portraying aggressors and victims in a clear-cut fashion. Attempting to discern the expectations that people had from these encounters, while at the same time forming an understanding of the experiences they related, was often an exhausting process. On top of this, it often revealed my own biases, to the point where I seldom felt able to challenge militant viewpoints or historical inaccuracy.

Ironically, maintaining a conscious stance of empathy resulted in my sometimes feeling ambivalent about peace and violence. Many long-term peacebuilders told me that they thought a return to war was inevitable, and that the work they were doing was personally fulfilling but politically futile. Others struggled with and occasionally abandoned efforts at dialogue. In August 2014, the region experienced the most serious escalation of violence in 20 years. There were dozens of fatalities on both sides, and rumours of impending war abounded. During this period, only a small number of my acquaintances publicly declared their outright opposition to war as feminists and anti-militarists. Some made patriotic arguments, stating, for example, that there was a time for peacebuilding and a time for self-defence. Others remained silent, which could have been a refusal to condone war *or* to condemn it, or even an expression of paralysis in the face of 'too many or conflicting claims on our sense of empathy and moral obligation' (Crawford, 2014, p 452).

Understanding how people respond to violence and polarisation requires an awareness of pressures they face from family, friends and society at large. For people who are affected by conflict on a daily basis, including in ways that threaten their right to existence, empathising with the other group is a luxury they may not always be able to afford. Failure to empathise with one's own group, on the other hand, carries a similar cost of 'social exclusion, shame of embarrassment' (Head, 2016, p 181). Head identifies material and embodied risks associated with (the wrong kind of) empathy, including physical violence and intimidation, and feelings of vulnerability and exhaustion (Head, 2016, p 184). On several occasions, women told me they kept their peacebuilding activities secret from neighbours and colleagues for fear of endangering their families or losing their jobs. Others spoke about receiving hate mail or threats, and some were explicit about government surveillance of cross-border dialogue groups. Silence requires its own form of reflexive listening, and as with the other elements of fieldwork discussed here, can continue to echo across the later stages of the research process.

Emotions, ethics and representation

While fieldwork is usually an emotionally exhausting experience, it would be disingenuous to suggest that the affective weight of fieldwork disappears if and when the researcher returns to the secure folds of academic life – in another word, home. Although researchers are often reluctant to name their emotions or describe the way they impact on daily life, it is not uncommon to acknowledge an aversion to reading over one's field notes, transcribing interviews, or pushing ahead with a line of analysis (Hoglund, 2011, p 126). Some have described being overwhelmed by confidential data, haunted by the memories of intense or violent encounters, and too anxious or upset to discuss the experience with family, friends and colleagues (Drozdzewski, 2015; Emerald and Carpenter, 2015). While some researchers find ways to readjust, others desire nothing more than to leave again as quickly as possible. Given that peace research often does entail recurring visits to a particular site, and sometimes leads to non-academic employment opportunities in the field, the period of analysis and representation might well be considered an opportunity for personal and professional growth.

Academic conferences can be a site of performance where novice researchers attempt to resolve some of the confusion and challenges they experienced during fieldwork. Presenting an analysis in front of our peers and more senior academics forces us to make decisions about the representation of ourselves and others that go to the heart of research relationships. My experience of this was marked by contradictions, as each opportunity to discuss my work seemed to bring increasing anxiety about the prospect of doing so. A recurring concern was that few academics in feminist international relations or peace studies specialise in the South Caucasus or even the former Soviet Union, and that this lack of awareness contributes to the tensions between post-socialism and transnational feminism (Koobak and Marling, 2014). Rather than focusing on my application of feminist theory, my presentations often dwelt on the dynamics of conflict and ongoing, or imminent, political crises. Quoting at length from interviews and including images such as the ruined villages close to the border, I hoped that my listeners would engage with the data on an emotional level (Scheper-Hughes, 1995), recognise the agency of the speakers and identify with their efforts to resist Russian and Western forms of imperialism.

Representing our research in a way that does not attempt to mask emotional attachment to the field raises feelings of vulnerability (Behar, 1997). It causes us to relive distressing memories, and raises concerns about our ability to manage a complex range of emotions. These can include fear that we will not be taken seriously, guilt at potentially misrepresenting participants, shame at having left the field without making a real difference and desire to either return at once or abandon it altogether. Given the pervasive myth of the 'superhuman feminist researcher' (Marshall, 2011), it is important to acknowledge that:

> Emotion in (and as) research is an experience shared by all researchers. Some deny it. Some embrace it. Some of us cannot sort it out. Some need therapy about it or fall into more than one (or even all) of those categories. There are also interrelated emotions about disciplinary reactions to the research: the situated and contextual risk of doing the work and sharing it. (Sjoberg, 2011, p 699)

Connecting this observation to the concept of empathetic cooperation reflecting on the emotional aspect of our academic performances can give us an indication of how far our subjectivities have travelled during fieldwork (Sylvester, 1994, p 325), allowing us to be more honest about what is needed to sustain that relational commitment. However, finishing a PhD thesis and defending it, publishing papers and cultivating an academic network – all of these are daunting and time-consuming tasks, which may gradually diminish the attention given to research relations.

This was brought home to me shortly after my thesis defence, when violence between Armenia and Azerbaijan reached a new peak in what was called the 'four-day war'. Discussing our feelings in the aftermath of this event, one friend told me over Skype that she was "in the process of giving up". Although it cannot be said with any certainty that my response would have been different if we had been having the conversation in person, I was struck by my own resignation and even indifference in the face of renewed violence. When another friend from the region reminded me that at least I now had the "luxury" of walking away, the prospect of doing so suddenly seemed not only reasonable but perhaps preferable to re-engaging with the conflict. Seeing myself through the eyes of my friends at these moments was a reminder of the limits of empathetic solidarity, but also suggested a 'point of departure' for future research endeavours (Gray, 2011, p 226).

Even when no follow-up research has been planned, it is important to take note of how empathy can be carried over from the fieldwork context to the writing up phase, creating challenges in interpretation and representation (Jones and Ficklin, 2012, p 111). Researchers are also writers who must do justice to the humanity of those who gave their time and expertise to the research. A responsible imaginative effort is needed to depict traumatic events from multiple perspectives, and to interpret and in some instances sustain the silences that arise around certain topics (Ackerly and True, 2008, p 696). These challenges often evolve in tandem with political events and personal developments in the lives of participants. The existing data needs to be evaluated in light of what the researcher has learned as well as unfolding political situations. In my case, this helped to make sense of some of the early data which had been recorded without an awareness of political context, but equally led to the realisation that it would be unethical to share this data with a wider audience.

The challenges of peace and conflict research often require a departure from conventional ethical codes (Clark, 2012, p 825; Brewer, 2016, p 4). While it is possible to ensure that people and organisations are anonymous in a text, it is harder to guarantee that they will not be implicitly identifiable to readers with local knowledge. This is of major consequence in settings where the researcher knows or suspects that they or their participants were subject to government surveillance, as was the case in some of my fieldwork. From rich and complex data, generalisations may have to be made, not in order to prove a rule, but to safeguard confidentiality and trust. When portraying participants' views on sensitive topics, such as political violence or the potential parameters of a conflict settlement, my analysis referred mainly to data that was already in the public domain. When such data was unavailable, I often resorted to measures such as sketching background material without directly referencing my sources. Another tactic was to list the positions adopted by a wide range of organisations, emphasising the diversity of civil society rather than highlighting underlying unity. This shifted the focus to pragmatic activism rather than critical positions (vis-à-vis the government's handling of peace and human rights issues) that had often been made known to me through subtle references, gestures, jokes and silences.

Many peace and conflict researchers desire to 'make a difference', often understood as influencing policy (Smyth and Darby, 2001). However, whether or not a researcher aims to achieve a broad impact through immediate publications will depend on the risks inherent in making their analysis known. For the researcher, this can result in arrest, deportation or future visa bans. For research participants, the consequences can be far worse (Koch, 2013). While we should recognise that there are contexts in which it is impossible to conduct research ethically (Wood, 2006, p 374), there are also a multitude of grey areas that cannot necessarily be identified in advance. Ultimately, individuals decide whether to talk to a researcher and how much they reveal – but between the messiness of informal relationships and shifting political circumstances, much can be said that is of a potentially harmful nature. The closeness of some relationships might suggest the possibility for research collaboration or co-authorship, allowing participants maximum say over what is included in the final product. However, faced with project deadlines, funding cycles and other logistical challenges, it may be less time-consuming and involve fewer risks to aim in the short term for deniability and detachment.

It is in the nature of interpretive ethnography to reveal the structures and meanings of a social world that are taken for granted by insiders and impenetrable to casual observers (Geertz, 1973). In places that are badly affected by the legacies of past violence, the risk of current violence, or the fear of future violence, this task may be require particular efforts. It should be no surprise that researchers leave the field only to become paralysed by emotional weight as they endeavour to distinguish between reasonable concern and mere paranoia. Despite the fear and mistrust that characterise violent research settings (Green, 1995), I usually felt more comfortable making decisions about representation while still in the field, where it was easier to be guided by unspoken moods and social cues, and to consult informally with participants. In other words, it is not necessarily detachment that is key in writing up violent research, but the art of keeping a safe distance while maintaining an empathetic stance towards the positions of all participants. Those whose research subjects may lead them into a similar conundrum – or who are perhaps already there – would do well to consider the social supports they could use in different stages and locations throughout the research process.

Conclusion

This chapter has argued that empathy constitutes a methodological tool insofar as it serves as the basis for relationships that influence the objectives and scope of data collection and the ways that data is subsequently analysed. However, far from having a neutral value, empathy is replete with ethical and emotional risks that can potentially outweigh the benefits of engaging in empathetic encounters. Viewing empathy as a skill that can be controlled or manipulated offers only a partial understanding of its contingent and relational nature. Instead, as a reflexive narrative on my own research process has shown, critical reflection on how empathetic relationships cut across the fieldwork and its aftermath reveals its role in challenging power relations and contributing to the (co-)construction of knowledge.

Empathy can be anticipated but is also fundamentally unpredictable in nature. Although my research in Azerbaijan and Armenia was based on a strong attachment to post-Soviet culture and a desire to get to know feminist activists and peacebuilders, the friendships I developed in a group setting and on a one-to-one basis were barely accounted for in my initial plans. Rather than viewing friendships as somehow peripheral to research concerns, the fieldwork design could have been more attentive to potential ethical issues arising from interpersonal as well as inter-organisational relationships, situating myself within the transnational networks being studied.

In the wider fieldwork context, empathetic encounters create insight into the embodied, daily realities of people surviving and living in conflict settings. However, emotional affinity may not always be the primary or even the desirable response. Sometimes our efforts to provide a supportive presence can lead to emotional fragmentation. At other times, understanding how and why people tell stories means acknowledging that empathy can sometimes be a discomforting or confrontational experience (Pedwell, 2013), or a 'horrific prospect' (Hemmings, 2012, p 153). The ambivalence I felt relating to some of these situations carried over into my efforts to represent them faithfully in an external context, along with other heightened emotional responses. As uncomfortable as it may be, I have suggested that working through these emotions is an important part of ethical reflection and representation.

Finally, whenever empathy is discussed, privilege must also be accounted for. Those who have the luxury of walking away from violent settings may want to ask themselves why it is they don't avail of this option. It may be that we have already invested too much in establishing an academic career to walk away from the risks, but it may be that we have experienced a 'positional slippage' (Sylvester, 1994, p 317) that draws us toward affective solidarity (Hemmings, 2012). Although this chapter has focused on some of the more negative aspects of fieldwork, we should never forget that fieldwork can include joy, or assume that the personal cost of researching violence is automatically higher than the benefits. In fact, fieldwork may represent both the best and the worst in what the research experience has to offer, and provide incentives for personal and political transformation.

Note
[1] Martyrs' Alley in Baku is a memorial to, and burial site of, civilians massacred by the Soviet army in January 1990, as well as thousands of victims of the Karabakh war and of conflicts which occurred between 1918 and 1920. The genocide memorial complex in Yerevan includes a monument, museum and research institute dedicated to the memories of more than a million Armenians who died in the Ottoman Empire between 1915 and 1922.

References
Ackerly, B. and True, J. (2008) 'Reflexivity in practice: power and ethics in feminist research on International Relations', *International Studies Review*, vol 10, pp 693–707.

Ahmed, S. (2004) 'Affective economies', *Social Text*, vol 79, no 2, pp 117–39.

Bartky, S. (1996) 'Sympathy and solidarity: on a tightrope with Scheler', in D. Meyers (ed) *Feminists rethink the self*, Boulder, CA: Westview Press, pp 177–96.

Behar, R. (1996) *The vulnerable observer: Anthropology that breaks your heart*, Boston MA: Beacon Press.

Bell, P. (2001) 'The ethics of conducting psychiatric research in war-torn contexts', in M. Smyth and G. Robinson (eds) *Researching violently divided societies: Ethical and methodological issues*, London: UN University Press and Pluto Press, pp 184–92.

Bloor, M., Fincham, B. and Sampson, H. (2007) *Quality (NCRM) commissioned inquiry into the risk to well-being of researchers in qualitative research*, Cardiff: School of Social Sciences (www.cf.ac.uk/socsi/qualiti/CIReport.pdf).

Brewer, J. (2016) 'The ethics of ethical debates in peace and conflict research: Notes towards the development of a research covenant', *Methodological Innovations*, vol 9, pp 1–11.

Brounéus, K. (2011) 'In depth interviewing: the process, skill and ethics of interviews in peace research', in K. Hoglund and M. Oberg (eds) *Understanding peace research: Methods and challenges*, Abingdon: Routledge, pp 130–45.

Browne, B. and McBride, R. (2015) 'Politically sensitive encounters: Ethnography, access, and the benefits of "hanging out"', *Qualitative Sociology Review*, vol 11, no 1, pp 34–48.

Browne, K. (2003) 'Negotiations and fieldworkings: Friendship and feminist research', *ACME: An International E-Journal for Critical Geographies*, vol 2, no 2, pp 132–46.

Clark, J. (2012) 'Fieldwork and its ethical challenges: Reflections from research in Bosnia', *Human Rights Quarterly*, vol 34, no 3, pp 823–39.

Cohn, C. (2008) 'Mainstreaming gender in UN security policy: A path to political transformation?', in S. Rai and G. Waylen (eds) *Global governance: Feminist perspectives*, Basingstoke and New York: Palgrave MacMillan, pp 185–216.

Crawford, N. (2014) 'Institutionalizing passion in world politics: Fear and empathy', *International Theory*, vol 6, no 3, pp 535–5.

de Waal, T. (2003) *Black garden: Armenia and Azerbaijan through peace and war*, New York and London: New York University Press.

Dickson-Swift, V., James, E., Kippen, S. and Liamputtong, P. (2007) 'Doing sensitive research: What challenges do qualitative researchers face?', *Qualitative Research*, vol 7, pp 327–53.

Drozdzewski, D. (2015) 'Retrospective reflexivity: The residual and subliminal repercussions of researching war', *Emotion, Space and Society*, vol 17, pp 30–6.

Emerald, E. and Carpenter, L. (2015) 'Vulnerability and emotions in research: Risks, dilemmas, and doubt', *Qualitative Inquiry*, vol 21, no 8, pp 741–50.

England, K. (1994) 'Getting personal: Reflexivity, positionality, and feminist research', *Professional Geographer*, vol 46, no 1, pp 80–9.

Galtung, J. (1969) 'Violence, peace and peace research', *Journal of Peace Research*, vol 6, no 3, pp 167–91.

Geertz, C. (1973) *The interpretation of cultures: Selected essays*, New York: Basic Books.

Gibbings, S. (2011) 'No angry women at the United Nations: Political dreams and the cultural politics of United Nations Security Council Resolution 1325', *International Feminist Journal of Politics*, vol 13, no 4, pp 522–38.

Gray, B. (2011) 'Empathy, emotion and feminist solidarities', in W. Ruberg and K. Steenbergh (eds) *Sexed sentiments: Interdisciplinary perspectives on gender and emotion*, Amsterdam: Rodopi, pp 207–33.

Green, L. (1995) 'Living in a state of fear', in C. Nordstrom and A. Robben (eds) *Fieldwork under fire: Contemporary studies of violence and survival*, Berkeley CA: University of California Press, pp 105–27.

Grewal, I. and Kaplan, C. (eds) (1994) *Scattered hegemonies: Postmodernity and transnational feminist practices*, Minneapolis, MN: University of Minnesota Press.

Head, N. (2016) 'Costly encounters of the empathic kind: A typology', *International Theory*, vol 8, no 1, pp 171–99.

Hemmings, C. (2012) 'Affective solidarity: feminist reflexivity and political transformation', *Feminist Theory*, vol 12, no 2, pp 147–61.

Hoglund, K. (2011) 'Comparative field research in war-torn societies', in K. Hoglund and M. Oberg (eds) *Understanding peace research: Methods and challenges*, Abingdon: Routledge, pp 114–29.

Ishkanian, A. (2004) 'Working at the local-global intersection: The challenges facing women in Armenia's nongovernmental organisation sector', in K. Kuehnast and C. Nechemias (eds) *Post-Soviet women encountering transition: Nation building, economic survival, and civic activism*, Washington, DC: Woodrow Wilson Centre Press, pp 262–87.

Jacoby, T. (2006) 'From the trenches: Dilemmas of feminist IR fieldwork', in B. Ackerly, M. Stern and J. True (eds) *Feminist methodologies for International Relations*, Cambridge: Cambridge University Press, pp 153–73.

Jones, B. and Ficklin, L. (2012) 'To walk in their shoes: Recognising the expression of empathy as a research reality', *Emotion, Space and Society*, vol 5, pp 103–12.

Koch, N. (2013) 'Introduction – Field methods in "closed" contexts: Undertaking research in authoritarian states and places', *Area*, vol 45, no 4, pp 390–5.

Koobak, R. and Marling, R. (2014) 'The decolonial challenge: Framing post-socialist Central and Eastern Europe within transnational feminist studies', *European Journal of Women's Studies*, vol 21, no 4, pp 330–43.

Marshall, S. (2011) 'Super-human researchers in feminist International Relations' narratives', in C. Sylvester (ed) 'The forum: Emotion and the feminist IR researcher', *International Studies Review*, vol 13, no 4, pp 688–90.

Mohanty, C. (2003) *Feminism without borders: Decolonizing theory, practicing solidarity*, Durham, NC: Duke University Press.

Moser, S. (2008) 'Personality: A new positionality?', *Area*, vol 40, no 3, pp 383–92.

Parashar, S. (2011) 'Embodied "otherness" and negotiations of difference', in C. Sylvester (ed) *The forum: Emotion and the feminist IR researcher*, *International Studies Review*, vol 13, no 4, pp 696–9.

Pedwell, C. (2012a) 'Economies of empathy: Obama, neoliberalism, and social justice', *Environment and Planning D: Society and Space*, vol 30, pp 280–97.

Pedwell, C. (2012b) 'Affective (self-)transformations: empathy, neoliberalism and international development', *Feminist Theory*, vol 13, no 2, pp 163–79.

Pedwell, C. (2013) 'Affect at the margins: alternative empathies in *A Small Place*', *Emotion, Space and Society*, vol 8, pp 18–26.

Robinson, F. (2006) 'Methods of feminist normative theory: A political ethic of care for International Relations', in B. Ackerly, M. Stern and J. True (eds) *Feminist methodologies for International Relations*, Cambridge: Cambridge University Press, pp 221–40.

Sjoberg, L. (2011) 'Emotion, risk, and feminist research in IR', in C. Sylvester (ed) 'The forum: Emotion and the feminist IR researcher', *International Studies Review*, vol 13, no 4, pp 699–703.

Scheper-Hughes, N. (1995) 'The primacy of the ethical: Propositions for a militant anthropology', *Current Anthropology*, vol 36, no 3, pp 409–40.

Smyth, M. and Darby, J. (2001) 'Does research make any difference? The case of Northern Ireland', in M. Smyth and G. Robinson (eds) *Researching violently divided societies: Ethical and methodological issues*, London: Pluto Press, pp 34–54.

Spelman, E. (1997) *Fruits of sorrow: Framing our attention to suffering*, Boston, MA: Beacon Press.

Suchland, J. (2011) 'Is postsocialism transnational?', *Signs*, vol 36, no 4, pp 837–62.

Sylvester, C. (1994) 'Empathetic cooperation: A feminist method for IR', *Millennium: Journal of International Studies*, vol 23, no 2, pp 315–34.

Tohidi, N. (2004) 'Women, building civil society, and democratization in post-Soviet Azerbaijan', in K. Kuehnast and C. Nechemias (eds) *Post-Soviet women encountering transition: Nation building, economic survival, and civic activism*, Washington, DC: Woodrow Wilson Centre Press, pp 149–71.

Wallensteen, P. (2001) *The growing peace research agenda*, Occasional Paper No 21, San Diego, CA: Joan B. Kroc Institute for International Studies.

Walsh, S. (2015) 'One step forward, two steps back: Developing a women's peace agenda in post-Soviet Armenia and Azerbaijan', in M. Flaherty, T. Matyok, J. Senehi, S. Byrne and H. Tuso (eds) *Gender and peacebuilding: All hands required*, Lanham MD: Rowman & Littlefield.

Wood, E. (2006) 'The ethical challenges of field research in conflict zones', *Qualitative Sociology*, vol 29, pp 373–86.

Yuval-Davis, N. (1997) *Gender and nation*, London: Sage Publications.

Vignette 5: The limits of a part-time political ethnographer

John Heathershaw

In the summer of 2011, residents of the Central Asian republic of Kyrgyzstan were living in the aftermath of the political violence of 2010. The events of the previous year had included the violent removal of the authoritarian regime and an ethnic conflict that irrupted from the political uncertainty that the fall of the regime had elicited. I had previously spent over two years living and working in Kyrgyzstan's capital Bishkek, largely as a lecturer at the American University in Central Asia (AUCA) over most of the period from 2001–05. AUCA is a private university that was launched in 1997 not long after the end of the Soviet Union and situated – until it moved to a new campus in 2015 – in the former building of the republican Soviet (council) in the centre of the capital.

In 2011, having recently been appointed to a senior lectureship and granted a six-month period of academic leave by my UK institution, I returned to study the new settlements surrounding Bishkek. While AUCA was at the centre of the city, the new settlements were at its margins. Residents of the settlements were dismissed as 'land-grabbers' by many city dwellers and officials, a familiar refrain to a familiar problem in urban centres throughout the world. They had purchased land from brokers who had occupied public and private land in the aftermath of the 2010 'revolution', but found their right to settle either contested or wholly denied. Such places lacked clear property rights and public goods such as roads, utilities, school provision and access to other basic services.

In my research, I was interested in the many protests that were being undertaken by settlers in order to demand legal recognition of their property rights. The literature of the dominant 'resource mobilisation' and 'political opportunity structure' approaches suggested that such protests were typically elite-led and, where they took place in unstable political environments of chronically weak states like Kyrgyzstan, tended to turn violent (Tarrow, 2011). Kyrgyzstan's protests, some of which had turned violent and had led to deaths in 2010 in the settlement of Maevka, seems to bear witness to these theoretical propositions (McGlinchey, 2009; Radnitz, 2010). Few specialists on the region dissented from this view (cf Sanghera and Satybaldieva, 2012).

Soon after I arrived, in August 2011, I met with my research assistant, a Kazakh who was a research fellow at another local university, in the cafe at AUCA. While we were meeting, we heard of a protest occurring between the university building and that of the mayoralty. Venturing outside, we observed around 25 protestors from the new settlement of Tets-2 (named after the abbreviated name of Hydro-Electric Power Station number 2, on whose land they had built their homes). We began chatting with several protestors, particularly Cholpon, a middle-aged woman who was speaking confidently to others and may, from our perspective, have been one of the leaders. However, Cholpon refuted the categories that were applied to her, not just by academic researchers, but also by politicians and public opinion in Bishkek.

> 'I am not a protestor [Russian: *Ya ni piketchika*]', she repeated several times during our first meeting.

Our discussion eventually led to questions about how the 'protest' occurred, with Cholpon declaring that "we decided between ourselves." She denied that there was a leader who had ordered the protest and financed the protestors' transport, as the Political Science literature may expect. Rather, one of the new settlers had used their own *marshrutka* (minibus public transport vehicle) to bring the new settlers into the capital. Finally, our conversation ended as the mayor of the capital appeared at his office steps and reassured the protestors that their petition was being considered by the city council. Soon after, the protest broke up.

Over the next few weeks we began to make more and more connections with Cholpon and other residents from around 400 people who lived in Tets-2. Sceptical of Cholpon's narrative, we eventually found a man who had designated himself leader and had met with the city authorities on multiple occasions, based on an unclear business relationship with one or more of the officials. Our findings were beginning to correspond with what may be expected in the literature, particularly regarding 'political opportunity'. Violence, however, was entirely absent among this small group of unemployed and middle-aged professionals who had been educated in the late-Soviet era.

In October 2011, as the residents of Tets-2 were preparing for the coming and quite extreme Kyrgyzstani winter, we witnessed a further collective action. While we were having tea with Cholpon and two of her young grandchildren in the back room of her home, a truck arrived on site. It turned out that the truck was carrying rough gravel and broken masonry that had been purchased cheaply and was to be used to pave the mud roads of the new settlement prior to the snowy months. Rather than this being organised by the leader or financed by a political patron, the gravel had been arranged by the group who lived on a particular street, including Cholpon, who had each contributed a roughly equal share to pay the costs. The truck poured the gravel on to the mud track which, over the coming days, the residents worked together to disperse across the track to create a make-shift road.

In effect, this collective act provided public goods that neither the state nor the absent patron was delivering. It occurred, like the protest, unbeknownst to the self-appointed leader about whom many residents spoke disdainfully. Examples such as this demonstrated that this leader had very little control over the protests and collective activities of the residents, many of whom were able to work together intermittently as a substitute for the lack of patronal leadership. These practices of self-organisation and non-violent protest were witnessed and narrated in interviews in the new settlements over the four months of fieldwork.

A complex picture emerged of collective action in an insecure environment (Kalyvas, 2006). In the three settlements we studied comparatively, we found that intermittent state investment was taking place in the semi-legal settlements, often in direct responses to protests. However, patronal relations had only become stable in one of these two (that which was the longest serving settlement, with origins in the late-1980s during the last years of the Soviet Union). Tets-2 was largely forsaken by the state, but its residents continued a legal process to protect their right to settlement while organising some basic public goods for the community. Our initial research findings suggested that mobilisation in the two most recent new settlements was not explained by patronal relations and 'resource mobilisation', as may have been expected. A more bottom-up, non-violent and inconsistent process was apparent in these two cases.

Without ethnographic research, these findings may have been unobtainable. However, my Kazakh colleague and I also realised our limits as ethnographers. If I had been single, or it had been the time of my PhD studies, I may have sought to live in a new settlement. However, with my partner and two infant children accompanying me, and various academic responsibilities that required a good internet connection, it was not an option to live in a place without heating or electric. I chose to study Kyrgyz – the first language of all three of the settlements we studied – alongside the fieldwork while based at a warm apartment in the city centre as the harsh winter approached. Equally, my colleague had a young family and other tasks to complete. As part-time or 'day-trip' ethnographers with limited language skills, we relied on Russian, spoken more or less competently as a second language by our research participants, as our primary medium of communication during our twice-weekly visits. The 'insider' or emic perspective was lacking or was at least limited from our political ethnographic study (Schatz, 2009).

This period of 'ethnographic research' told me of my limits as a political ethnographer while also demonstrating the value of ethnography and the co-production of knowledge between a mixed research team and participants. It also told me of the structural constraints of a faculty member at a Western university seeking to reorient his research to an unfamiliar setting in the space of a six-month period of academic leave. During my leave I also completed and eventually won a large research grant to continue research on conflict in Central Asia, albeit in the quite different settings of southern Kyrgyzstan and Tajikistan. This new project, which ran from 2012–16, distracted me from the completion and writing up of the new settlements study. Moreover, we found that the freedom to conduct research that was present in Bishkek was no longer present in other previously open parts of the region. In Khorog, Tajikistan, in 2014, our research team were targeted by the Tajik security services, and one of our local colleagues was detained for over a month. The ethnographic co-production of knowledge, which had been so promising in the new settlements, became a liability. My own privileges, relatively reduced vulnerabilities and partial perspectives were thrown into sharp relief.

In retrospect, the new settlements research in 2011 demonstrated my personal deficits as an aspiring part-time political ethnographer of Kyrgyz settlers as well as my structural constraints, both familial and professional. I learned that the ethnography of conflict requires an immense amount of time and patience that is often in tension with the realities of tenured academic life and research funding. The ethical and political questions raised by such research are multiple and often at cross-purposes. Most of all, weighed down by both the academic literature and external funding imperatives, I learned of the value of humility when faced by research contexts that simply fail to conform to our expectations.

References

Kalyvas, S. (2006) *The logic of violence in civil wars*, Cambridge: Cambridge University Press.

McGlinchey, E. (2009) 'Central Asian protest movements. Social forces or state resources?', in A.E. Wooden and C.H. Stefes (eds) *The politics of transition in Central Asia and the Caucasus. Enduring legacies and emerging challenges*, London: Routledge, p 133.

Radnitz, S. (2010) *Weapons of the wealthy: Predatory regimes and elite-led protests in Central Asia*, Ithaca, NY: Cornell University Press.

Sanghera, B. and Satybaldieva, E. (2012) 'Ethics of property, illegal settlements and the right to subsistence', *International Journal of Sociology and Social Policy*, vol 32, issue 1/2, pp 96–114.

Schatz, E. (ed) *Political ethnography: What immersion contributes to the study of power*, Chicago, IL: University of Chicago Press.

Tarrow, S. (2011) *Power in movement: Social movements and contentious politics* (3rd edn), Cambridge: Cambridge University Press.

Index